The
Weaving Explorer

The
Weaving Explorer

Ingenious Techniques,
Accessible Tools &
Creative Projects with
YARN, PAPER, WIRE & More

Deborah Jarchow &
Gwen W. Steege

Storey Publishing

*The mission of Storey Publishing is to serve our customers by
publishing practical information that encourages
personal independence in harmony with the environment.*

Edited by Michal Lumsden
Art direction and book design by Alethea Morrison
Text production by Jennifer Jepson Smith
Indexed by Nancy D. Wood

Cover and interior photography by Mars Vilaubi
Additional photography by © Andrew Neuhart,
    134; Chris Autio Photo, 52 & 53; Private
    CollectionPhoto © Christie's Images/
    Bridgeman Images, 15 top; © Emily Weaving,
    38 & 39; © Friedrich Stark/Alamy Stock Photo,
    144; © Gregory Case, 132; © Helen Hiebert, 245;
    © John Mullarkey, 166 & 167; © Kara Saxby,
    105; © Mark LaMoreaux, 137; © Michael F.
    Rohde, 135; © Michele and Tom Grimm/Alamy
    Stock Photo, 145; © PHAS/Getty Images, 159;
    © Rachel Hine, 138 & 139; © Rebecca Mezoff,
    133; © Sarah C. Swett, 136
Prop styling by Sally Staub
Diagrams and charts by Ilona Sherratt, based on
    reference provided by the authors

Text © 2019 by Deborah Jarchow and Gwen W.
    Steege

Storey books are available at special discounts
when purchased in bulk for premiums and
sales promotions as well as for fund-raising
or educational use. Special editions or book
excerpts can also be created to specification.
For details, please call 800-827-8673, or send
an email to sales@storey.com.

Storey Publishing
210 MASS MoCA Way
North Adams, MA 01247
storey.com

Printed in China through World Print
10 9 8 7 6 5 4 3 2 1

LIBRARY OF CONGRESS CATALOGING-IN-PUBLICATION
DATA

Names: Jarchow, Deborah, author. | Steege, Gwen,
    1940– author.
Title: The weaving explorer : ingenious techniques,
    accessible tools & creative projects with yarn, paper,
    wire & more / Deborah Jarchow & Gwen W. Steege.
Description: North Adams, MA : Storey Publishing,
    [2019] | Includes index. | Summary: "The Weaving
    Explorer takes inspiration from the world of folk
    weaving traditions, adding a contemporary spin by
    introducing an unexpected range of materials and
    home dec projects" — Provided by publisher.
Identifiers: LCCN 2019033543 | ISBN 9781635860283
    (hardcover) | ISBN 9781635860290 (ebook)
Subjects: LCSH: Hand weaving. | Hand weaving
    — Patterns.
Classification: LCC TT848 .J36 2019 | DDC 746.1/4—dc23
LC record available at https://lccn.loc.gov/2019033543

To all
the weavers and
other fiber enthusiasts
who have enriched our lives
with the beauty and skill of their
art and provided us with inspiration.
And to our families, who have put up
with piles of yarn, stacks of looms,
and endless hours of distrac-
tion — we thank you and
love you!

PART 2: **WEAVING BEYOND THE FRAME** 141

IT'S A WOVEN WORLD

From the sublime medieval Unicorn Tapestries created with luxury fibers and metallic threads to our perfectly practical, ubiquitous blue jeans, woven fabrics have enriched and protected us for millennia. We wear woven items, we carry our belongings in them, we use them to store our stuff, we walk on them. Our windows and furniture, and sometimes even our walls, are covered with woven fabric. Whether functional or decorative, held together by weaving, twisting, braiding, or wrapping, the interlacement of the weaving materials is universal and the process is ancient. Some researchers cite evidence of woven textiles from as long ago as 20,000 to 25,000 years. Modern tools have made the weaving process easier, but the concept of weaving one set of threads over and under another set placed at right angles to it remains the same.

Examining Over/Under

The simple genius of weaving is this over/under interlacing of threads. Warp threads are generally stretched vertically between two fixed horizontals, such as the top and bottom pieces of a frame. The weaver ensures there is enough tension in the warp threads to let the weft travel smoothly and at a right angle through the raised and lowered warp threads. As you will see throughout this book, a weaver can provide warp tension in many ways, including with his or her own body.

Perhaps the most familiar way of providing warp tension is with a loom. Looms can be as simple as a bowed stick made of notched wood; others are small enough to tuck in a pocket. Some weavers use 60-inch floor looms with multiple shafts that carry the warp threads, and computer-operated looms churn out miles of fabric in giant factories. Without any loom at all, nonhuman creatures such as spiders, birds, and even weaver ants weave intricate structures to attract prey and offer themselves protection.

Often the weft is wound onto a shuttle so that it easily passes through the warp threads. Shuttles can be as elementary as a flat piece of wood with notches in the ends to contain the threads; this tool is called a stick shuttle (see page 151). A more complex tool known as a boat shuttle (since it's shaped like a little boat) holds a bobbin loaded with weft thread. Weavers can even use their fingers as shuttles to carry the weft, or they can wind the yarn into little packages called butterflies to keep the weft in order.

Diversity of Weaving Materials

Weaving materials range from the finest silk threads to sturdy wools, linens, and cottons, from fragile papers and plant leaves to precious metals. Whatever the material, the warp must be strong enough to hold up under tension and not break or shred when you weave the weft through it. You have more flexibility in choosing weft, as it is not under tension, so strength doesn't need to be the determining factor. The materials list we include with each project gives specifications for warp and weft materials that will work best as you explore each new technique.

In this book we have used some conventional yarns such as different weights of wool spun from a variety of animal fibers, and even pin roving (an unspun length of cleaned, unaligned fiber). The versatility of wool allows you to weave a sturdy floor mat as well as a luxurious cashmere pillow! Linen threads of different weights provide a strong, reliable warp, and pearl cottons, with their exciting range of colors and lovely sheen, are ideal for card-weaving projects. If you are a knitter or a crocheter, weaving is a sensational way to make use of odds and ends left over from other projects.

Ready, Set, Go for It!

Weaving can be incredibly complex, but it can also be exquisitely simple. In this book, we explore a variety of weave structures as well as weaving materials. Many projects are based on ancient weaving traditions, updated for contemporary looks and purposes. We sometimes combine traditional techniques with nontraditional materials. Some projects require no loom at all, while others use a simple frame to hold the warp that is interlaced with weft to create fabric, and still others are woven around an object — such as a stone, branch, or ring — that remains part of the completed item. We use common materials, such as paper, ribbon, fabric strips, and, of course, yarn, along with wire, plastic, and even parachute cord, sometimes in unexpected ways.

A few of the projects — for example, kumihimo and lucet braiding, knotless netting, and Viking knitting — are not technically woven, but because they involve interlacing yarn or wire, we feel weavers will enjoy stretching the definition.

You can follow the instructions we offer to learn new techniques and create the projects just as shown in this book. Or, use the Design Notebook feature to understand the design inspiration and process behind each project

SPOTLIGHT ON THE ARTISTS

The world of weaving is diverse, with endless ways of expressing form and ideas, limited only by the imagination of the weaver. To bring some of that diversity to our book, we invited a number of weaving artists whom we especially admire to share their work. As you examine their weavings and read their stories, we hope they will inspire you, as they do us, to take the basic ideas that we offer in new and exciting directions. Our deep gratitude to each artist for being willing to contribute to our book! See page 303 for a complete list of the artists and their websites.

and to take the concept in your own new and unique direction. The glossary will assist you with unfamiliar terms, and the appendix offers a useful foundation in forging your own path for the projects. Appendix instructions will guide you through procedures that will help you master necessary skills and also tell you how to make some of the tools used in the projects.

Many of the projects in this book require no weaving experience, though we hope dedicated weavers, as well as fiber lovers who have never woven, will be inspired to explore unfamiliar techniques and approaches to their passion. Although we are both long-time weavers, we made many new discoveries about our craft, both its history and its possibilities, as we developed the book. These discoveries have inspired us to learn and experiment, and above all, they have reignited our love of the ever-absorbing art and craft of weaving. We hope that what we offer here will inspire you in the same way. Be a weaving explorer!

WE INVITE YOU TO WEAVE!

For each of us, one of the true pleasures of writing this book has been developing a deep friendship with a new weaving friend, our coauthor. While we designed and created our projects independently, we always shared our frustrations and successes over long Facetime sessions linking California with Massachusetts. You'll find our initials (DJ or GS) at the end of the introductions to each of our projects.

OPENING UP

For many years I was a production weaver, working at floor looms making structured, evenly woven cloth for garments and accessories that I sold. My personal definition of weaving was pretty narrow since I focused on floor-loom woven fabrics and didn't give much thought to any other types of weaving.

But I learned that weaving can be many things. The first definition of *weave* in Dictionary.com is "to interlace (threads, yarn, strips, fibrous material, etc.) so as to form a fabric or material." This open definition offers many possibilities in materials and tools. In this book we incorporate traditional thread and yarn as well as wire, cord, paper, twigs, and ribbon. We hope to get you weaving around peg looms, pins, rings, hoops, mat board, and more. Stepping away from my usual looms allowed me to appreciate and explore the inventiveness that's possible using simple equipment. I'm thrilled to be able to share my weaving journey with you.

Deborah Jarchow

TAKING YARN FOR A WALK

For many of us, the tactile experience of working with our hands is as necessary as eating and sleeping. To knitters, spinners, crocheters, sewists, embroiderers, and other fiber lovers, the allure of fiber in all its myriad forms is irresistible. But there is something additionally mesmerizing about the process of weaving — watching colors interact as the fabric develops, noticing the relationship of warp and weft, taking pleasure in the simple repetition of under, over, under, over. One of my weaving heroines is the Bauhaus weaver Anni Albers. Inspired by Paul Klee's advice that drawing was like "taking a line for a walk," Albers applied that idea to weaving and devoted herself to it for decades, becoming a major influence on textile design in the mid-twentieth century. I love the image of taking *yarn* for a walk and invite you to come along.

Gwen Steege

shed stick

warp

weft

tapestry shuttle

PART 1

WEAVING ON FRAMES

Weaving on a frame is a simple way to keep tension on warp threads. The frame can be any form, including a circle, square, triangle, or hexagon, or even a free-form shape, such as a tree branch.

What's important is that the frame is rigid enough to keep the warp threads aligned and under tension. You can wrap the warp around the frame itself or around notches, nails, slits, pegs, pins, or even alligator clips that are on the frame. As you will see, keeping the warp taut enables you to pass the weft over and under the warp without tangling the threads.

Generally, the warp threads are evenly spaced between two sides of the frame. The number of threads per inch of space on the frame is referred to as the sett of the warp (sometimes also called ends per inch or epi). So if your warp is 10" wide and has 40 warp threads total, that would be a sett of 4, or 4 epi.

You may see a row of weft referred to as a pick or shot of weft. When weaving in the weft, it is up to you how tightly to beat, or push each row into place against the previous row. If you want to weave a fabric with a flowing drape, you will want to beat the weft rows somewhat loosely. If you are making a floor mat or any textile that needs to stand up to rough use, tightly beat the weft so the weave is dense. The density of the weft is called picks per inch, or ppi.

Have fun playing with the various techniques to see how the same yarns and techniques can produce very different results based on how close together or far apart your warp and weft threads are.

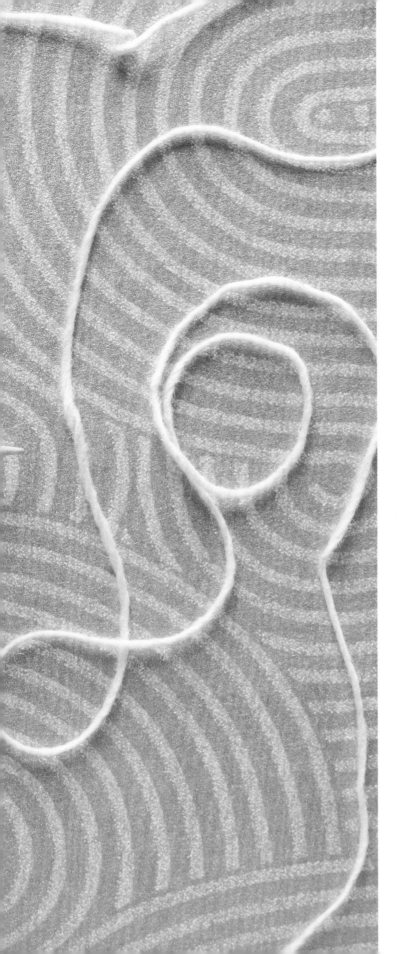

WEAVING IN CIRCLES

Circles have a unique place in the traditions and beliefs of many cultures. They variously symbolize perfection, infinity, protection, completeness, and fidelity. Some are part of religious rituals, such as the mandalas of Buddhism and Hinduism. They appear in both ancient and contemporary art, often representing those ever-present circles, the sun, moon, and planets, including Earth. From the wheel to the bowl, circles serve everyday practical purposes, but they can project fun and whimsy too! The next few projects show off beautiful, creative ways to work circular frames into your weaving.

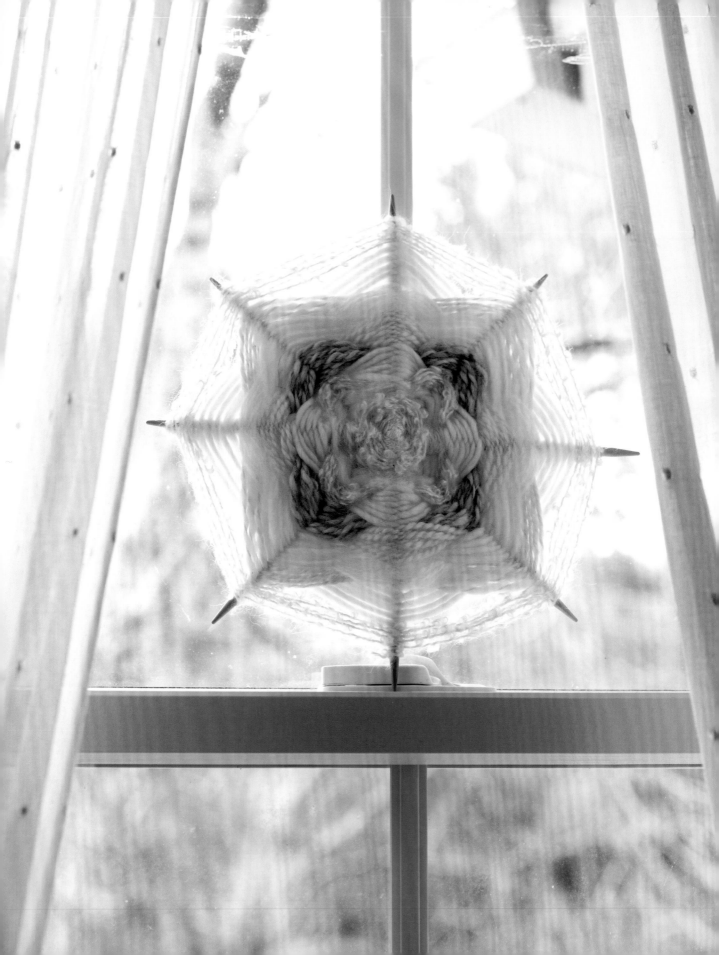

God's Eye

The woven object we call a God's eye originated with the Huichol people of the Sierra Madre mountains in what is now western Mexico. Traditionally, the four spokes of the crossed-stick frame represented the elements: fire, water, wind, and earth. The Huichol people believed these sacred objects offered protection and the power to see the unseeable and unknowable. When the Spanish came to the region in the 1500s, they called the weavings *ojos de Dios*, or "God's eyes." The religious significance of these objects has largely been lost over the years, but the infinite ways to weave them remain fascinating. —GS

DESIGN NOTEBOOK

The most common method of making a God's eye is to cross two sticks and weave yarn around them in a spiral, but the project shown here uses four sticks, so that you have eight "arms" to weave around. This results in a more three-dimensional object. For my sticks, I used 10"-long double-pointed knitting needles. You can use knitting needles of any length or width, depending on how large or small you want your finished God's eye. If you use skewers instead of knitting needles, trim off the pointed ends.

Also traditional is to work with many colors, often bright primaries and other vibrant hues. When I created the mostly white design shown opposite and above, however, I was influenced by the weather — a cold, snowy December day in New England. Working with one color and many kinds of yarns gave me the opportunity to explore my love of texture. In this God's eye, I used bamboo, wool bouclé, and both singles and two-ply wool yarns, including some handspun. Although you could say they are all white, the actual hues vary and the different yarn weights and textures add to the effect.

This project is a great way to use small bits of yarn left over from other knitting, crochet, or weaving projects. The yarns don't have to be all the same weight, although you may want to double or triple any that are very fine.

God's Eye

YOU WILL NEED

- Ruler
- Pencil or pen
- Four double-pointed knitting needles or bamboo skewers
- Hot glue gun
- Assortment of yarn of different textures and colors

1. Measure and mark the center on each needle. Place a dab of hot glue at the center of one needle, and position another needle on the glue at a right angle to the first. Hold the two needles together until the glue sets. Repeat for the second pair of needles and set that pair aside.

2. Holding a 3" tail of yarn under the point where the two needles cross, lash the needles together by drawing the yarn diagonally over the center of the cross, starting at the upper left and moving to the lower right. Take the yarn under the bottom needle to the lower left and come up across the front to the upper right, under the top needle to the upper left where you started, as shown below. Rotate the needles one-quarter turn clockwise, as you take the yarn under the next needle to the left. Continue to rotate the needles and repeat the lashing in this manner as many times as necessary to establish a firm cross.

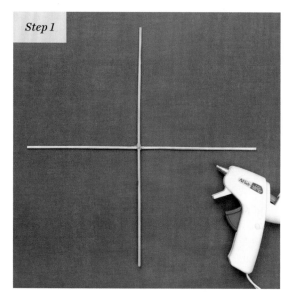

Step 1

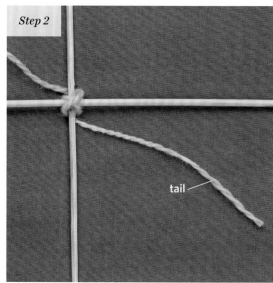

Step 2

tail

3. Continuing with the same yarn, draw the yarn over and around the needle arm to the right. Turn the crossed needles counterclockwise and draw the yarn over and around the next arm to the right. Continue in this manner until the width of the weaving measures about 1" from the center. You may find it more natural to turn the crossed needles clockwise. If so, draw the yarn over and around the needle arm to the left.

4. Repeat steps 2 and 3 with the second pair of needles to create the other half of the God's eye. Make the weaving on this second cross slightly wider than that of the first.

5. To join the two halves, place the first God's eye you wove on top of the second as shown, so that the eight arms of the needles are evenly spaced. Join a new length of yarn with a sliding knot (see page 293) and weave around each of the eight arms as you did in step 3. (Hide the tail ends of the knot in subsequent rounds.) Adjust as necessary to keep the symmetry of the design. Weave around until this section is about ½" wide (or as desired).

TIPS FOR SUCCESS

- You can simply begin lashing the two needles together without gluing, but the glue makes it easier to get started and helps maintain the symmetry as you weave.

- Snug each length of yarn neatly up against the previous round, but do not overlap it.

- Keep a firm tension on the yarn in order to maintain the integrity of the structure.

- Check often to see that the crossed sections remain symmetrical, and adjust if necessary.

- When changing to a new length of yarn, use a sliding knot (see page 293) to tie the two ends together on the back, leaving tails that you can weave in as you continue to work.

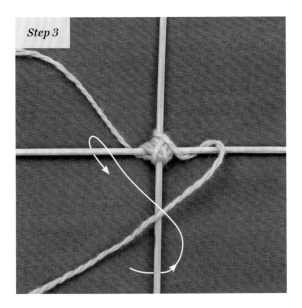

Step 3

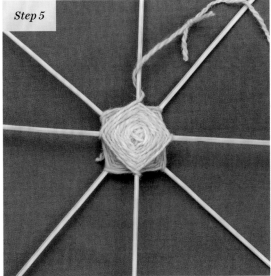

Step 5

6. After a few rounds of weaving around each of the eight arms, you can increase the three-dimensional effect by weaving around every other arm for several rounds (four arms in all; see photo 6a) and then weaving several rounds around the alternate four arms. (see photo 6b). Mix it up further by weaving around each arm again. Change colors as desired, using a sliding knot for each join. Play with it!

7. When about 1" of each arm remains, weave around each of the eight arms again for about ½". Using all of the arms for the last band creates a border that completes the design. (You may wish to have a wider border — your choice!)

8. Cut the yarn, leaving an 8" tail. Wrap the tail several times around the last arm, make a loop for hanging, and finish off with a double half-hitch knot (see page 292) at the base of the loop.

Step 6a

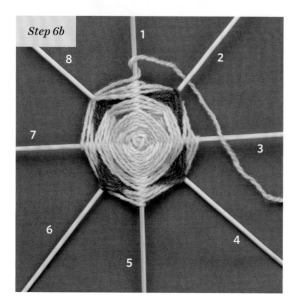

Step 6b

I wove bands ½" to ¾" wide, each one going around only every other arm and alternating the sets of four. In other words, for one band, I wove around arms 1, 3, 5, and 7, and for the next band, I wove around arms 2, 4, 6, and 8. Take care to draw the yarn under the yarns in the previous section.

ALTERNATIVE WEAVE

The weaving method described in step 3 creates a smooth surface on top of the God's eye, with a clean line down the center of each needle where the yarn has been wrapped. I used that method for the entire God's eye shown on page 8. To create even more dimensionality in your God's eye, experiment with this alternate weave:

1. Take the yarn under the arm to the left of where you start, up and over it, and then under the next arm on the left.

2. Rotate the God's eye clockwise and repeat step 1. (Note that you can also turn the arms counterclockwise and wrap the arm to the right.) With this alternative weave, the wrap is visible on top of the arms and the length of yarn between each arm is set back slightly.

You can alternate between this approach and the one described in step 3 (page 11).

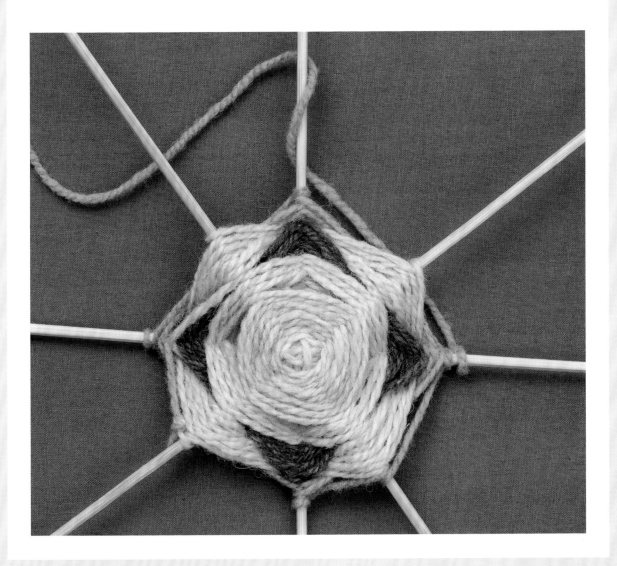

Handcrafted Dorset buttons were used on European formal wear throughout the seventeenth and eighteenth centuries.

Crosswheel Ornament (page 21)

Delicate Dorset Buttons

Dorset buttons were first made commercially in the English county of Dorset in the seventeenth century. For the next 200 years, making buttons by hand was a thriving cottage industry in the region; anyone not capable of or interested in working in the fields could survive by making buttons. In one day, successful button makers could create as many as six or seven dozen buttons, which amazes me!

The invention in the mid-1800s of the button-making machine put an end to the Dorset cottage industry, but fortunately, Dorset-style buttons are still admired and the technique has survived through the centuries. In addition to buttons, the disks can be made into beautiful accessories — including necklaces, bracelets, hair clips, and rings — and adornments (see Crosswheel Ornaments at left and on page 21).

No matter how I end up using these small creations, I find making them fun — and a bit addictive. —DJ

DESIGN NOTEBOOK

The buttons I've made are based on the basic Dorset crosswheel pattern, but there are many styles and patterns of varying complexity. You can also create a huge variety of buttons simply by changing the size of your base ring, the thread you use, and the pattern in which you wrap the thread. I chose rings with ⅝" diameters, and used about 4 yards of yarn to complete each button. For a kaleidoscopic effect, use different colors of thread or a variegated thread when wrapping the ring and/or the spokes.

I used a blunt-tip embroidery needle 1⅝" long with a ⅜" eye. Since the project is very small, I prefer using a needle with a blunt tip so I don't prick my fingers while wrapping the threads. If I need to sew in any tails, I use a sharp-tipped 1⅝" embroidery needle.

Delicate Dorset Buttons

YOU WILL NEED

- Size 10 crochet cotton or similar-size yarn
- Blunt-tip embroidery needle
- Plastic cabone rings the diameter of your desired buttons

- Scissors
- Sharp-tip embroidery needle

TIPS FOR SUCCESS

- Avoid working with long threads that tangle easily. Use lengths of thread no longer than a yard.

- Every so often, allow the needle and thread to dangle from the button so the thread can untwist itself.

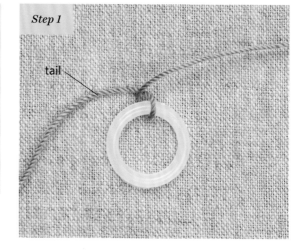

Step 1

tail

Wrapping the Ring

1. Thread the crochet cotton on the blunt-tip needle. Position the tail alongside the top of the ring, with the tail pointing to the left.

2. Put the needle through the ring from front to back and right to left. Continue bringing the needle up through the inside of the loop of thread above the ring, forming a buttonhole stitch or half hitch (see page 292) on the ring. This first stitch may seem a bit unstable, but you will be able to snug it into place after you work a few loops and the stitches are settled.

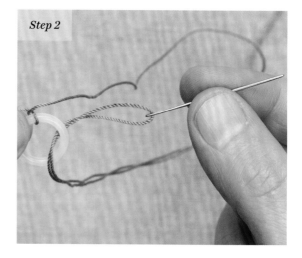

Step 2

3. Continue moving around the ring clockwise, repeating the wrap described in step 2. When approaching the part of the ring that is already wrapped, catch the beginning tail inside the wrapping threads. To do this, hold the tail against the ring and complete the wrapping over it.

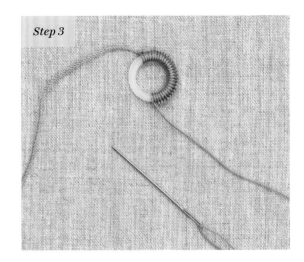

Step 3

4. When the ring is completely wrapped, trim the beginning tail if any of it protrudes through the wrappings. If you are using a different color for the inside part of the button, thread the ending tail under the wrapped area using the sharp-tip needle. If you are continuing with the same color, just continue on using the same thread.

5. There will be a ridge around the outside edge of the ring. Slide that ridge to the back of the ring.

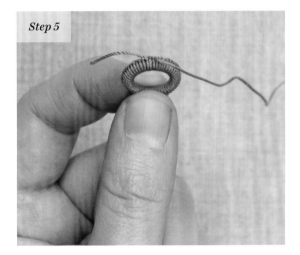

Step 5

Creating the Spokes

6. Now wrap the thread completely around the ring like the spokes of a bicycle wheel so you have a total of eight spokes on the top and eight spokes on the bottom of the button. It will be a bit messy at this point. If you are using the same color, continue with the thread you were using to wrap the ring. If you are starting a new color, begin by securing the new thread under a section of the thread wrapping the ring. Try to keep the spokes evenly spaced around the ring.

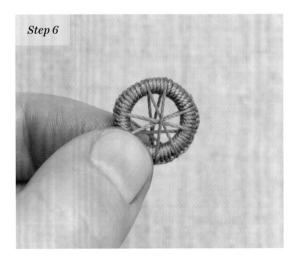

Step 6

7. Tighten and straighten the spokes by wrapping the thread a few times around the center hub of the wheel, between the spokes. The wrapping will form a cross shape and will gather the center of the spokes together. End with the thread coming out the back of the button. Tug the hub until it is positioned in the center of the ring.

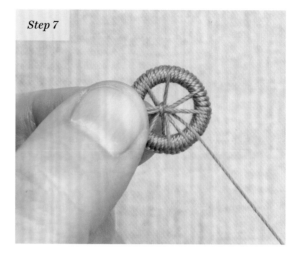

Step 7

Each spoke will consist of a pair of threads, one thread on the back of the button and one on the front. The spokes you create will not line up directly on top of each other. This is okay; they will be straightened out in the next step.

Wrapping the Spokes

8. Bring the needle up between spokes A and B. Move the needle to the right, over spoke B. Then take the needle down between spokes B and C. Tug the thread inward toward the wheel's central hub. From underneath, bring the needle up between the spokes A and H.

9. Repeat the wrapping pattern in step 8, moving one spoke to the right and down, then under two spokes to the left and up. Continue until the space between all the spokes is completely filled in.

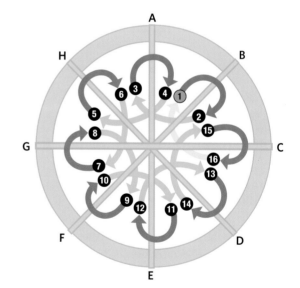

Finishing

10. Using the sharp-tip needle, bury the tail in the threads on the back side of the ring and trim off the excess.

11. If you need to add more thread or change colors, use the sharp-tip needle to bury the ends of the previous tail and the beginning tail of the new yarn.

USE YOUR BUTTONS ON A HANDMADE GARMENT

After searching all over for buttons for a sweater that I was particularly proud of knitting, I eventually made my own Dorset buttons. I needed buttons that were very small and elegant but didn't steal the spotlight from the lace patterns in the sweater. Commercial buttons I found were either too plain or too thick. My handmade buttons turned out to be exactly the right look. It is such fun to render the perfect closure for a handcrafted garment.

Sew the finished button(s) on the garment as follows:

1. Catch your sewing thread around the hub of the button's wheel to create a shank, making sure to allow enough room for the fabric around the buttonhole to lie flat and not bunch up.

2. As you sew the button on, wrap the thread around the shank to make the connection more secure.

Crosswheel Ornaments

The basic Dorset button crosswheel pattern makes a perfect holiday ornament.
Use these festive embellishments on trees, wreaths, candles, centerpieces,
or wherever you want a bit of holiday sparkle. —DJ

DESIGN NOTEBOOK

Try using various ring sizes to fashion a variety of ornaments. I chose a coordinated color palette of greens, blues, white, and silver to give my ornaments the cohesive look of a set, but you could use a variety of colorful threads to make very merry holiday decorations.

To create the ornaments shown here I used an assortment of welded rings ranging in size from 1" to 3"; several different Kreinik Metallic threads, sizes 8–16; some size 5 crochet cottons with shiny finishes; and some lightweight yarns and crochet cottons with sparkle.

YOU WILL NEED

- Plastic and metal rings in various sizes: ¾"–1½" plastic rings and 1"–2" metal washers or 1"–2" welded metal rings
- Assortment of threads, some with glitter; amount will depend on size of ring
- Small tapestry needle
- Scissors
- Pliers

Follow the instructions for Delicate Dorset Buttons (page 16), making anywhere between six and ten spokes.

Make a hanging loop by taking the final thread under some of the wrapping threads around the outer ring. Bring the working thread up, make a loop about ½" long, and bring the thread back into the wrapping threads. Wrap the working thread around the loop a couple of times to stiffen the base of the loop. Slip the needle under some of the wrapping threads and then backstitch (see page 297) to anchor the tail. Trim any excess.

TIPS FOR SUCCESS

- Create distinct and individual ornaments by using different threads for each button or ornament.

- For some ornaments, continue around the spokes until all the space is filled in up to the ring. For others, try leaving some open space between the threads and the ring.

- Work several rounds using one color, then switch to a different thread. Simply bury the beginning and ending tails in the previous woven area. To make sure the tail is really buried, try pulling the needle with a pair of pliers. Just make sure to pull away from your face and body.

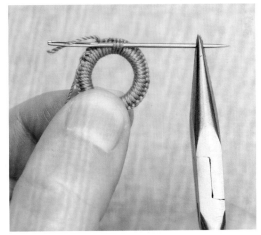

- Add some extra sparkle to your ornaments with beads. Slip several beads on the thread before threading the needle, then slide each bead into place where you want it on your ornament. (To easily thread the beads onto the needle, use a dental floss threader. Place one end of the thread through the loop of the threader. Pick up the beads with the single end of the threader and slide them down over the loop onto the thread. Slip the end of the thread out of the threader and onto your needle. For another method of threading beads, see page 178.)

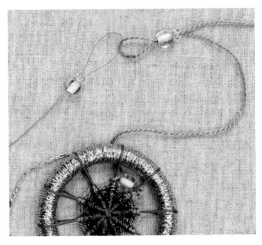

16-Cord Kumihimo Braid

Kumihimo is a Japanese method of braiding threads together to make decorative cords. The technique has been around for 1,500 years, and the cords — which samurai once used to lace up their armor — are used today as ties for *haori* jackets and as part of traditional kimono sashes.

The cords can have extremely complex designs woven into them or can be quite simple. Traditional Japanese cords are woven with fine silk threads on beautiful specialty looms called *marudai*, but many modern kumihimo disks are made of thick foam. The foam disks are inexpensive, portable, and easy to use. Although this is technically braiding, the working threads are referred to as warp threads, and they are kept under tension as they would be if you were weaving fabric on a loom.

This cord can be used as a closure for the Stitched Project Bag (page 229) or the Small Treasure Bag with Twisted Draw Cord (page 207), or you can make a shorter version onto which you can string your Free-Form Pendants (page 55). —DJ

16-Cord Kumihimo Braid

YOU WILL NEED

- **Warp:** size 3 crochet cotton (3/2 pearl cotton), 8 yards in each of 4 colors
- 16 EZ Bobs
- Kumihimo disk with 32 notches
- Weight (This can be a large washer, a fishing weight, or an actual kumihimo weight.)

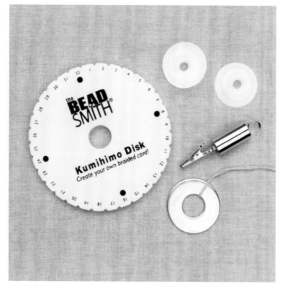

In this project you will wrap the long warp threads around the core of weighted plastic bobbins. The top layer of the bobbin is then flipped down over the threads to keep them from unwinding. The two layers of plastic keep the warp threads from coming off the bobbin as they dangle from the disk. The bobbins keep the long warp threads from tangling as you work.

1. Cut four pieces of warp thread from each of the four colors. Each warp thread should be twice as long as you want your finished cord.

2. Wind all but about 10" of each warp onto an EZ Bob.

3. Spread out the warp threads on the disk following the diagram below. Leave two empty notches between each group of two adjacent threads.

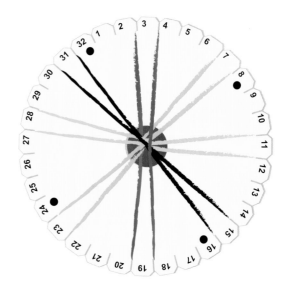

4. Pull the ends of all the warp threads through the center hole from top to bottom, making sure to keep the ends of the tails even, and tie a square knot (see page 291) on the bottom side of the disk.

5. Attach the weight around the knot to keep tension on the cord.

6. Adjust the length of the threads in the EZ Bobs so they hang evenly over the edges of the disk.

7. Beginning with the group of threads at the 6 o'clock position, lift the left warp thread and move it over the disk and position it in the notch to the left side of the two threads at the 12 o'clock position. Then lift the thread on the right side of the 12 o'clock position, and move it over the disk and position it in the notch to the right of the threads at the 6 o'clock position.

8. Turn the disk slightly counterclockwise so the threads that were in the 7 o'clock position are now in the 6 o'clock position, and move the threads as you did in step 7. As you use up the available thread, unwind more thread from the EZ Bobs and continue weaving.

9. Repeat steps 7 and 8 until your cord is the desired length. Remove the threads from the disk, and tie an overhand knot (see page 291) in each end of the bundles.

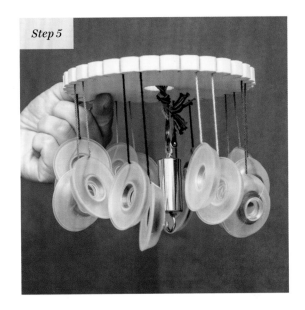

Step 5

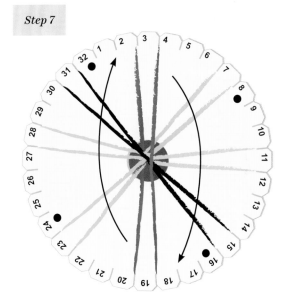

Step 7

What a Lot of Hoopla!

An embroidery hoop makes a perfect loom for a circular weaving, and once the weaving is complete, it also provides the frame. Available in a wide range of sizes, hoops are lightweight and portable. Be sure to use a wooden hoop: plastic does not grip the warp yarns as securely as wood and is less attractive as a frame. —GS

DESIGN NOTEBOOK

I wove this project on a 14" embroidery hoop. You can use a larger or smaller hoop, depending on how big you want your finished project to be. If you wish, you can paint or stain the hoop before warping.

For the warp, you could use cotton, wool, or other fibers, but I like the strength of the linen, as well as its slightly toothy texture, which helps it stay in place on the wooden frame. I wrapped my warp over the inner ring of the embroidery hoop and then locked it in place with the outer ring.

For the weft yarns, I dove into my stash to find as many variations as possible in the palette I chose. This is an ideal project for using up what you have on hand,

as it's perfectly acceptable (in fact, I believe preferable) to feature yarns of different weights, textures, fibers, and fiber blends. The project shown includes 2 rounds of roving near the center. For advice on how to create the gradient effect, see Preparing a Color-Blended Weft on page 36.

I chose to create an asymmetrical design because I felt it had more energy than strict symmetry. It was also more fun to weave, as I found that the spiraling colors seemed to have a mind of their own as the weaving progressed.

It took about 9½ yards of linen thread to make the warp and about 5 ounces total of yarns for the weft.

What a Lot of Hoopla!

YOU WILL NEED

- Wooden embroidery hoop
- Tape measure
- Pencil or pen
- **Warp:** 8/2 soft-finish linen warp, 100% linen

- **Weft:** Yarn in a variety of colors, weights, textures, fibers, and fiber blends
- Long blunt-tip tapestry needle, table fork, or tapestry beater

Warping the Loom

1. Decide how many warp threads you would like your weaving to have. Note that you must have an odd number of warps so that you can weave in a spiral fashion and maintain the under/over sequence. See Go Figure (below) for advice on how to determine the warp intervals, or spacing between each warp.

2. Set the outer hoop aside. The warp is wound over only the inner hoop. With a pencil, lightly mark the warp intervals all the way around the inner loop.

Go Figure

Using a tape measure, I determined that the distance around the inner hoop (circumference) was 45". I wanted my weaving to have 21 warp threads. To get my warp interval, I divided the circumference by the number of warp threads.

$$45" \div 21 = 2.14" \text{ intervals}$$

I wasn't fastidious about making sure I got the inch fraction the same on every interval. Instead, I marked each warp interval just a tiny bit more than 2" from the previous one.

3. Use a square knot (see page 291) to tie the linen warp around the inner hoop at one of the marks. Draw the yarn straight across the hoop to a mark on the opposite side. It won't be exactly opposite; choose the mark to the right of where the first warp is tied. Wrap the warp thread over the hoop and back to the opposite side to the next mark just left of where you tied the first warp. Again wrap the warp thread over the hoop and take it back to the opposite side to the right of the first wrap. Continue in this manner, criss-crossing the warp threads at the center, until you reach the last mark.

Step 3

Don't be concerned if the threads aren't precisely matched up at the center; you will take care of that in step 4. Keep an even tension as you wrap the thread around the hoop. The tension should be consistently moderate rather than extremely tight.

4. When you get to the last warp mark, there will be no corresponding mark on the opposite side of the hoop. Take this last warp to the center, and loop it around all the other warp threads to gather them together. You can position this gathering point either at the center of your circle or off-center, for an even more asymmetrical design. Take care to catch them all; you may have to go around the center a few times to secure them (a). Secure with a half-hitch knot (see page 292), loop the warp again around the gathered warps, tie another half-hitch knot, and then take the yarn back along the only single warp and tie it to the hoop (b). Trim the end. Note that you now have 21 doubled warps. You may need to adjust them a bit to get them evenly spaced.

Step 4a

Each warp consists of two threads, one in front and one in back.

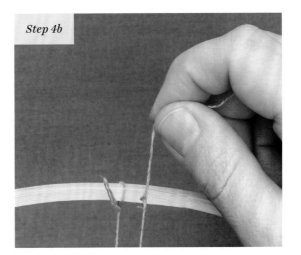

Step 4b

5. Slide the outer hoop over the inner and tighten the adjusting screw firmly to secure the warp.

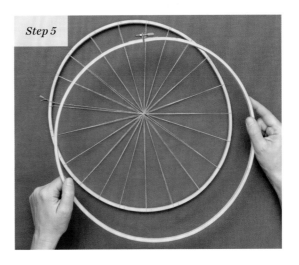

Step 5

Weaving

6. Prepare your weft yarns as described in Preparing a Color-Blended Weft (see page 36).

7. Leaving a 4" tail, use the weft to cover the center warp in this manner: draw the weft directly over the center, down into the space opposite, under the center, and then up into the space to the left of where you began. Repeat this process until you have worked around the entire center, or until the warp is entirely covered.

8. Weave about 8 rounds in plain weave (weaving under and over adjacent doubled warp threads). Continue to spiral out without stopping. As the weaving progresses, pack each round down with a tapestry needle, table fork, or tapestry beater to completely cover the warp.

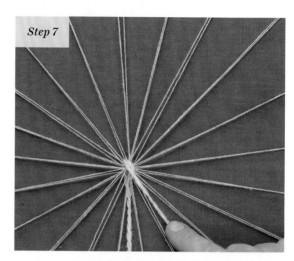

Step 7

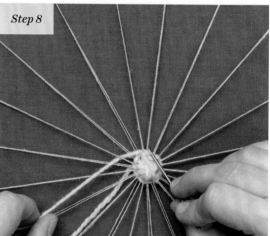

Step 8

HIDDEN ENDS

It's a bit difficult to hide ends in this weaving, so I like to tie on each new color and push the tails to the back. A sliding knot (see page 293) is useful for this purpose, since it is very secure, as well as relatively small.

The best way to weave the first couple of rounds is to work a bit away from the center, where it's easier to see which warp pairs belong together. After 2 rounds, tease the weaving down toward the center, pulling the working yarn and the tail to get close to the center and cover as much of the warp as possible.

9. When the weaving is about 2½" wide, the warps are now far enough apart that the under/over approach is not as attractive or as stable. At that point, switch to a technique similar to that used for weaving a God's eye (see page 9): Wrap the yarn around each warp and then move to the next warp. Take care not to weave too tightly, and periodically use a table fork, tapestry beater, or your fingers to pack in the weft so that no warp shows. Note that you can achieve a different effect if you wrap from front to back (a) as opposed to wrapping from back to front (b). You may occasionally want to wrap the weft yarn more than once around a warp before moving to the next one (c). This creates little yarn "beads" along the warp.

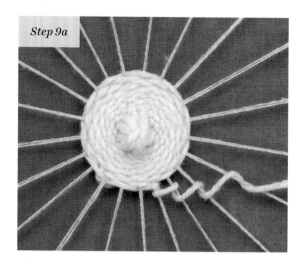

Step 9a

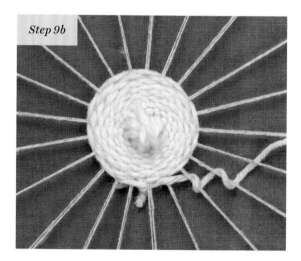

Step 9b

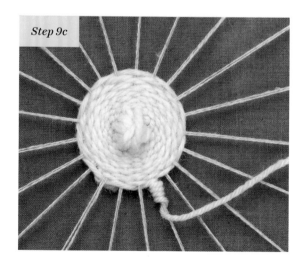

Step 9c

10. To achieve asymmetry, weave only partway around, then turn and weave back in the direction you just came from. To soften the contours of these bump outs, make each turn one warp short of the one before. For example, weave across eight warps, turn and weave across 7 (a), turn and weave across 6, and so on. When the bump is as deep as you want it (b), weave the next round all the way around.

11. Your weaving is complete when you reach the rim. Tie off the weft yarn, leaving a tail to weave in on the wrong side. Weave in all remaining tails. Use the rim to hang the piece, or make a hanger by tying a loop of strong yarn around the rim.

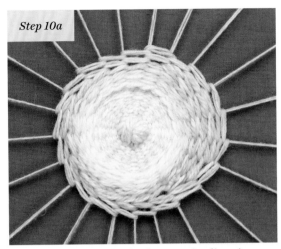

Turn and start weaving in the opposite direction.

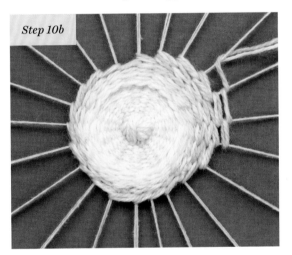

PREPARING A COLOR-BLENDED WEFT

Use the color wheel to achieve a wash of color like that shown in the project on page 28.

You probably learned about primary colors — red, blue, and yellow — at a very early age. If you arrange the primary colors in a traditional color wheel, what sits between them are secondary colors. For example, purple sits between red and blue because purple is the color you get if you mix red and blue pigments together. Similarly, blue and yellow make green, and red and yellow make orange. You can mix secondary colors with primaries in varying ratios to get more and more subtle and interesting hues. We can use this blending phenomenon in weaving without touching paints or dyes; instead, we'll let our eyes do the mixing.

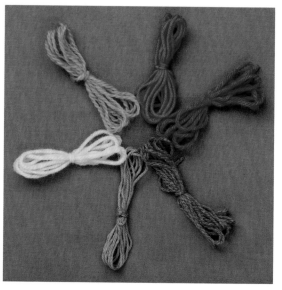

It is often quite effective to weave with colors that lie next to each other on the color wheel. Known as analogous colors, they have a natural affinity toward one another.

For the project on page 28, I chose beginning and ending colors that I particularly like, a light greenish blue for the center and purple for the outer edge. I then searched my stash for yarns in colors that lie along the color wheel between those two hues: teal, blue, blue-purple, moving finally to a darker, reddish purple. You might decide to start with yellow, then move through oranges, to reds, perhaps ending with a purple-red. Or, you could start with yellow as shown below and go the opposite direction on the wheel, through greens and end up with blue. The possibilities are endless! In addition to considering the hues (colors), pay attention to the value of the colors — that is, how dark or light they are.

Arranging My Color Sequence

For the weaving shown on the following pages, I started by making a pile of several blues, yellows, and greens from my yarn stash. I laid out several dozen yarns in a long line, with light blue at one end and pale yellow at the other end. I tried to imagine how each one related to those next to it. For the center of the weaving, I planned to use only one strand of yarn, but as the circle widened, I wanted to use fatter wefts, and so I planned to double or even triple the number of yarns in each round of the weaving. I often mixed yarn textures in the bundles.

The next step was to make yarn butterflies to help make the weaving go faster. To create a more gradual color blending, I used two or three yarns of different colors in each bundle and varied the number of strands according to the thickness of each yarn:

A. Four strands of bright yellow
B. Two strands of bright yellow and two strands of light yellow
C. Two strands of light yellow and two strands of variegated green
D. Three strands of variegated green and one strand of light yellow
E. Four strands of variegated green

By gradually increasing and decreasing the proportions of color in each package, I achieved the subtle changes I was looking for.

I was careful to keep my butterfly packages in the order I created them. Although preparing all the yarns in advance is time-consuming, it makes the weaving process pure pleasure. It goes quickly, leaving you the luxury of concentrating on the shape of the weaving you are creating, without having to stop and decide what yarn to use next. I made a few adjustments as I wove, particularly as I neared the edge of the circle and saw that if I didn't eliminate some of the prepared packages, I wouldn't have the pale blue that I wanted at the edge. It's a bit difficult to prepare exactly the right amount of yarn, but it's always better to have too much than not enough.

WINDING A BUTTERFLY

Yarn butterflies are a useful way to manage small amounts of weft.

1. Cut lengths of yarn about 3 yards long, then start with a 4"–5" tail. This will be the working end that you draw out of the center of the bundle while you're weaving.

2. Anchor the tail across your palm with your fingers, then wind the yarn figure-8 fashion around your thumb and little finger 15 to 20 times: heavier yarn limits the length of yarn that makes a manageable bundle; you can have more wraps if you're using a finer yarn.

3. Pinch the bundle at the center, and cut the yarn, leaving a 4" tail. Wrap this tail tightly around the center ("waist") of the butterfly several times, and secure it firmly with a half-hitch knot (see page 292).

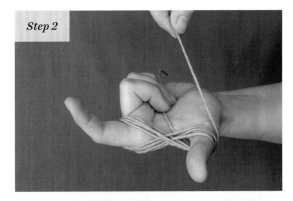

Step 2

Step 3

TAMMY KANAT

Tammy Kanat's weaving journey began in 2011, when she enrolled in the highly regarded Australian Tapestry Workshop to learn and refine the complex skill of tapestry weaving. Her 2014 exhibition, *The Spirit*, consisted of handwoven wall art, vessels, and sculptures that established her as an intuitive and original textile artist. Tammy has gained international recognition through social media for her vibrant, uplifting work and has since produced commissions for local and international clients.

She believes weaving is an ever-evolving, timeless art and an enchanting way to share the impact of her surroundings. I particularly love the way Tammy uses a variety of textures to enhance her wonderful choice of color in each of her pieces.

About her work in general, Tammy says, "There is always so much control in our lives, so it is important for me that my works are not forced or contrived. They are always a free-flowing, genuine, natural process. They come from a deep place within me, and this is a therapeutic way for me to express myself, similar to the way one may write in a personal journal or gratitude diary."

WILDERNESS, 2018

Wool, linen, silk, and other exotic fibers; copper frame
150 cm diameter

Wilderness evolved from her love of Australia's nature — the undulating landscapes and rich, earthy colors. Tammy says that "working on a larger circular scale created a sense of freedom and space similar to my experience in the Australian bush. I wanted the completed piece to be one that makes you feel calm and peaceful."

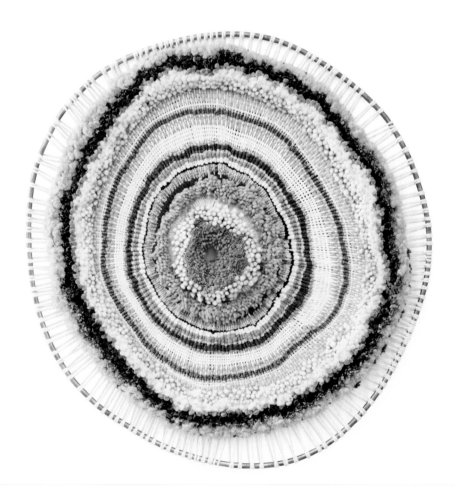

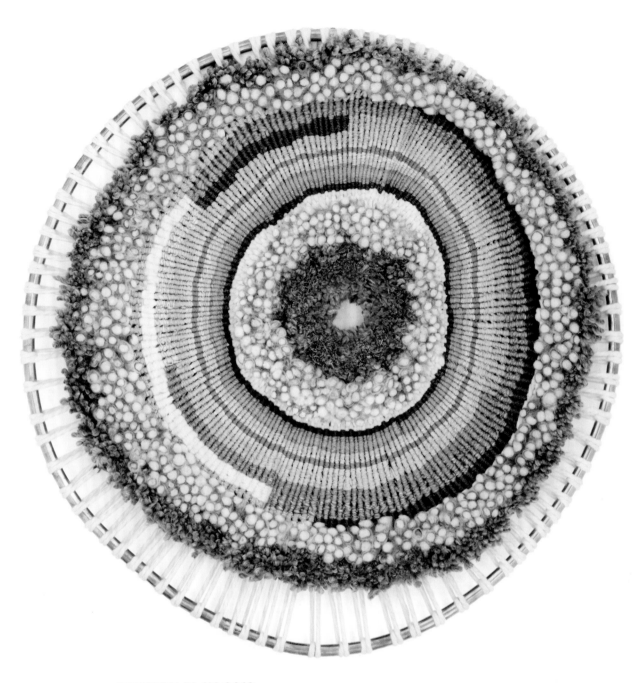

PATTERN PLAY, 2018

Wool, linen, silk, and other exotic fibers; copper frame 100 cm diameter

In this joyful piece, Tammy explains that she "was experimenting with color and shapes and how they play and interact with each other. It was a spontaneous work, and there was no plan as to which direction the piece would take. The process of creating this work was freeing, as there were no limits or rules — it just happened instinctively. I just knew I wanted the end result to be a happy piece that makes you feel good."

PIN-LOOM WEAVING

Small looms with "pins" on all four sides have been around for a long time, but the pin arrangement that Donald R. Simmons designed and patented in the 1930s is especially inventive and fun to use. This design arranges the pins in groups of three, which makes it easier to set up the layers of warp threads. His Bakelite version was marketed as a Weave-It, and the concept was re-introduced in the 1990s by Licia Conforti, who called her looms Weavettes (at right, opposite). More recently, the Schacht Spindle Company offered a newly designed version called the Zoom Loom (at left, opposite). The most common size creates a 4" square, and once you've woven a few, you may find yourself going down a rabbit hole of discovery as you invent new ways to use these squares.

To make a square on a pin loom, you wrap yarn around the pins sequentially, back and forth, to create a layer of parallel threads. You then turn the loom and wrap the yarn around a different set of pins, making a second layer of threads that are perpendicular to the first. Pivot the loom again and wrap the yarn to create a third layer of threads on top, parallel to but off-set from the bottom layer of threads. The final step is to needle-weave the yarn through the three layers using the traditional over/under weaving motion and securing all the threads in place. Once you get the rhythm of the pattern, it's satisfying to see the squares develop.

Color-Play Pillow

Making squares on a small square pin loom is great fun — and very addictive. Each one is relatively quick to make, and I find myself thinking that I will start just one more before I move on to other tasks. So when I start making squares on my small loom, I can keep going until there are piles of them waiting to be assembled. Then the real work begins: figuring out what to make with them and how to put them together in a pleasing pattern. —DJ

DESIGN NOTEBOOK

For the pillow shown opposite, I used cashmere yarn that I had purchased previously and had been waiting for the perfect project to use it on; the idea of making a pillow cover from this ultrasoft yarn seemed dreamy. Each of the six ombré skeins had slightly more than 50 yards, and I used almost all of the yarn in each skein. I wove on a 4" × 4" square Schacht Zoom Loom. The pillow form I used is 15" × 15".

Color-Play Pillow

YOU WILL NEED

- **_Warp and weft:_** light worsted weight yarn, about 325 yards total of six colors
- 4" square pin loom
- 5"-long needle for weaving
- Bent-tip tapestry needle to sew squares together
- Scissors
- Pillow form to fit finished pillow cover

1. Choose six colors of yarn, then designate them as A through F. My color scheme is monochromatic but by no means dull! These six varieties of purple represent a range of values, which is the art world's way of describing the lightness and darkness of a color. There are many ways you can choose your combination of colors. For more information about the color wheel, see page 36. If you are insecure about making color choices, your combination can be based on a painting you like or any colored design that appeals to you. This piece uses almost equal amounts of the six colors, so have fun selecting your own hues!

2. According to the instructions for your pin loom, weave the number of squares indicated below for each color, for a total of 40 squares. When weaving, do not trim the tails of the yarn. Leave them to be used for sewing the squares together.

COLOR	NUMBER OF SQUARES
A	7
B	6
C	7
D	7
E	6
F	7

3. Join each long strip starting with the square in the bottom row and moving up the column.

4. With the beginning tail in the lower left corner and the longer ending tail in the upper right corner, lay out two squares to be attached. Match the bumps and dips on the edges as if they were puzzle pieces. Note that each bump consists of four threads.

5. Thread the long ending tail of the bottom square onto a tapestry needle. Bring the needle through the two crossed threads in the lower right corner of the top square. Pull the working thread to snug up the two squares, but do not pull so tight that the fabric puckers.

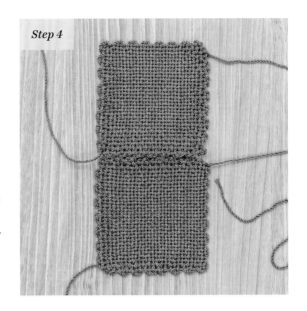

Step 4

ASSEMBLY CHART

Use this chart as your pattern for laying out the squares. You will join squares together to make four long strips of 10 squares each. Then you will join the four strips.

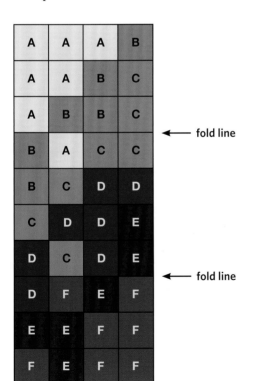

← fold line

← fold line

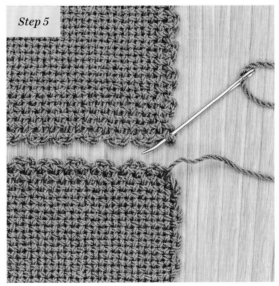

Step 5

TIPS FOR SUCCESS

- As you finish weaving each square, leave the tails loose. You will use these later to sew the squares together.

- Sew together all of the squares before wet finishing or steaming any of them.

Color-Play Pillow

6. At the first bump in the bottom square, insert the needle over the rightmost thread, under the two center (crossed) threads, and over the leftmost thread.

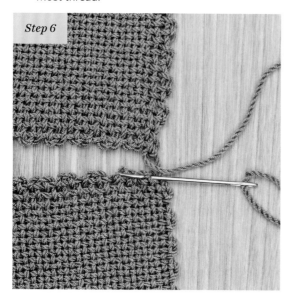

Step 6

7. Alternating bumps on the top and bottom squares, continue the stitching pattern described in step 6 to finish connecting the two squares. End by bringing the needle through the top square's left corner bump. Pull the yarn tight enough so the seam is even.

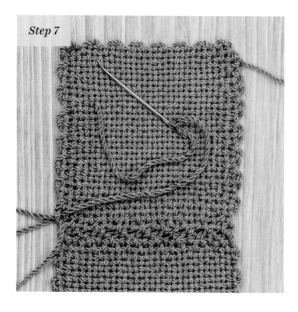

Step 7

8. Repeat steps 5–7 until you have four strips of 10 squares each. Leave all of the tails hanging out for now.

9. Using the existing tails and the alternating bumps process described in steps 6 and 7, sew together the strips following the Assembly Chart on page 45. Weave in the tails as you go.

10. Steam-iron the assembled fabric to even out any puckers. You may want to use a damp press cloth to protect your yarn. After seaming and steaming, my piece measured 15" wide × 39" long.

11. Lay out the fabric with the wrong side facing up and fold up the bottom front end just shy of three squares from the bottom. The seam between the 3rd and 4th rows will be positioned just on the front side of the pillow.

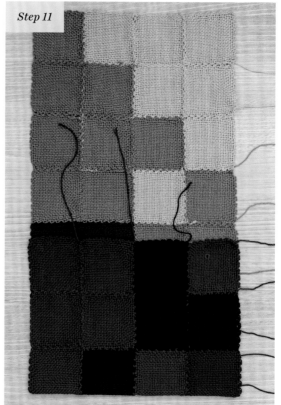

Step 11

12. The top edge of the folded-up bottom front will end four and one-fourth squares from the top of the fabric. Stitch together the sides with the hanging tails using the method described in steps 6 and 7.

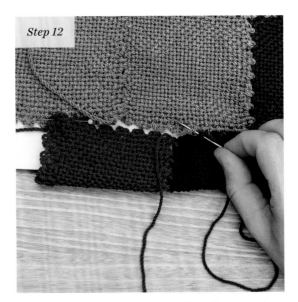

Insert a hard, flat surface inside the pillow cover so that you can stitch together the sides without catching fabric that shouldn't be in the seam.

13. Fold the top front down a little less than three squares. It will overlap the bottom panel by about one and a half squares. Stitch the side seams as described in steps 6 and 7, but do not sew the final overlapping square closed. Weave in any additional tails.

14. Carefully insert a pillow form into the pillow cover. It can be a bit difficult to get the form into the cover, but just be patient and wiggle it into place.

15. If desired, stitch the sides of the front flap to the side seams after inserting the pillow form.

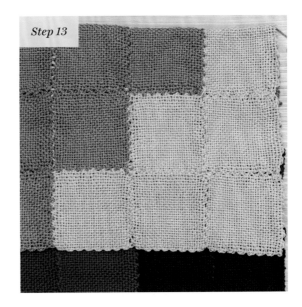

Patchwork Pin-Loom Scarf

I often like to wear a scarf simply for decoration and not for warmth. A long, narrow piece like this can be a lovely adornment that offers a variety of looks: I can wear it draped around the back of my neck and hanging down loosely, or I can wrap it around my neck a couple of times. Whatever your preferred style is, piecing together pin-loom squares is a fun way to create a fanciful neckpiece. —DJ

DESIGN NOTEBOOK

For this project, I chose a lightweight yarn that drapes nicely and is still comfortable in warm weather. I used three colors of rayon slub yarn from Yarn Barn of Kansas. For the scarf shown opposite, I used light gray, dark gray, and pink-and-gray variegated as A, B, and C, respectively. For the version shown being made on the following pages, I used green, blue, and variegated as A, B, and C, respectively, in the following quantities:

- Color A, 90 yards
- Color B, 100 yards
- Color C, 70 yards

Patchwork Pin-Loom Scarf

YOU WILL NEED

- 4" square pin loom
- 5"-long needle for weaving
- **_Warp and weft:_** sport weight rayon yarn, about 260 yards total of three colors

- Scissors
- Bent-tip tapestry needle to sew squares together

1. Following the instructions for your pin loom, weave 10 squares in color A, 12 squares in color B, and 8 squares in color C, for a total of 30 squares. Do not weave in the tails, as you can use those to seam the squares together.

2. Assemble the squares following the diagram opposite. I found it easiest to sew the horizontal pairs together and then sew the pairs together to form the long scarf.

3. To attach the squares on this project, I chose a looser stitch than for the pillow in the previous project. I wanted the area between each square to be slightly open, giving a lacy look to the scarf, so I used a simple whipstitch seam (see page 302).

4. Line up the two squares next to each other with the bumps and indentations interlocking. Thread the long tail onto your tapestry needle.

5. With your needle, go into the bump on the square to the right and then into the indentation on the square on the left. Do not pull the thread too tight as you want a loose join for these seams.

6. Continue up the seam with your needle going from right to left, catching the bump on one side and the indentation on the other side.

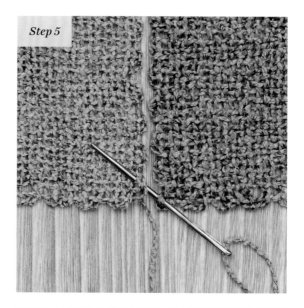

Step 5

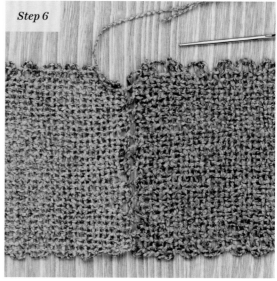

Step 6

7. After the squares are sewn together in pairs, begin at one end and whipstitch the pairs together. Offset each square 1" from the square above.

8. Weave in all tails and steam-press using a press cloth.

Step 7

ASSEMBLY DIAGRAM

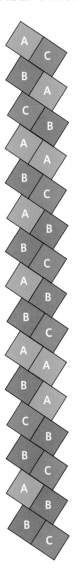

DEB ESSEN

Deb Essen was nine years old when she saw a handweaver at work for the first time. She decided that weaving was magic, and she has been studying that magic combination of color and structure for more than 25 years.

Now Deb lives, works, and weaves in western Montana. She runs a business selling kits for a wide range of weavers: some kits introduce new weavers to simple pin looms; others encourage weavers to stretch themselves with new techniques and looms. When Schacht Spindle Company first asked Deb to create a kit, she agreed, but decided a scarf, runner, or shawl — while easy — also felt uninspired. As she was weaving a green square on her pin loom, she thought, "Can I make a turtle?" The first one looked like an armadillo, but after a little trial and error, her Swatch Critters were born.

After a couple of years of working with small critters like the unicorn (bottom right) and fiber fairy, she started playing with making bigger animals. The macaw (left) and bison (top right) both take between 50 and 70 squares and have become Deb's booth mascots at events, showing off what's possible using just 4" squares. She now offers kits for a teddy bear, dog, and cat big enough to hug and snuggle.

Deb travels and teaches all over the country, helping others to develop the creativity and skill to create handwoven heirlooms. In 2004, the Handweavers Guild of America awarded her the Certificate of Excellence in Handweaving, Level I. She has been recognized by the Montana Arts Council and writes feature articles for national weaving magazines.

SCOBY THE SCARLET MACAW, 2016
Hand-painted wool yarns, metal hoop, and polyester stuffing; 27" × 5" × 4"

Deb Essen's kit designs range from whimsical critters to scarves, table runners, and napkins. These imaginative and fun kits spark ideas about what weavers can make with the squares woven on small pin looms.

TATONKA THE BISON, 2016
Hand-painted wool yarns, polyester stuffing; 19" × 12" × 6"

EUREKA THE UNICORN, 2015
Hand-painted wool yarns, polyester stuffing, metallic thread, and pipe cleaner; 8" × 8" × 2"

Touch of Glass Pendant (page 61)

Free-Form Pendants

After weaving with my purchased pin looms, I wondered how I could make different shapes by constructing my own loom out of . . . pins! Having a small piece of weaving peeking out from under the collar of my shirt makes me happy, and crafting my own loom lets me decide what shape I want my pendant to be. —DJ

DESIGN NOTEBOOK

For my design, I chose simple trapezoids with a curved bottom slightly wider than the top. You can attach your pendant to any kind of metal or cord choker — or to a Viking knitted chain (see page 193) or 16-Cord Kumihimo Braid (see page 25)!

Choose your weft yarn based on what kind of look you want for your finished pendant. Anything from lace weight yarn to 3/2 pearl cotton works nicely for this project.

Free-Form Pendants

YOU WILL NEED

- Pencil or pen
- Graph paper
- Two 8" × 10" pieces of mat board ⅛" thick
- Painter's tape
- 9 straight pins
- *Warp:* size 8 or 10 pearl cotton or mercerized crochet cotton, 2 yards
- *Weft:* yarn, about 12 yards (The length will vary depending on how thick your weft yarn is.)

- 5"-long tapestry needle for weaving
- Embroidery needle
- Three 6/0 Czech glass beads or similar
- Sewing needle and thread to match the weft yarn
- Choker necklace

---

1. Draw your full-scale design on graph paper.

2. Tape two thicknesses of mat board together, then tape the graph paper with your design onto the board.

3. With straight pins, mark where the eight warp threads will begin and end. Angle the pins away from where the warp threads will go.

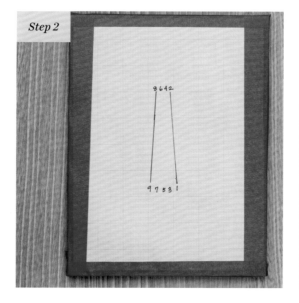

Step 2

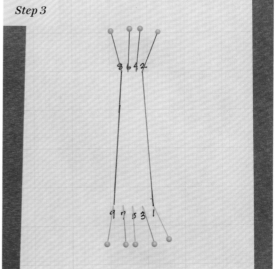

Step 3

4. Start creating the warp by tying the cotton thread onto the pin in the lower right corner, leaving a 4" tail (a). Bring the cotton upward and loop it over the pin in the upper right corner, then take the cotton down to the lower pin that is second from the right (b). Loop the thread around the bottom of that pin, then bring the thread upward, repeating this pattern until you reach the lower left pin. Tie off the warp thread on the lower left pin (c), leaving a 4" tail.

5. Cut a piece of the weft yarn that is 1½–2 yards long, and thread it onto the 5"-long tapestry needle.

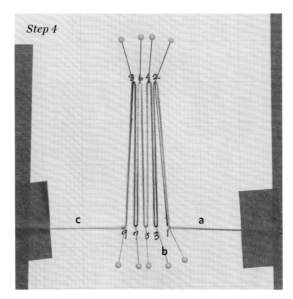

Step 4

To help keep the thread taut while winding on and when tying off, use painter's tape to secure the tails.

TIPS FOR SUCCESS

- Use painter's tape to secure loose thread tails to the mat board so they do not get in your way. Painter's tape works well for securing the ends because it comes off easily when you are finished with the project and does not leave a sticky residue.

- As you put in each row of weft, use the tip of the needle to pull the yarn snug up to the outside warp thread. Insert the needle tip at the inside edge of the outside warp thread, and pull the yarn so it passes around the edge of the warp leaving no slack loop, but also not pulling the warp thread in toward the center. You'll soon get the feel of how to tug it "just right" so the edges are smooth and even.

- Use the side of the tapestry needle to push each row of weft into place as you weave.

- If you are using a variegated yarn, try to match up the color when adding additional weft.

6. Starting at the top pins, weave the weft as follows: with the tapestry needle, go under the first warp thread, over the next warp thread, under the next, and so forth across all eight warp threads.

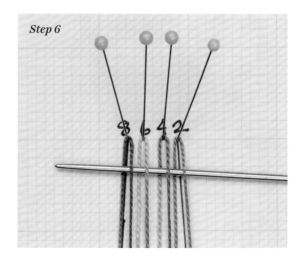

Step 6

7. When working the next row of weft, insert the tapestry needle under and over the appropriate warp threads, then push the needle up to pack the previous row firmly into place. The weft in this row will go under the threads that it traveled over in the first row, and over the threads it went under. You will always work opposite of the pattern in the previous row. Snug up the edge loops of the weft so they are even with the side of the piece. After finishing each row of weft, use your fingers or the weaving needle to push the weft in place more densely.

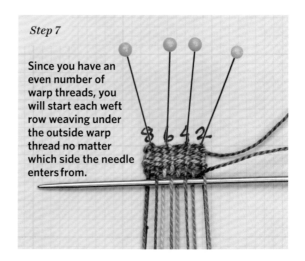

Step 7

Since you have an even number of warp threads, you will start each weft row weaving under the outside warp thread no matter which side the needle enters from.

8. When you run out of weft yarn, leave a 4"–5" tail hanging from the side of the piece to weave in later. Then begin weaving from the opposite side, working the opposite over/under pattern that you established with your first weft yarn. Leave the tail hanging from that side to be woven in later. Now each weft row will start by weaving over the outside warp thread no matter which side the needle enters from.

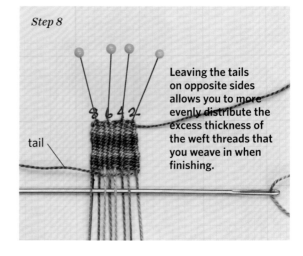

Step 8

tail

Leaving the tails on opposite sides allows you to more evenly distribute the excess thickness of the weft threads that you weave in when finishing.

9. As you get toward the bottom of the piece, it will become difficult to get the needle through the warp threads. Push the weft up toward the already woven area as tightly as it will go. Adjust the pins holding the bottom of the warp threads so they are angled toward the top of the mat board; this allows a little more room to get the tapestry needle through.

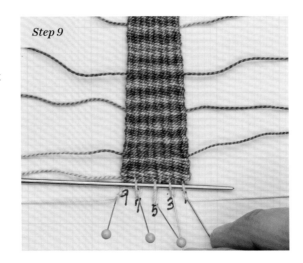

Step 9

10. To create the shaped edge along the bottom of the pendant, stop working the weft through all eight warp threads when the piece measures ⅜" less than you want the total length of the pendant. Instead, work the weft through the central six warp threads for several rows. For the final 2 or 3 rows, work the weft through only the two center warp threads. Leave the weft tail hanging from the center when you have finished weaving.

11. Remove the pins and take the piece off the mat board.

12. Using an embroidery needle, weave the loose weft tails into the back of the piece. Follow the path of the warp thread as you weave in tails to make them less noticeable.

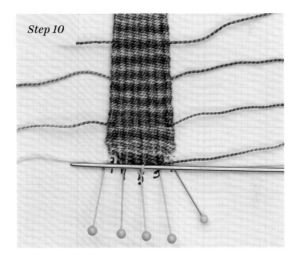

Step 10

Free-Form Pendants

13. Thread a bead onto the weft tail that is hanging from the center bottom. Slide the bead up to the bottom edge of the weaving, and bury the tail in the fabric along the warp threads. Repeat, adding beads on each of the two warp tails at the outside edges.

14. Fold down the top ¾" to make a casing for the choker ring. Using the sewing thread and tiny stitches, hand-stitch across the edge.

15. Slide the pendant onto the choker necklace or chain.

Step 13

Step 14

TOUCH OF GLASS PENDANT

This version of the pendant uses the same yarn for both warp and weft — plus beads worked into the warp throughout the project. (See page 55 for a photo of a finished version.) The length will vary depending on how thick your weft yarn is.

You will need the same materials list on page 56 except for about 15 yards of lace weight yarn for the warp and weft and 18 small beads. Depending on the look you want, you can use anything from seed beads to 6/0 Czech glass beads. In addition, a dental floss threader will be helpful as you thread the beads onto the yarn.

Follow the instructions starting on page 56 with the following additions:

1. On the graph paper design, mark where to place the beads in the pendant.

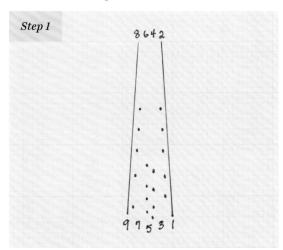

Step 1

This version has five beads on the warp threads adjacent to the selvage warp threads and four beads on each of the two center warp threads.

2. Slip four or five beads onto the straight end of the dental floss threader. Place the end of the warp thread through the loop of the dental floss threader, leaving a 5"–6" tail. Slip the beads over the dental floss loop and onto the working thread, then pull the tail out of the loop. Repeat

this whole process until all 18 beads are threaded onto the warp. As you stretch the warp thread around the straight pins, place the beads in the appropriate section of the warp as marked on the graph paper.

3. Move the beads down to the bottom of the warp until you are weaving the row where they will be inserted.

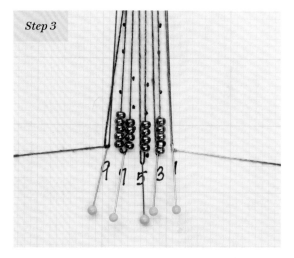

Step 3

4. As each bead is required, slide it into place and continue weaving.

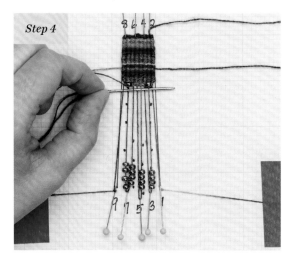

Step 4

FRAMED!

If you're one of the many people who, as a child, made a pot holder from strips or loops of fabric on a small square loom, then you've used a frame loom. Weaving with a pot holder loom is a time-honored tradition, and whether it was at school or camp, making a pot holder on a frame loom is how many of us were introduced to weaving.

A frame loom is exactly what its name implies: a simple, usually four-sided frame (even a picture frame will work) with or without nails or pegs along the sides to wind the warp around. For directions on how to make your own frame loom, see page 285.

Biased Hemp Washcloth

One thing I enjoy about knitting is that the resulting fabric is stretchy and can be pulled in different directions. Generally woven fabric is firmer and doesn't have the same elasticity. When the weaving is done on a diagonal, however, it makes a textile that returns to its original shape after being stretched. It's the perfect structure for a washcloth that will get lots of hard use. —DJ

DESIGN NOTEBOOK

I wanted to make a functional washcloth that, when combined with handmade soap, could be part of a gift. Initially I used soft light-weight yarn that made a delightful lace-like square, which perhaps would be perfect if fashioning a shawl, but for a washcloth I needed something more sturdy. I tested several other yarns, and it was great fun seeing how the results differed depending on the fibers and sizes of yarn. I decided to use hardworking yarns like linen, cotton, and hemp that would stand up to the hard wear and repeated washing and drying required for a washcloth. To make a firmer wash-cloth, try doubling the yarn as I did for the finished versions shown opposite and on page 69. (Single strands of yarn draw in more and make a smaller finished cloth. To make the how-to photos clearer, though, only one strand was used.)

You have several options for the loom for this project: Use a frame loom with nails or pegs evenly spaced around all four sides, or as I did, use a Harrisville Designs pot holder loom and add an alligator clip in each corner as the corner "pegs." You can also make your own loom from a square box by attaching alligator clips around all four sides of the top edge. The pegs should be spaced at regular intervals around the edge. The size of those intervals depends on the yarn you'll use to weave: place four or five pegs per inch if you're using worsted weight yarn; space the pegs farther apart if you're using thicker yarn or a double strand of yarn.

Biased Hemp Washcloth

YOU WILL NEED

- Frame loom with pegs around all sides
- 4 alligator clips, one for each corner of the pot holder loom
- ***Warp and weft:*** worsted weight yarn, 80–160 yards (depending on whether you use a single or double strand)
- Crochet hook or long needle with hook on one end (This needs to be the length of your loom from one corner to the opposite corner. You can create this hook from a wire hanger.)
- Scissors
- Long blunt-tip tapestry needle

TIP FOR SUCCESS

- When using two or more strands held together, make sure to keep even tension on both strands when pulling the yarn across the frame and around the pegs.

- After you have woven more than 50 percent of the piece, it may get difficult to insert the crochet hook through the entire width of the piece. Try inserting the hook starting about halfway across, making sure to keep on track with the over/under pattern. Then reinsert the hook at the right side and finish that row.

1. If using a loom that does not have corner pegs, place an alligator clip at each corner. Place the loom on your lap with one corner facing you. Make a slip knot (see page 293) around the bottom corner peg. Bring the yarn from that peg up to the opposite top corner peg.

2. Wind the yarn clockwise around that top corner peg, from left to right.

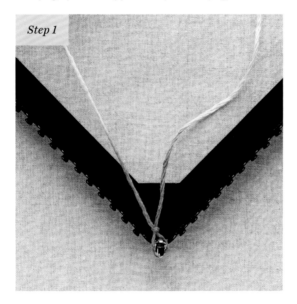

Step 1

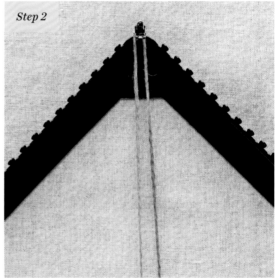

Step 2

3. Bring the yarn down to the first peg on the right of the bottom corner peg. Wind the yarn around that peg from right to left, then over to the first bottom peg left of the corner peg. Go around that peg from right to left.

4. Bring the yarn up to the top corner and wind it clockwise around the first open peg to the left of the corner peg. Then bring the yarn down on the right side of the peg about 1".

5. With the long crochet hook, go over the right strand of yarn coming from the top corner, under the middle strand, and grab the 1" section of your working yarn and pull it to the right through the vertical strands.

6. Hook the working yarn over the first open peg to the right of the top corner peg.

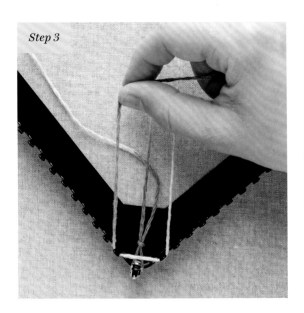

Step 3

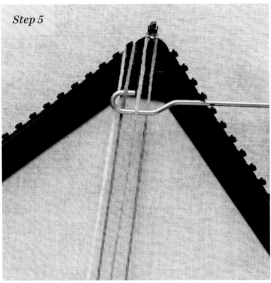

Step 5

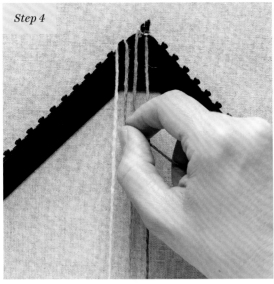

Step 4

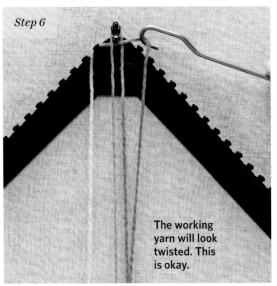

Step 6

The working yarn will look twisted. This is okay.

Biased Hemp Washcloth

7. Stretch the working yarn down from that peg to the first open peg on the right of the bottom corner. Wind the working yarn around that peg from right to left, then pull the yarn across the bottom to the left and hook it over the first open peg to the left of the bottom starting corner. Since you are pulling the top of the strand across the threads at the top of the loom, the bottom part of the strand will automatically weave through the vertical threads as you pull the loop to the right side. The bottom of the loop becomes the horizontal thread that goes across the bottom of the loom as seen in photo 9b.

8. After each pass, snug the most recent additional row into place with your fingers.

9. Continue following the pattern described in steps 4–7: winding around the next peg, weaving the crochet hook through at the top by entering over the first vertical thread, under the next, over, then under all the way across, grabbing the

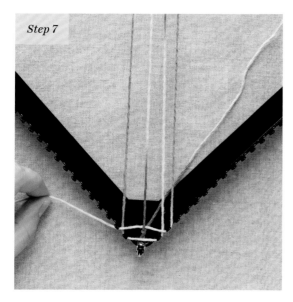

Step 7

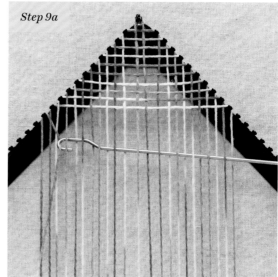

Step 9a

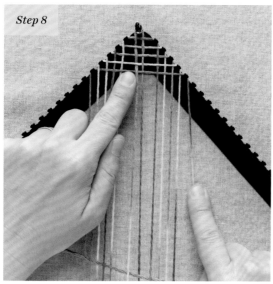

Step 8

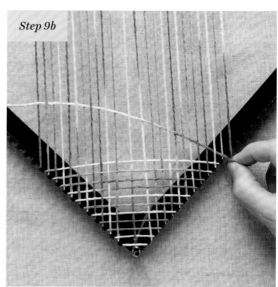

Step 9b

working yarn and pulling it through (a). Bring the yarn down the right side and around the next open peg at the bottom (b). Pull yarn from the left to adjust tension, and wind around the first open peg on the left. Repeat until all pegs are wrapped and the square is made.

10. After the final pass, cut a long tail and use the long tapestry needle to weave the tail back between the last two (middle) threads.

11. Slip the edges off the pegs.

12. Use the tapestry needle to weave in the tails. If there are any loops that are not caught properly, secure them with a yarn tail.

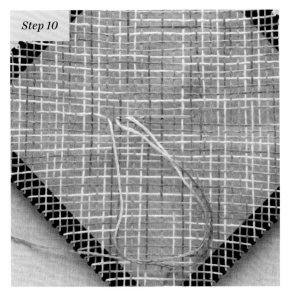

Step 10

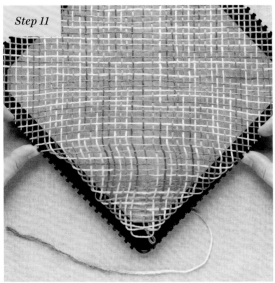

Step 11

Pretty Plain-Weave Bracelet
(page 72)

Woven Wristlets

Most jewelry is made from metal or ceramic materials. But as a weaver, I enjoy decorative pieces made from fibers. It's especially satisfying when I can weave something to wear as jewelry.

The company Purl & Loop makes weaving tools with helpful uses such as determining the correct weaving density for your projects and making sure the color combinations you see in your mind will work together in reality. The following projects use a small Purl & Loop loom that's designed to make bracelets. —DJ

Beaded Gap Wristlet (page 76)

Pretty Plain-Weave Bracelet

This bracelet is a wonderful introduction to needle weaving. I used variegated yarn for both my warp and weft. The little loom makes it easy to maintain the shape of the bracelet, and the project is small enough to tote around and work on as you have a chance. I find it delightful to be able to use the needle to both carry the weft thread through the warp and to pack in the weft threads. This project is a fabulous way to use up bits of yarn, and it makes a great gift!

DESIGN NOTEBOOK

- The Purl & Loop loom comes with a tapestry needle for inserting the weft and a comb to pack in the weft, but I found that a 3" tapestry needle worked for both purposes.

- For jewelry findings, I used two 1" flat crimp jewelry closures on each end of the bracelet, two ⅜" jump rings, and one small lobster claw fastener. Note that the jewelry findings you use to open and close the bracelet will take up some space. The amount of space will vary based on what findings you plan to use, so it is best to make that decision before beginning the project so you get a proper fit.

YOU WILL NEED

- Tape measure
- Painter's tape
- **Warp and weft:** 3/2 pearl cotton, 100% cotton, or size 3 crochet cotton, about 11 yards for a 7" bracelet
- Purl & Loop Stash Blaster Birch Bracelet Loom in 10 ends per inch
- Scissors
- Long blunt-tip tapestry needle
- 2 pairs of small round-nose or needle-nose pliers to attach jewelry findings
- Jewelry findings

1. Measure your wrist to determine how long you want your finished bracelet to be.

Step 1

The opening from the findings I chose was 1". Therefore, when figuring how long to weave my piece, I subtracted 1" from the total length I needed the bracelet to be.

2. Tape the tail end of the warp yarn to the back of the loom and place the working end through the fifth slot from one side at the top of the loom.

   Note: There are 24 slots on the loom; each slot alternates with a prong. You will use 15 slots for this project, so there will be 5 empty slots on one side of the warp threads and 4 empty slots on the other side of the warp threads.

3. Take the warp thread down to the bottom of the loom, through the matching bottom slot and around the prong, and back to the front of the loom. Bring the working thread up to the top of the loom, through the next open slot and around the prong.

4. Repeat step 3 until there are a total of 16 warp threads on the loom. All warp threads will be on the front side of the loom.

5. Leaving about a 6" tail, cut the warp thread. Tape the tail to the back of the loom.

6. Thread the tapestry needle with a 24"–30" length of the weft yarn.

7. Weave the weft yarn by going over the first warp thread, under the next, over the next, and so on until you have reached the opposite side. Leave a 5"–6" tail at the beginning of the first row of weaving.

8. After weaving each row and before removing the needle from between the warp threads, use the needle to push the weft threads down to the bottom of the loom. (Alternatively, you can push the weft into place using the comb that comes with the loom.)

9. Continue weaving, repeating the same over/under pattern that you established in step 7, until you've reached the desired length.

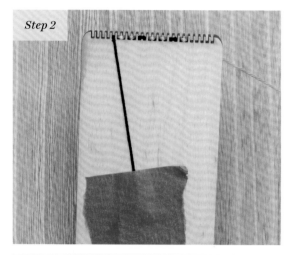
Step 2

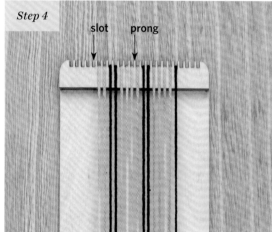
Step 4
slot   prong

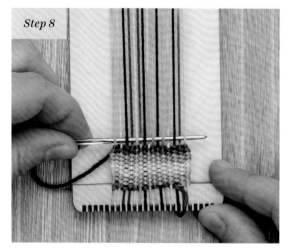
Step 8

On each row, go *over* the threads you went *under* in the previous row and *under* the threads you went *over*.

Pretty Plain-Weave Bracelet

ADDING NEW WEFT YARN

When you run out of weft yarn on the needle, leave a 5"–6" tail hanging out the side of the weaving. Begin weaving on the opposite side with a new length of weft yarn, leaving a 5"–6" tail. Remember to go *over* the threads you went *under* in the previous row, making sure you go *under* the first edge thread at the beginning of each row. Since there are an uneven number of warp threads, you can always start a weft row by going *over* the first warp thread and end that row going *under* the last warp thread, no matter which side you enter from.

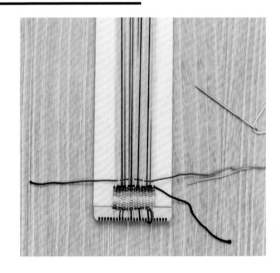

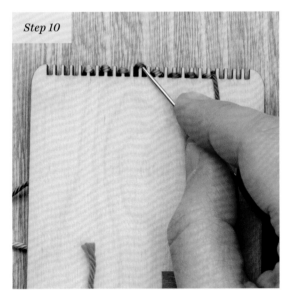

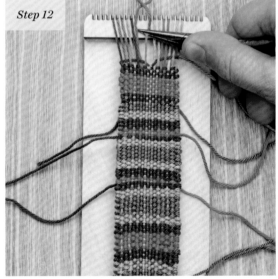

10. When you finish weaving, turn the loom over and slip the middle warp thread off the prong on both ends of the loom.

11. Carefully pull the loop on one end to tighten the loop on the opposite end so it is even with the edge of the weaving.

12. Working outward from the center warp thread and alternating end to end, remove the loop from the prongs at both ends of the loom. Tighten the loops on the opposite ends as described in step 11. This will move the excess warp thread to the outside edges of the project.

13. Cut the long warp tails to measure 5"–6".

14. Using the tapestry needle, weave all the tails from both the warp and weft into the back of the bracelet. Trim excess thread.

15. Using pliers, crimp the flat closures onto the ends of the bracelet strip.

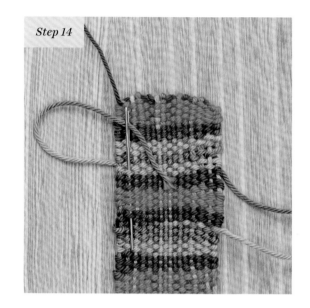

16. Attach a jump ring to each crimp closure.

17. Attach the lobster claw to one jump ring.

To open a jump ring, hold one side with pliers and push the other side in the opposite direction. Do not pull the opposite sides apart. Slip the open jump ring onto the circle on the crimp closure. Close the jump ring by pushing the two sides toward each other.

Beaded Gap Wristlet

This bracelet is also an easy take-along project, but the beads add a bit of glamour and shine. (See page 71 for a photo of a finished version.) Try using beads of different sizes and shapes to vary the results. Alter the colors to give your bracelets individual appeal!

DESIGN NOTEBOOK

I used a 3.2 mm magnetic tube clasp. Note that some space in the length will be taken up by the clasp. This amount of space will vary based on what size clasp you plan to use, so it is best to make that decision *before* beginning the project so you get a proper fit.

YOU WILL NEED

- Tape measure
- Painter's tape
- **Warp:** 10/2 cotton, 100% cotton, about 5 yards
- Purl & Loop Stash Blaster Birch Bracelet Loom in 10 ends per inch
- 5 size 2/0 Czech glass E beads
- 6 size 6/0 Czech glass E beads
- Dental floss threader
- Pencil
- Waste yarn
- Scissors
- Two 3" tapestry needles
- **Weft:** 3/2 cotton, in same color as warp, about 15 yards
- C-Lon beading thread, 24"
- Sewing needle
- Wax paper
- Fiber glue
- Magnetic tube clasp
- Toothpick
- Epoxy glue

1. Measure your wrist to determine how long you want your finished bracelet to be.

2. Tape one end of the warp thread to the back of the loom near the center. Leaving the first seven slots on the loom empty, wrap the working end of the warp thread through the eighth slot on the top, going from back to front. It doesn't matter if you wrap the warp from right to left or from left to right.

   Note: There are 24 slots on the loom. You will use 9 for this project, so there will be 7 empty slots on one side of the warp threads and 8 empty slots on the other side of the warp.

3. Take the warp thread down to the bottom of the loom, through the eighth slot on the bottom and up the back of the loom and into the next top slot. You'll be wrapping the warp thread around both sides of the loom.

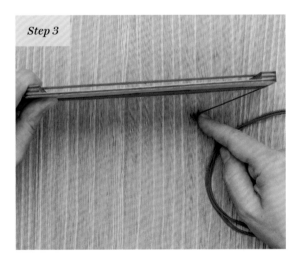
Step 3

4. After the first four slots are filled, slip the beads onto the warp. Put the beads on a non-slippery surface, thread the end of the warp thread through the opening in the dental floss threader, leaving a short tail. Using the other end of the threader, pick up the beads in the order you want them on the bracelet. Slide the beads down the threader and over the warp thread.

5. Once all the beads are on the warp thread, slide them down the warp length until they are in position on the loom. They will be centered on the front of the loom on the fifth (center) warp thread.

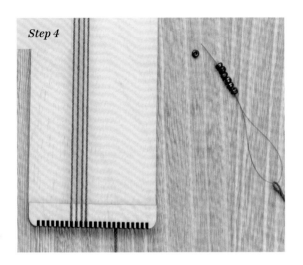

Step 4

6. Continue wrapping the warp around the loom until you have a total of nine warp threads on the front. The beads will rest on the center thread as the construction of this loom keeps them from moving off that thread.

7. Trim the warp tail to about 5". Pull it tight and tape it to the center back of the loom.

8. Place a piece of painter's tape on the face of the loom parallel to the warp threads. Measure and mark where you will start and stop weaving and where you will center the beads. To center your beads along the warp, measure how much height your beads take up. Subtract that figure from the total woven length of your bracelet. Divide that figure by 2. This is the length you will weave all the way across the weft before and after working in the beads.

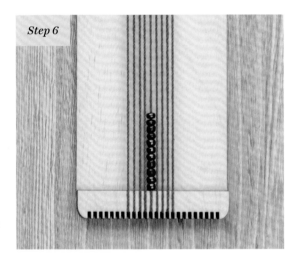

Step 6

Go Figure

The total woven length of my bracelet is 5½". My beads take up 1¼", so in order to center them, I'll weave 2⅛" all the way across the piece, then weave for 1¼" with the beads in the center, then weave for a final 2⅛".

5½" bracelet length − 1¼" beads = 4¼"

4¼" ÷ 2 = 2⅛" to weave above and below the beads

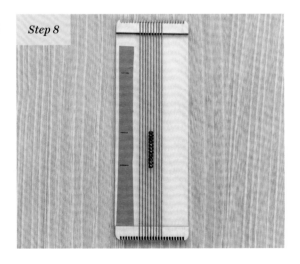

Step 8

9. Begin weaving with some waste yarn to create a solid base to weave against. End the waste yarn weaving at the marker for the beginning of the project.

10. Thread a tapestry needle with the 3/2 cotton and weave across the warp, leaving a 10" tail.

11. Weave for 2⅛" (or the length you've determined for this section on your bracelet), pushing the weft very close together, at 50 ends per inch. Use the long needle to push the weft into place and pack it down after each row.

12. After weaving the appropriate beginning length, slide the beads into place, pressing them to the edge of the woven area.

13. Weave the four warp threads on one side of the beads with the existing weft thread. Thread the second tapestry needle with a new length of weft thread, and use that to weave the four warp threads on the other side of the beads. Do not weave the center warp thread the beads are on.

14. Continue weaving up the sides of the split in this manner until you reach the top of the beads.

15. Leave a weft tail hanging out from one side and use the other weft thread to begin weaving all the way across again.

ALTERNATIVE LOOM

Make your own loom from mat board and straight pins like in the Free-Form Pendants (page 55). This is a flexible (and inexpensive) option, but your homemade loom will not be as sturdy as the Purl & Loop version.

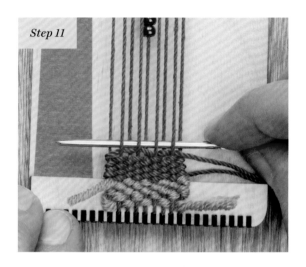

Step 11

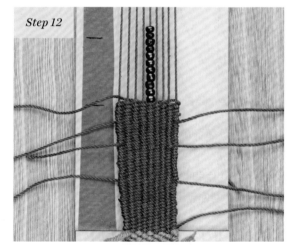

Step 12

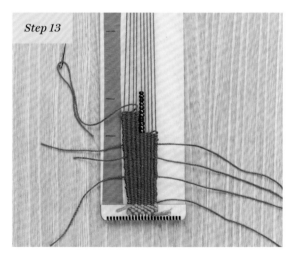

Step 13

- When you run out of thread on the needle, leave a 5"–6" tail hanging out the side of the weaving. Begin weaving on the opposite side, again leaving a 5"–6" tail.

- Prevent the edges of your bracelet from pulling in by pressing the tapestry needle downward as shown at right, while adjusting the tension of the weft thread.

- Wrap very tightly when making the bundles that go into the clasps.

- Use the adhesives in a well-ventilated area.

16. Continue weaving across the full width of the bracelet for the final 2⅛" (or designated length for your bracelet).

17. Cut the warp threads in the center of the back of the loom. Weave in the weft tails.

Adding the Clasp

18. Fold in the end edges, angling them slightly to form a triangle that tapers from the body of the bracelet to the center of the warp threads.

19. With the C-Lon thread and the sewing needle, stitch the tapered edges down and tightly wrap the warp threads into a very small round bundle coming out of the center of the bracelet width.

20. Working over a protective surface such as wax paper, add a few drops of fiber glue on the bundle of threads.

21. Allow bundles to dry and then trim them shorter than the tube clasp.

22. Using a toothpick, apply epoxy on the bundles according to package directions. Stuff the bundles into the tube clasps. Allow to dry as directed.

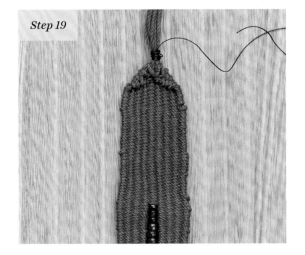

Step 19

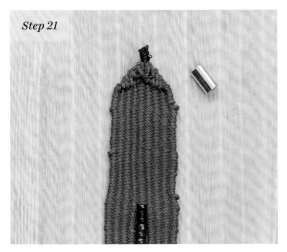

Step 21

Twined Parachute-Cord Mat

Parachute cord (or paracord) was first used in the military for a variety of practical purposes, including suspension lines for parachutes. In the years since World War II, the versatility of this slim nylon rope has made it popular with civilians; it is now commonly used in camping and other outdoor activities, as well as for crafting bracelets, pet leashes, and belts. Its impressive strength comes from its design, which is a braided sheath made up of tightly woven strands surrounding an inner core of nylon filaments. Because of its sturdiness, resistance to mold and mildew, and quick-drying properties, paracord is an ideal material for weaving a doormat.

Once you understand the twining process and master the trick of fusing one length of paracord to another (which is where the small lighter comes into the picture) this project goes quickly. —GS

DESIGN NOTEBOOK

This mat features a weaving technique called twining, which is often used as a heading (or reinforced edge) for tapestries and rugs. Instead of twining only to provide a firm edge to a weaving, here I used it to weave the entire mat. To ensure that the fabric would be sturdy enough to use as a doormat, I used paracord for both the warp and weft.

I used about 250 feet each of two different paracord colors (moss and cream). Although I twined the two colors around each other in each row to create this design, you can also twine the entire mat in one color, or alternate rows for a different striped pattern. I wove from the top down, but you could also weave from the bottom up.

Twined Parachute-Cord Mat

YOU WILL NEED

- Frame loom 32" square (see page 285)
- 550 paracord, about 500 feet total
- Scissors
- Wooden slat about 34" long
- Multipurpose lighter
- Needle-nose pliers
- Bent-tip tapestry needle

FINISHED MEASUREMENTS

15" wide × 23" long

TIPS FOR SUCCESS

- Pull up on the working end of the twining as you make each twist to tighten and smooth the twist. Every few twists, insert your fingers between two warps to help maintain the spacing and to snug the row up against the row above, just as you would snug in yarn in other types of weaving. (You can also use a tool such as a tapestry bobbin for this purpose.)

- Measure, measure, measure. Measure the mat's width and length after completing each row, one or two twists after you turn. The paracord's flexibility and consistency make it relatively easy to maintain straight rows and even edges. In spite of that, it's important to frequently measure the width of the mat as you weave. Measure the length at both the left and right sides of the mat to ensure that your rows stay straight from one side to the other. It's nearly impossible to correct uneven edges or rows once you've gone a row or two beyond, but not at all difficult to adjust inconsistencies if you catch them soon enough.

- Determine a good working length of paracord. When you run out of cord, cut new lengths of about 3 yards. This should allow you to weave about 4 rows. You can work with shorter or longer lengths of cord, but I find that anything longer is awkward to work with; shorter lengths mean that you have to make more joins. Try to stagger the joins on the two working weft ends so that they are at least a warp or two apart.

Warping the Loom

1. To center your mat on your frame and determine where to tie the first warp, measure the width of the frame opening and subtract the width you want for your finished mat. Divide the difference by 2. See Go Figure below for an example of how to set up your warp. (You do not need to measure the paracord before winding on the warp.)

Go Figure

I wanted my mat to be 15" wide, so I subtracted that figure from the width of the frame opening, 29", then divided that by 2.

29" loom opening **− 15"** mat width =

14" ÷ 2 = 7"

Use a double half-hitch knot (see page 292) to tie the paracord securely around the top of the frame 7" from the side of the frame.

2. Take the cord to the opposite side of the frame and wrap it around the frame bottom from front to back, 7" from the inside edge. Take the cord up to the top and again wrap it around the frame from front to back. Continue in this manner until you have 29 warp threads (counting threads on the front and back of the loom individually), spaced about 1" apart; the last warp thread should be 7" from the inside edge on the far side from where you started. Cut the cord, leaving a 10" tail. Use a double half-hitch knot to temporarily tie the tail to the frame.

3. Return to the first warp and, working one by one across the warp and following the same path you used when you wound it on, pull each warp to tighten it. Do this at least one more time across the entire warp. The goal is to have all the warps at about the same tension as well as fairly taut. (If you had to join on extra cord, you may have to adjust the location of the knot in order to keep it outside of the weaving area.) Retie the double half-hitch knot when you're satisfied that the warp is consistent.

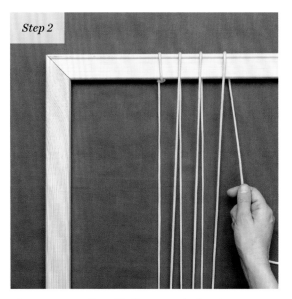

Step 2

If you run out of cord before completing the warp, tie on a new length with an overhand knot (see page 291). Be sure to tie this knot at the top or bottom frame edge, not in the weaving area.

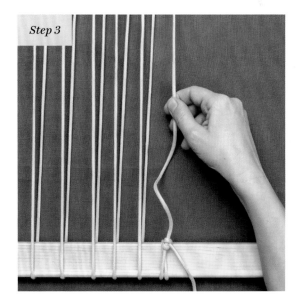

Step 3

Twined Parachute-Cord Mat

4. Before you begin weaving the weft, insert the wooden slat. This will help you reserve warp length at the top of the mat where you can weave in the ends when the mat is complete. Weave the slat over the warps that lie on top of the frame and under the warps that lie on the bottom of the frame. This draws the warps together so that they lie flat across the width of the mat, creating a sett of about 2 ends per inch. With the slat ends lying on top of the side edges of the frame, push the slat up to the top of the frame. This will provide a firm edge against which to push up the first few rows of twining.

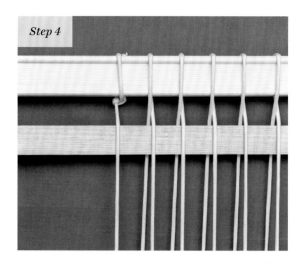

Twining

5. Cut one 3-yard piece of paracord of each color and tie the ends together in an overhand knot. Center the knot under the first warp on the left. Take the end that is on top (white) and lay it over the end that is on the bottom (green) and then under the second warp. Note that you are creating a twist between the first and second warps.

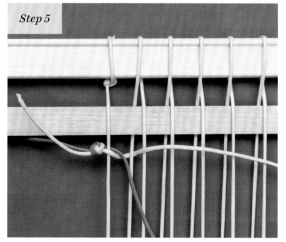

6. Lay the green weft over the next warp over the white weft, and under the next warp.

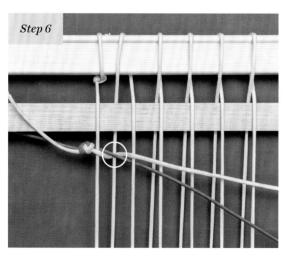

7. Lay the white weft over the next warp, over the green weft, and under the next warp.

8. Repeat steps 6 and 7 until you get to the last warp.

9. To turn, fold down the end that is on the bottom (green) so that it is parallel with the last warp. Take the end that is on top (white) and wrap it twice around both the last warp and the green weft. Bring the green weft over the next warp; bring the white weft over the green weft and under the next warp. Make sure that as you weave back, the same color weft is over the same warp as in the previous row. Note that when the pattern changes (in step 10 below), you'll need to fudge the turn to change the color order. Note, too, that the color used for wrapping changes in each section of the pattern.

10. Continue to twine as in steps 6 and 7. Whenever your paracord weft is about 4" long, cut another piece about 3 yards long and fuse it to the old working end (see page 87). Notice that when you complete each return row, you have created a series of horizontal Vs that look much like stockinette stitches in knitting. You have also created vertical stripes. Weave 8 rows in this manner, and then switch the colors so that the stripes are staggered. Weave 8 more rows.

11. Cut one of the cords near the edge of the mat, leaving a 4" tail, and fuse a new length of the other color to it. (You will weave the left-behind weft into the back of the mat when you have completed the weaving.) Weave 2 rows using the same color weft for both ends.

12. Repeat steps 6–11, this time using the opposite color for the solid-color rows.

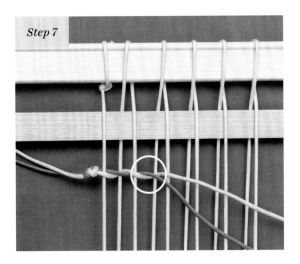

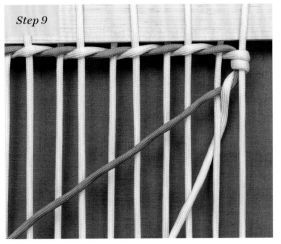

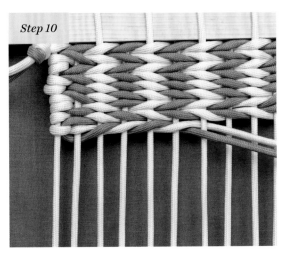

13. Continue repeating steps 6–12, maintaining the established color pattern until you reach the end of the mat. Five pairs of solid-colored rows divide the six vertical-striped sections. Be sure to leave enough room at the bottom of the mat both to get your fingers in to do the twining and to have warp ends that are long enough to weave into the back.

Securing the Ends

14. When the mat is the desired length, remove it from the loom by cutting the warps along the outside of the top and bottom bars.

15. Working with one warp at a time, reach inside the outer sheath of the paracord, pull out about 2" of the inner strands, and cut them off. (Take care not to cut the sheath.) Pull the sheath back out so that the remaining strands are drawn back inside the sheath, leaving a flat, empty tail that you can thread through a tapestry needle.

16. Working on the back of the mat, use the needle to weave the tail down through the backs of 4 or 5 rows of twining. Pull to even out the edge of the weaving and trim the tail end close to the mat. Weave in any other remaining ends in the same manner.

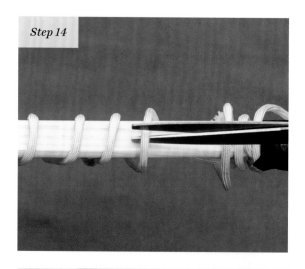

Step 14

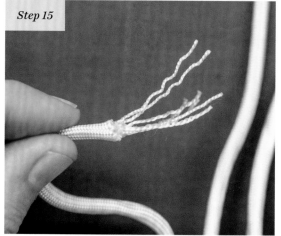

Step 15

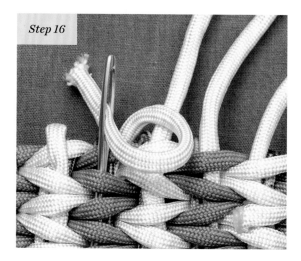

Step 16

FUSING THE ENDS OF PARACORD

There are several ways to fuse paracord, and until you settle on a method that works for you — one that is firm but also fairly quick to execute — you may find this action a bit challenging. In addition to a small multipurpose lighter, have a small bowl of water and needle-nose pliers nearby.

To get a relatively smooth join, butt the paracord end to end. Paracord melts, so to join two ends, trim them with sharp scissors, hold them parallel to each other, and insert them into the flame of a lighter until both the sheath and the inner strands begin to melt (a). Quickly push the ends firmly together until they are cool and fused (b). You may wish to use needle-nose pliers to hold them in place and help smooth the small bump at the point of fusion.

For the flame, use a small multipurpose lighter, rather than a candle, as it provides the right amount of heat and extinguishes immediately when you lay it down to focus on joining the ends. Position the paracord ends in the blue part of the flame, which is hotter than the orange part. It takes only

a couple of seconds to melt the material: you want to melt it, not burn it! As with any technique that involves working with flame, take care to direct the flame on the ends of the paracord only and keep other flammable objects (including your hair and clothing!) out of the way. *If the paracord itself catches fire, instead of just melting, quickly blow it out or extinguish it in water.*

Although the paracord cools relatively quickly, you can easily burn your fingers if you're not careful. The needle-nose pliers provide protection while also ensuring a tight join. Place a small bowl of cold water nearby to dip your fingers in before touching the melted paracord.

When twining, hide the join under the other weft or under a warp. Sometimes you're lucky and that happens naturally. If not, rather than making the weft looser, I find it easier to tighten up on the weft so that I can pull the join forward into a hidden position.

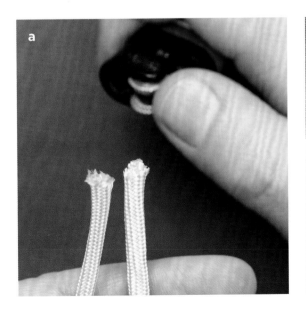

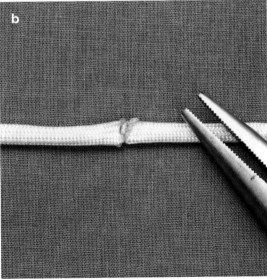

Carry-All

I believe one can never have too many bags, and this sturdy tote will serve just as well for a trip to the store as for an outing at the beach. Like the Twined Parachute-Cord Mat (see page 81), this is a twining project, here done with fabric strips; it is lined and features card-woven straps and trim. (If you prefer, you could use purchased 1"-wide woven tape for the straps.) As in rag rug weaving, the woven fabric completely fills the area between the top and bottom of the loom. —GS

DESIGN NOTEBOOK

This project started with a raid of my fabric stash, which included a dress that I wore on my first date with my husband, leftovers from a dress I made my granddaughter when she was about four years old, and more leftovers of a lovely batik fabric that that same granddaughter sewed for herself when she was a teenager. Memories are one of the best things about weaving with "rags"! As I started to weave, I realized that twining eats up fabric rather quickly, so I had to supplemented my stash with additional yardage from my local fabric store.

I wove this bag from the bottom up on the same loom I used for the Twined Parachute-Cord Mat. For this project, I enhanced that loom by adding a row of finishing nails along the top and bottom, spaced ½" apart and offset to avoid splitting the wood. For the 28" opening, I used 116 nails. (See page 285 for more information about building the frame.)

For the weft, I used the following amounts of 45"-wide fabric in three color "families": 1¼ yards each of reds and purples and 1½ yards of midnight blues. If you have an assortment of colors within each of the fabric families, try to use them unevenly within the design. I also recommend twining strips of two slightly different colors within each of the color families around each other. Both of these approaches give the fabric a blended rather than a striped look. Designing as you go makes the weaving process more interesting!

For the trim and handles, I used the following quantities of 3/2 Halcyon pearl cotton for each color: #1720 (red), 104 yards; #1270 (purple), 56 yards; and #1700 (midnight blue), 32 yards.

Carry-All

- **Weft:** 45"-wide, pre-washed 100% cotton fabric, about 4 yards total
- Scissors
- Pencil and ruler or tape measure
- Iron and ironing board
- Self-healing mat (optional)
- Clear plastic ruler (optional)
- Rotary cutter (optional)
- Frame loom (see page 285), with nails set ½" apart at the top and bottom
- 4 eye hooks large enough to accommodate the steel rods
- Two 36"-long, ⅜"-diameter steel rods
- **Warp:** Halcyon's 8/4 Soft Finish Linen Warp Yarn, 100% linen, about 35 yards
- Permanent marker

- **For lining:** 45"-wide, pre-washed 100% cotton fabric and matching thread, ½ yard
- Hand-sewing needle and heavy-duty sewing thread or sewing machine
- **For tape trim and handles:** 3/2 Halcyon pearl cotton, 100% cotton, about 192 yards
- 12 card-weaving cards
- Band lock and backstrap (see page 287)

> ## MEASUREMENTS
> *Bag on the loom:* 15" wide × 30" long
> *Finished bag:* 14" wide × 15" long
> *Card-woven tape:* 72" long

Preparing the Fabric Strips

Cut 1"-wide strips across the weft fabric, selvage to selvage. Fold and iron each strip in half lengthwise with wrong sides facing. While this step is time-consuming, it makes the weaving go faster, with less fiddling to keep the wrong side and frayed edges from showing. You can measure and cut fabric strips with scissors, but if you have a self-healing mat, a clear plastic ruler, and a rotary cutter, the job will go faster.

Setting Up the Loom

Because this project features a continuous warp, you do not need to measure it before winding it on, but you do need to center it on the loom.

To determine where to tie on the first warp, subtract the width of your project from the width of the frame's opening, and divide the result by 2 to get the distance between the side of the frame and the first warp.

Go Figure

I subtracted the bag width I planned, 15", from the 29" loom opening, and then divided the result by 2 to determine that I should start the warp 7" from the side of the frame.

29" loom opening **– 15"** bag width **=**

14" ÷ 2 = 7"

Start tying the warp 7" from the side of the frame.

Make light marks on the loom 7" in from each side, on both the bottom and top of the loom, to indicate where to begin and end the warp. Measure the distance between these marks to make sure the width is what you planned for your project.

To ensure straight edges that don't pull in, you must make one more adjustment to the loom. At both the top and bottom of the frame, screw in the eye hooks just outside the marks you made to indicate the side edges of the bag. Insert the steel rods through the eye hooks. You will weave around each edge warp and its paired rod, treating them as one.

Winding on the Warp

1. Tie the end of the warp thread to the designated nail, and then take the thread down to the nail directly opposite at the bottom of the loom. Continue to wind the warp onto the loom from top to bottom and back until you reach the mark at the other side. Instead of tying the warp thread to the last nail, wind it several times figure-8 style between the last nail and the one next to it to secure it temporarily.

2. It's important to tension the warp firmly and consistently before making the final tie. To do so, beginning at the first nail, trace each warp thread with your fingers, pulling it taut as you go. Follow the path you took to wind it on. You'll find that a fair amount of slack has developed. When you get to the last warp, unfasten the figure 8, then redo it, taking up the additional length. Repeat this process two or three more times, until very little slack remains in the warp threads and they are consistently tensioned. Tie the end securely to the last nail, using a double half-hitch knot (see page 292).

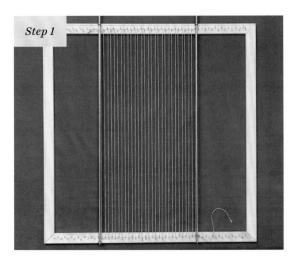

Step 1

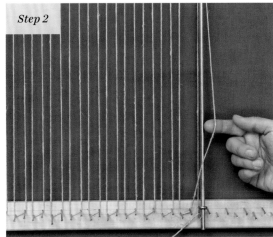

Step 2

3. Using a permanent marker, color the ninth warp thread in from each edge. This is where you will change colors.

Step 3

5. Take strip B over strip A and then under the next warp thread, again twisting the strips between warps.

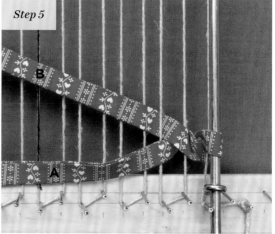

Step 5

Weaving the Bag

4. Beginning at the right-hand side of the loom, fold one red fabric strip in half widthwise and lay it around the steel rod and the first warp thread. Place both ends on top of the warp side by side. Take fabric strip A that is coming from beneath the rod and wrap it over fabric strip B and under the second warp thread, and lay it out to the left. Take strip B over the second warp thread. Strips A and B should now be twisted between the first and second warp threads.

6. Continue in this manner, taking each strip over the other strip, over the next warp thread, and then under the next warp thread. The two strips will be twisted between each warp thread. End this color with one of the strips going under the ninth warp thread from the beginning edge; leave the other strip where it emerges from under the eighth warp thread. Push the twined row firmly down against the line of nails.

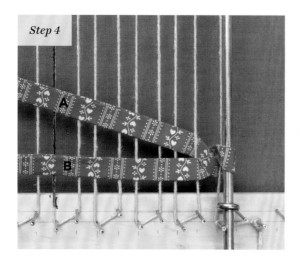

Step 4

Step 6

7. Repeat steps 4–6 using a midnight blue fabric strip and starting by wrapping it around the ninth warp thread until you come to the next marked warp thread.

8. Repeat steps 4–6 using a purple fabric strip and starting by wrapping it around the ninth warp thread from the other edge until you come to the end of the row.

Turning

9. Draw the fabric strip A that is lying over the next-to-last warp thread under the last warp and the steel rod, and lay it horizontally on top of the warp to the right. Draw the other strip B over the last warp and steel rod from the back and tuck it under strip A.

10. Take strip A over strip B and under the second warp thread. The two strips are now twisted in the space between the edge warp thread (and rod) and the second warp thread. Take strip B over that same warp, over strip A, and under the next warp.

11. Continue in the same manner until you get to the marked thread. As before, take the appropriate strip under the marked warp thread and leave the other strip coming from under the previous warp thread. Place both of these wefts down vertically so that they are out of the way for the next step.

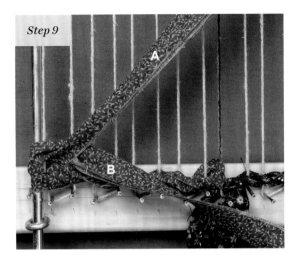

Step 9

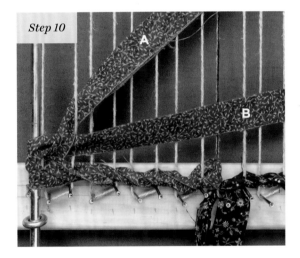

Step 10

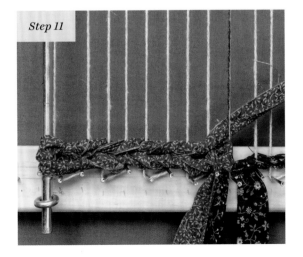

Step 11

Starting a New Color

12. Note which of the midnight blue strips lies under the marked thread and move it off to the left (A). Pick up the strip that hasn't yet been woven around the marked thread (B) and weave it from right to left under the marked thread. Lay it out to the right horizontally.

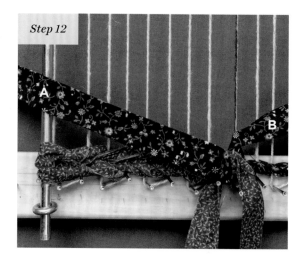

Step 12

13. Take strip A over strip B and then under the warp thread to the right of the marked thread. You can now pick up the same weaving sequence that you followed earlier. At the next marked warp, change to the red fabric strip in the same manner, and weave to the right-hand edge.

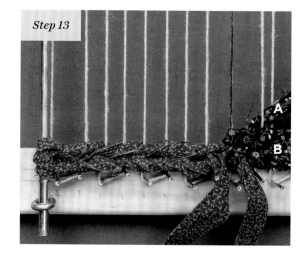

Step 13

14. To turn at the right edge, weave fabric strip A under the last warp and the rod, and lay it out to the right. Take strip B over the last warp and rod, then wrap it around the rod and last warp to come up and over the second warp from the edge. Bring strip A over the rod and last warp and under the second warp from the edge. Strips A and B are now twisted between the last warp and the second warp from the edge. Continue to twine across.

When you've woven all but about 2" of a fabric strip, join another strip. See Joining Fabric Strips (opposite) for how to do this.

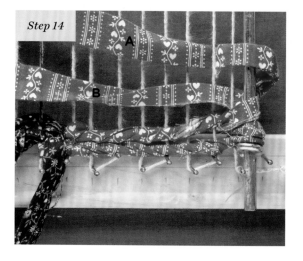

Step 14

JOINING FABRIC STRIPS

If you are using new fabric and have cut it from selvage to selvage, each strip is usually 45" long — and this turns out to be a comfortable length for twining. When you have only a few inches of a strip left, you must join it to another fabric strip.

When joining two pieces of yarn, weavers usually overlap the ends or splice the ends together for an inch or so. When working with fabric strips, though, you can transition to a new strip with this useful method.

1. Fold down about 1" at the end of the strip and make a small, vertical slit in the fabric. About ⅜" is usually fine. (Do not cut to the end of the strip.) Unfold the end and refold the strip along the vertical slit. Trim off the corners so that you have a point above the slit. Make another slit and point on the strip you are joining.

2. Lay the two strips against each other with the right side of the old strip facing the wrong side of the new and the slits aligned. Take the new strip first through the slit in the old strip and then through the slit in the new strip (a). Pull on both strips to slide the ends together and join them in a small knot (b).

When you get to the knot while twining, take extra care to keep the right side of the fabric out. You can push the knot to the back, or you may find that it is so inconspicuous (depending on the fabric and the colors) that it can sit right on top without objection. It's usually possible to tuck it in more when you weave the next row or even after the weaving is complete.

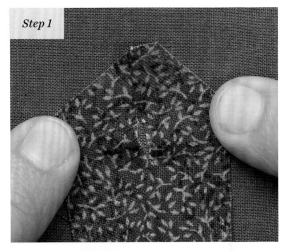

Step 1

Step 2a

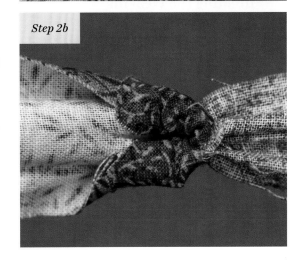

Step 2b

TIPS FOR SUCCESS

- Tuck in the raw edges of the fabric strips as much as possible as you weave. Inevitably, some threads will come to the surface. I pull out or cut off as many of these as I can, but I also believe that a reasonable amount of "fuzz" is part of the charm of weaving with fabric strips.

- Check your weaving for wrong sides showing. Although you folded and ironed the wrong sides of the fabric to the inside, you may have to fiddle a bit to keep the wrong side from showing at times. Of course, this will not be an issue if your fabric has no wrong side (such as with solid colors, as well as with plaids and stripes that were woven into the fabric, rather than printed). While using solid-color fabrics makes the weaving go faster, patterned fabric gives the design some extra sparkle.

- Pull on each of the ends to smooth them out as you finish each row in a color panel. This is also a good moment to push down the twined row.

- Make the join snug and smooth when you change colors by pulling the ends of both the new and old colors to tighten them and pushing down on the "seam." You will find wider spacing develops between the warp threads where you change colors: this is natural and does not affect the look or integrity of the finished fabric.

- Avoid loops of fabric at the edges and make the turn at the edges smooth and even by giving an extra tug on both strips after the first twist in the other direction. The metal rod prevents draw-in at the edges. In spite of this, when you remove the fabric from the loom, you will lose a little width due to shrinkage and weft take-up (see page 290).

- Try weaving in different directions. I find it easier to twine from the bottom up, but some weavers work from top to bottom, as I did for the Twined Parachute-Cord Mat (page 81).

Finishing the Weaving

15. When you have woven about one-half of the finished length of the bag, turn the loom 180 degrees to begin weaving from the other end. (This maneuver makes it easier to ensure that the warp will be completely covered at both ends of the weaving. You will complete the weaving near the center of the bag when the two woven sections meet.) Push the first row down against the nails as you did in step 6. Take care to maintain the same color pattern as at the first end. (The reds will now be at the left.)

16. Weave until the warp is completely covered, firmly pushing the weft rows both above and below the unwoven area so that you can fill the space as completely and evenly as possible. Tuck the remaining ends to the back.

17. To remove the fabric from the loom, first slide the steel rods out of the eye hooks. Next, beginning at one corner, push the warp loops off the nails at the top; repeat at the bottom of the loom. The continuous warp will have caught the first and last rows of weaving, so you don't need to worry about making fringe — or having the piece fall apart! You should, however, check the corners. You may have to adjust the warp or hand-stitch the weft to secure it at those points if you find any loose warps.

Lining the Bag

18. Measure the width and length of the rag-woven fabric. Add 2" to the width and 2½" to the length. Measure and cut the lining fabric to that size.

19. Fold the lining material in half widthwise with right sides together. Hand- or machine-stitch the side seams, using a 1" seam allowance. Trim the seam to ⅝" and trim the bottom corners. Fold the top edge to the wrong side ¼" and then 1", and press. Hand- or machine-stitch this hem in place. Leave the lining wrong side out.

20. Fold the rag-woven fabric in half widthwise with the right sides together. Use heavy-duty sewing thread and small whipstitches (see page 302) to sew the edges together. Turn the piece right side out.

21. Slip the lining into the bag with the wrong sides facing and the lining extending about ½" beyond the top edge of the rag-woven fabric. Fold the hemmed edge of the lining over the front of the bag. Slipstitch the lining to the bag.

Step 19

Step 20

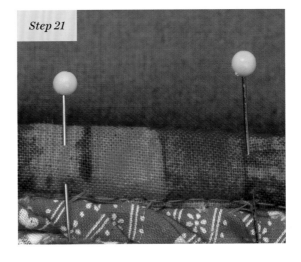
Step 21

Weaving the Tape

22. Follow the instructions on pages 161–165 for card weaving. Measure a 3-yard-long warp, with 26 red, 14 purple, and 8 midnight blue lengths of yarn. Follow the chart (at right) to thread the cards, and weave a 72"-long tape, using midnight blue as the weft.

Attaching the Tape

23. Measure the circumference at the top edge of the bag. Mark that measurement on the woven tape. To secure the weaving, hand- or machine-stitch across the tape at that point, as well as at both ends of the tape. Run another line of stitching across the tape about ¼" away from the first stitching (for the circumference). Cut the tape between these two lines of stitching. For the handles, fold the remainder of the tape in half, and run two lines of stitching across the tape about ¼" apart at that point. Cut between these stitching lines.

24. Pin the handle ends to the bag front at the color changes (or wherever you think best fits the design), extending the ends a little less than 1", or just long enough not to show when they're covered by the woven trim. Take care not to twist the tape when you position it. If possible, machine-stitch 2 rows of stitching across each end to secure it. If your sewing machine can't manage so thick a join and you need to do this step by hand, use a heavy-duty thread, such as upholstery thread, and be sure your stitching is secure.

25. Pin the remaining length of tape along the top of the bag. Position the ends at one of the side seams, turning each one under enough so that you can butt them together along the seam. Blind-stitch along both edges of the tape, taking care to tuck in any loose threads where the ends are folded over.

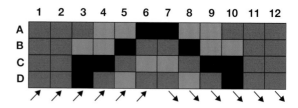

WEAVING THE TAPE

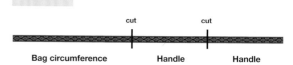

Step 23

cut   cut

Bag circumference   Handle   Handle

Cutting diagram for woven tape

Step 25

Rag-Woven Stool Seat

Stools and chair seats may be covered with a variety of materials, including rush, seagrass, twine, and wood splints. The Shakers even wove the narrow tapes that they then used to craft beautifully patterned seating. For this little stool, I used fabric strips.

Note that when completed, the seat on this stool is double thick. All the strips run over the rungs and are tied snugly on the underside, so that both the top and bottom of the seat are woven. —GS

DESIGN NOTEBOOK

For this project, you can use just about any chair or stool with four rungs framing the opening for the seat. Maybe you have a chair or stool with a worn or missing covering, or you can find something suitable at a secondhand store. I used a little stool that comes as an inexpensive, unpainted kit. Assembled, it is 12" × 9" × 8" high. I painted the version on the facing page with Glidden's Diamond interior paint/primer, using a 7-ounce can of Clipper Ship Blue in eggshell finish. I painted the stool shown in the step-by-step photos with Craft Smart's Satin Acrylic Paint in orange.

The cloth strips might come from your fabric stash, or you can have fun choosing favorite color combinations at a fabric store. For best results, choose plain-colored fabric or fabric with the pattern woven in, such as stripes or plaids. Printed fabrics are also acceptable, but unless you aren't concerned with the wrong (usually lighter) side showing, you have to take more care in keeping that side folded in. I used five different fabrics, but you could have fewer — or more!

Rag-Woven Stool Seat

YOU WILL NEED

- Stool or chair with a seat that has rungs on all 4 sides to weave over
- Paint or stain (optional)
- 45"-wide 100% cotton fabric, ¼ yard each in as many colors and patterns as you wish (This stool required about 1½ yards of fabric; you will need more for larger seats.)
- Scissors
- Ruler
- Iron and ironing board (optional)

TIP FOR SUCCESS

To make the weaving go more easily and to achieve a neater finished seat, fold each fabric strip in half lengthwise with the wrong sides facing and iron it in place. In traditional rag rug weaving, the strips are beaten in and therefore become coiled, rather than remaining flat, as in this project. The difference here is that the warp and weft show equally, so I preferred to keep all the strips relatively flat in order to highlight the design. As you can see, some of them shift a bit, but I like the wonkiness of that look.

Weaving the Seat

1. Prepare the stool or chair by refinishing and/or painting it, as desired.

2. Prepare the fabric by cutting it into 1"-wide strips. (If you are using fabric scraps, be sure they are at least as long as the longest lengthwise strips; see Go Figure, opposite.)

3. Lay out your fabric strips on a floor or table in your desired design. I opted for symmetry, using one darker-colored fabric as a contrast to the lighter ones. I also laid out all the strips in the same order for the warp and weft, so that the dark strips create a subtle grid.

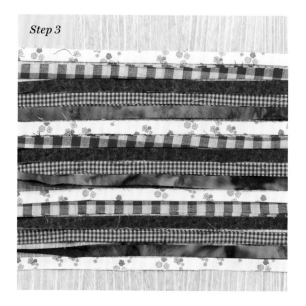

Step 3

4. Once you've decided on the order of your strips, calculate how long your warp and weft strips should be, and count how many you will need of each length.

   To determine the length of the strips that you'll use widthwise, multiply the width of the stool or chair seat by 2, then add approximately 8" for tying the ends together.

   To determine the length of the strips that you'll use lengthwise, multiply the length of the stool or chair seat by 2, then add approximately 8" for tying the ends together.

   To determine how many you need of each length, measure the length in inches of each rung that will serve as the "frame" of your loom, then multiple by 2 since the folded strips are ½" wide.

Go Figure

WIDTHWISE STRIPS
   (8½" [width of stool or chair] **× 2) + 8"** for tying ends together **= 25"** strip length
   10½" (length of the lengthwise rung) **× 2 = 21 strips**

LENGTHWISE STRIPS
   (11½" [length of stool or chair] **× 2) + 8"** for tying ends together **= 31"** strip length
   8" (length of the widthwise rung) **× 2 = 16 strips**

   For the widthwise strips I prepared twenty-one 25" strips (five dark and four of each of the other colors). For the lengthwise strips, I prepared sixteen 31" strips (four dark and three of each of the other colors).

5. Begin by tying the shorter strips around the lengthwise rungs of the stool, nudging each one up to the previous one as you go. Use a square knot (see page 291) to tie the ends together on the underside of the stool. This will be your warp and should be tied firmly so the seat won't sag. It's not difficult to weave through this warp, so don't worry about the weaving being too tight.

Step 5

To avoid lumpy knots all in one place, try to position the knots randomly over the bottom of the seat. You will eventually trim and tuck them up so that they are sandwiched between the top and bottom layers of the woven fabric. Keep the strips as smooth and evenly positioned as possible.

Rag-Woven Stool Seat

6. When all of the widthwise strips are in place, your warp is set and you can begin to weave the top of the seat. Weave the complete top, leaving the tails loose at each side, before moving to step 7, in which you weave and tie the bottom strips. Remember, if you would like a symmetrical grid, as in the stool shown, weave the weft strips in the same order as the warp strips.

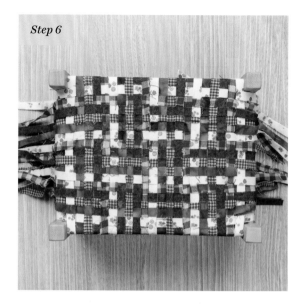

Step 6

7. Turn the stool over and weave through the bottom warp strips. This is the trickiest part of the project because the warp tails tend to get in the way at first. Trim them to about 1½" as you come to them and push them up above the bottom web of strips. Use a square knot to tie the newly woven-in strips firmly together, and trim and hide the ends between the layers as you weave.

8. Finish by adjusting any strips that are hidden or uneven, trim any threads that bother you, and tuck in all knots and tails so that the bottom is as neat as possible.

Step 7

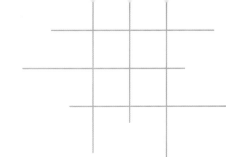

MARILYN MOORE

Marilyn Moore is a contemporary basket maker who fashions beautiful and stylish pieces that are nothing like the traditional items that come to mind when one thinks of a basket. After weaving baskets with natural fibers for many years, she was introduced to wire as a weaving medium. She was fascinated.

Today Marilyn creates vessels and then, with the same techniques she used in weaving baskets, translates those forms into wire jewelry with complex and sophisticated detail. Many of her pieces incorporate color blending, and she constantly experiments with new techniques and styles to keep her work fresh.

Marilyn has been teaching weaving across the country since 1979. In addition to classes on basketry, she also teaches jewelry making, using such varied materials as wire, wire cloth, pine needles, and raffia. She has contributed to several publications, books, and videos and has exhibited her work internationally.

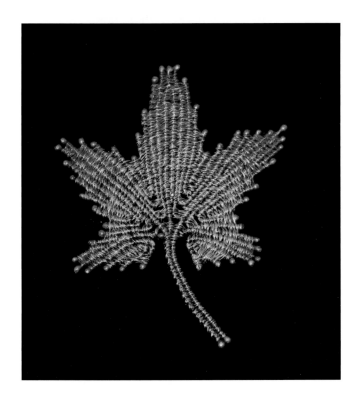

THE MAPLE LEAF, 2014
Coated copper wire twined over copper wire; 3½" × 3"

This important piece of Marilyn's work represents her grief over the loss of a loved one, and the cycle of life: just as trees get new leaves in the spring, life goes on. She made a grouping of leaves as an art statement, then turned her leaves into brooches.

Branching Out

Sometimes the simplest designs are the most satisfying to weave. Finding the "frame" for this project is half the fun! Unless you live on a prairie where trees are few and far between, you should be able to discover a forked branch perfect for the purpose, whether you're in a city, suburb, or out in the country. No two will be the same, of course, but look for something that is strong enough to withstand mild tension and with enough room between the two "arms" for the weaving. On your next morning walk or evening run, you're likely to find yourself seeing more than enough possibilities everywhere you look.

You may wish to prepare the branch by stripping the bark, as I did on the manzanita branch on the facing page; this step is optional, and I chose not to strip the bark from the branch shown in the step-by-step photos. Two or more layers of bark protect trees from sun, wind, and even some insects. If the branch you've chosen fell from the tree some time ago, all the bark layers may peel off quite easily. You can use a penknife to strip off the pieces that don't readily fall away, if necessary. For stubborn pieces, try soaking the branch in warm water with a bit of dish detergent to soften the bark. Finish your preparation with a light sanding. I like the small buds and imperfections that often appear when I get down to the bare wood. —GS

DESIGN NOTEBOOK

Because no two branches will ever be the same, each branch offers special challenges. One of these challenges is that the angle of the pieces you are warping may be so steep that the warp threads slip along the branch, especially if you've stripped the bark from it. It may also be difficult to space the warp threads evenly. To alleviate this problem, these weavings feature crocheted chains, which are lashed to the branches. The loops in the chain serve both to anchor and space the warp. Choose a crochet hook that is sized appropriately for your warp yarn; for my light worsted weight yarn, I used a size US 7 (4.5 mm) hook.

For the weft on the branches on page 106 and below, I used worsted weight handspun from Into the Whirled's "The Cat's Pyjamas," a blend of Bluefaced Leicester and tussah silk.

YOU WILL NEED

- Ruler or tape measure
- Tree or shrub branch
- **Warp:** unwashed worsted weight wool for large branch; 3/2 pearl cotton for small branch
- Crochet hook
- **Weft:** weaver's choice!
- Short blunt-tip tapestry needle

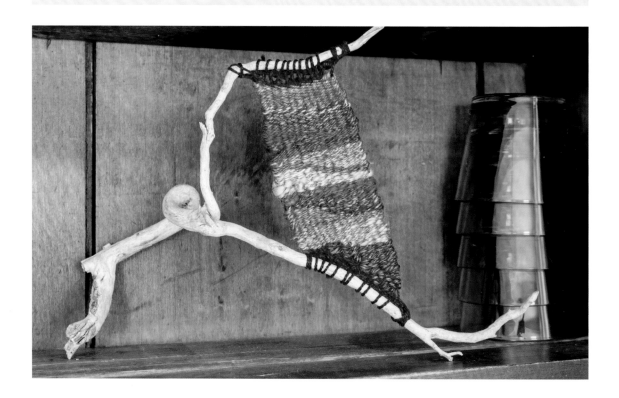

Step 2a

Warping

1. Measure the width you want to weave. (This is the measurement along the branch where you will be lashing on the warp in step 2.) With the warp yarn, make a slip knot (see page 293) and, leaving a 3" tail, crochet a chain (see page 111) the same length as that measurement. When the chain is complete, leave a tail 10 times the length of the chain for a branch with a ½" diameter. (If your branch is much narrower or wider, adjust the length of the chain accordingly.) You will use this tail to lash the chain to the branch.

2. Tie the short 3" tail of the chain to one of the branches near where it forks. Using a half-hitch knot (see page 292), tie the long tail to the end of the branch (a). Thread the long tail through a tapestry needle and, starting at the far end of the branch, lash the chain to the branch going through each crochet stitch in turn (b). When you reach the fork, use a square knot (see page 291) to tie the two tails together.

3. Repeat steps 1 and 2 for the opposite branch. Be sure to chain the same number of stitches as for the first chain.

Step 2b

4. Thread a long length of warp on a tapestry nee-
    dle. Starting at the fork, insert the needle into
    the first chain stitch on one of the branches.
    Move to the first chain stitch on the opposite
    branch and insert the needle, drawing the warp
    through. Go back to the first side and insert the
    needle into the third chain. You may insert the
    needle from either the front or from the back,
    but take care to be consistent whichever way
    you choose. Continue in this manner, alter-
    nating from branch to branch and using every
    other chain stitch, until you reach the outer end.
    (Depending on the weight of the yarn you are
    using, you may not need to skip chains to space
    the warp appropriately.)

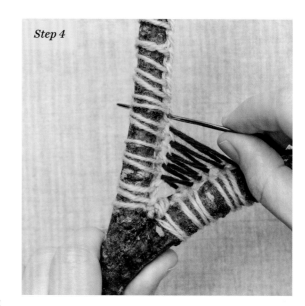

Step 4

5. Before tying the last warp to the branch, go back
    to the beginning and pull the warp threads into a
    consistent tension following the same path you
    took while warping. You may need to repeat this
    step to get a desirable tension.

Weaving

6. Begin weaving at the fork. You may weave the
    weft to create whatever design you like. You can
    create shapes by weaving shorter distances,
    then expand an area by weaving all the way
    across.

    When you begin a new yarn, in order to
    maintain the correct over/under sequence, it's
    important to stick to the pattern you've estab-
    lished. It's a bit magical, but as long as you
    follow that rule faithfully, you can meander from
    side to side, in short or long sequences, and
    always be in the correct position to go under or
    over the next warp. (For more information about
    this weaving technique, see Going Free-Form!,
    page 128).

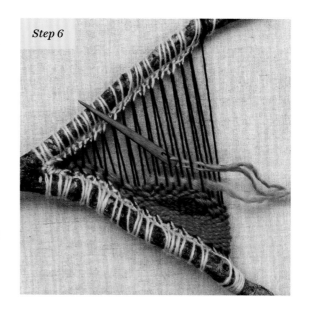

Step 6

7. When you are finished weaving, bury all the
    tails in the side you want to be the back of your
    weaving.

MAKING A CROCHET CHAIN

To crochet a chain, make a slip knot (see page 293) and place it on a crochet hook (a). Holding the hook in your right hand and the working yarn under tension in your left hand, scoop the hook down under the working yarn and pull a loop of it through the slip knot (b). You now have a new loop on the hook. Again draw the working yarn through the loop on the hook (c). Continue in this way to make a chain the length needed, taking care to keep the size of your loops consistent.

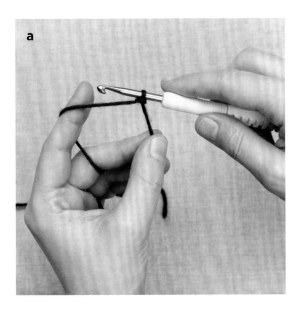

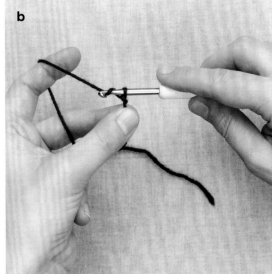

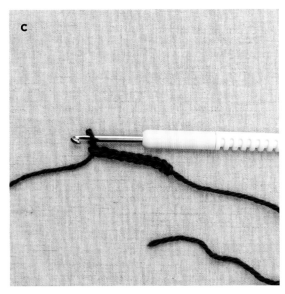

TAPPING INTO TAPESTRY

Tapestry weaving requires certain skills in order to accomplish the remarkable possibilities it offers. This shouldn't keep you from dipping your toes into that water, however, since many of those skills aren't difficult to learn. More important, those remarkable possibilities are so very intriguing!

There are two basic facts to understand about traditional tapestry: it is weft-faced (meaning that the weft yarn completely covers the warp threads) and it is plain weave (meaning you go over one thread and under the next, alternating that order in the next row). You can create realistic pictures or you can weave abstract patterns. You can play with the colors and textures that delight you, influenced by what you see around you, what you imagine, and what you want to express. You don't need to be an artist; you just need to love the feel of yarn in your hands and the pleasure of watching the play of colors as the tapestry unfolds.

Let your imagination and creativity soar as you explore tapestry weaving. Wall hangings with free-form designs, interesting textures, fringes, knots, and bubbles are a super-popular home decor look. At the more traditional and formal end of the spectrum, professional tapestry weavers create sophisticated pieces with subtly shaded colors and technically demanding imagery. Following a long history of pictorial weavings, some of today's weavers tell stories or make political statements with their work. See pages 132–139 to meet some contemporary tapestry weavers.

I wove the small tapestry at the left on a 12" frame loom using techniques that you will find in the four samplers that follow. Complete instructions for how to weave it are on page 131.

Beginning with Two Colors (see page 120)

Getting in Shape (see page 122)

Playing with Texture (see page 124)

Going Free-Form! (see page 128)

A Taste of Traditional Tapestry Techniques

On the following pages, I offer four small samplers (shown on the facing page) featuring several techniques that you can use to create your own tapestries, whether you prefer to weave traditional tapestry or go wildly free-form. These techniques are just the tip of the iceberg of what you can explore in tapestry weaving, but we hope they will whet your appetite.

The tool requirements are modest. In addition to a Hokett frame loom and a homemade frame loom (see page 285), I used small stick shuttles, yarn butterflies (see page 37), and blunt-tip tapestry needles to insert the weft; tapestry bobbins to insert and beat in the weft; a table fork and small tapestry beater to beat in the weft; a pickup stick to open the sheds as well as to beat in the weft; and a US 9 (5.5 mm) knitting needle to act as a shed stick.

Note that there are three common terms for one pass of weft yarn through the warp: *pick*, *shot*, and *row*. In this tapestry section, I use the word *pick*. —GS

Choosing the weft yarn and the sett (spacing of the warp threads) that ensures complete coverage of the warp can be challenging. One rule of thumb suggests that the weft, when laid parallel to the warp after the loom is warped, should just fill the space between two warps as shown here.

DESIGN NOTEBOOK

For the four small tapestries that follow, I used 16/2 linen for the warp and Harrisville's Highland yarn for the weft, in colors #4070 Oatmeal, #4910 Adobe, and #4930 Toffee. (I appreciate Rebecca Mezoff's recommendation to use this Harrisville yarn on the Hokett loom. Rebecca's work is shown on pages 132 and 133.)

I wove the featured tapestries on a 7"× 7¾" Hokett loom with 6 notches per inch. (My sett, therefore, was 6 ends per inch.) For the examples in the step-by-step photos on pages 117–131, I used the Hokett loom as well as a frame loom, which I built following the instructions on page 285. Although those directions are for a much larger frame, for this project, I used 12" stretcher bars, taking the same approach to bracing the corners and adding six finishing nails per inch along the top and bottom in order to achieve the same sett (6 epi) as those weavings I did on the Hokett.

  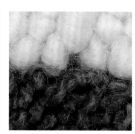 

YOU WILL NEED

- **Weft:** Harrisville's Highland (washed), 100% wool
- Stick shuttle (optional)
- **Warp:** 16/2 linen, 100% linen or cotton seine twine, 44 yards
- Frame loom with 6 pegs, notches, or nails per inch
- Shed sticks or knitting needles
- Piece of stiff cardboard, 1"–1½" wide and 2" longer than the width of your warp
- Pickup stick
- Table fork or small tapestry bobbin or beater

- Tapestry needles (short and long) or crochet hook (3 to 4 mm)
- **For Getting in Shape:** permanent marker
- **For Playing with Texture:** 100% wool pin roving, 1 yard, and a US 8 (5 mm) knitting needle
- **For Going Free-Form!:** Assorted handspun or different-textured yarns, unspun angora locks; white bouclé, 2 yards

FINISHED MEASUREMENTS
4 tapestries, each 6¼" wide × 4½" long

Weaving

1. Prepare your weft yarns by winding them on stick or tapestry shuttles or by creating yarn butterflies (see page 37). Take care not to make too thick a bundle or you will have difficulty pushing it through the shed. On a small loom like this one, they shouldn't be bulkier than about ¾".

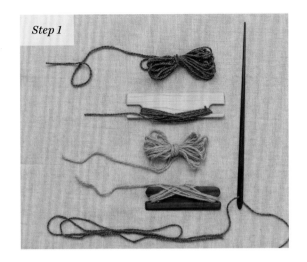

Step 1

2. Because the warp is continuous, you don't need to measure it before beginning, but it does need to be centered on the loom. Simply tie a warp thread to the first notch, peg, or nail at the top or bottom of the loom and wind back and forth between the top and bottom until the warp is the width you desire. When the warp is complete, increase and even the tension as necessary by running your fingers along each thread following the direction in which you first wound it. (See step 3 on page 83 for further information on how to do this.) If desired, double the edge warps for a firmer selvage.

3. Using a shed stick (or knitting needle), weave over, under, over, under across your warp threads to create the first shed. Slide this shed to the top of the loom and tie it to the frame at both ends to hold it in place. This remains throughout the weaving so that one shed is ready to weave every other pick. It also preserves warp at the top for weaving ends to the back when finishing your project.

4. To provide a base to weave against, as well as to preserve warp at the bottom for finishing, insert the cardboard strip at the bottom of the loom, in the same shed that you created in step 3.

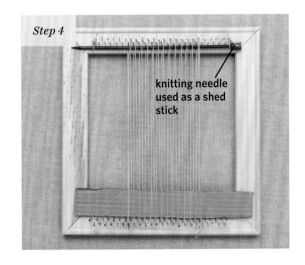

Step 4

knitting needle used as a shed stick

5. Use your pickup stick to weave under, over, under, over the warp threads, in the shed opposite to the shed you made in steps 3 and 4. Turn the pickup stick on its edge to widen the shed. You are ready to weave your first pick.

6. Insert the shuttle or butterfly through the open shed. Draw the weft all the way through the shed, leaving a 4" tail. Holding the tail, push about 2" of the weft into an arc about 1" tall: do this all the way across the warp. This is called bubbling. (For more about bubbling, see page 123.) Remove the pickup stick and beat in the weft with your fork or tapestry beater. Change to the next shed by using the pickup stick to increase the opening you created with the shed stick in step 3.

7. Insert the next pick of weft. Where the weft turns around the first warp thread, ensure that it just touches the warp: it shouldn't draw in, but neither should it form a loop; like Goldilocks's porridge, it should be just right. Pinch this turning point as you form the bubbles. Remove the pickup stick and beat the weft in. Change to the next shed and beat the weft in. Practice weaving for another inch or two until you feel that you understand the concepts and are pleased with the result. If everything looks good, you can go on to try some of the different techniques in the four tapestries shown.

Critique your work: Is the edge smooth but relaxed? Were your bubbles too big, resulting in loops along the weft? Does the warp show?

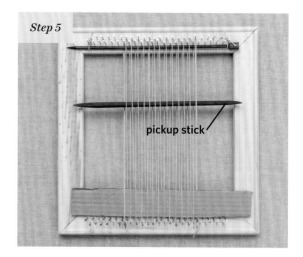

Step 5

pickup stick

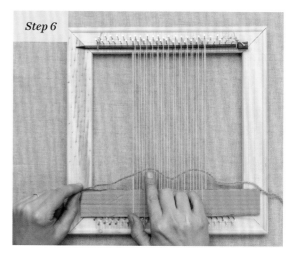

Step 6

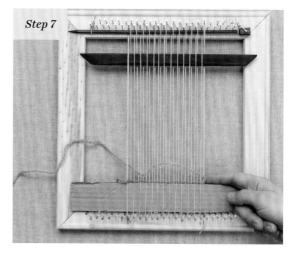

Step 7

Finishing

8. When you have completed your weaving, remove the tapestry from the loom by carefully cutting at the very top of the warp ends. Tie each pair of warp ends (the pair that formed a loop before you cut them) into square knots (see page 291). Keep the fell (edge) of the fabric as even as possible. You will find that tying the knots fairly tightly helps maintain a straight edge.

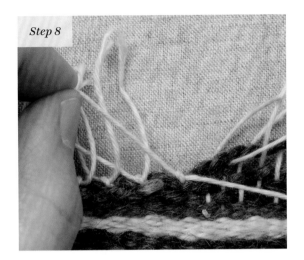

9. Note that the double warps at each corner of the piece emerge from inside the weft loop. At each corner, carefully slide one of the warp ends out of the loop, and tie a square knot to secure the weft at that point.

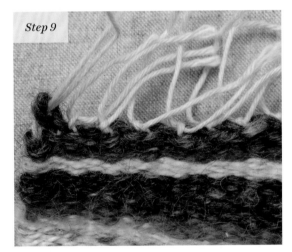

10. You can leave the tied-off ends as fringe or use a crochet hook or tapestry needle to weave them down on the back side of the tapestry, taking care that the ends don't show on the front.

Blocking Your Tapestry

Lay the tapestry face up on a work surface. Soak a dish towel in water, then wring it so that it is just damp, not dripping. Place the towel over your tapestry and hover an iron (set at woolen) over the towel until it is steaming. Do not press down on the towel with the iron or you will spoil all the lovely textures you've created in your tapestries.

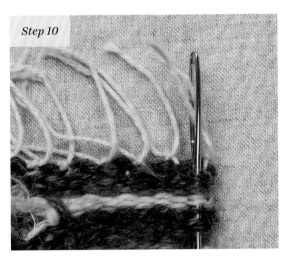

Beginning with Two Colors

This tapestry features three techniques: stripes, vertical columns, and meet and separate. Once you've explored these techniques using just two colors of yarn, try branching out with more. I've made suggestions along with the basic instructions. As you'll see, once you start experimenting, the possibilities are endless.

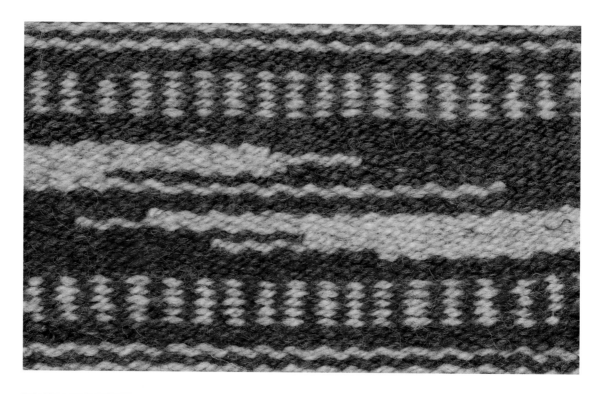

Stripes

Weave 2 picks of one color followed by 2 picks of the second color. By weaving 2 picks consecutively with the same color, you create slightly wavy lines.

Once you see how this works, try alternating a third color with one of the original colors, for example, 2 picks of Oatmeal, 2 picks of Adobe, 2 picks of Oatmeal, 2 picks of Toffee, and so on. Adding a fourth color would give you even more design opportunity.

STRIPES

Vertical Columns

Weave 1 pick with one color and the next pick with the second color, and continue alternating in the same way on subsequent picks. The result of this approach is that each color appears on the surface on alternate warp threads, the ones that are down when you weave, creating vertical columns of each color.

By weaving a variation of this technique, you can create checks. For example, weave 1 pick of Oatmeal and 1 pick of Toffee for 8 picks, then reverse the color order by starting with 1 pick of Toffee followed by 1 pick of Oatmeal. Continue to alternate as desired. You could also maintain one of the colors (Oatmeal?) and then use two or more other colors for the other vertical column.

Meet and Separate

This technique serves several purposes in traditional tapestry weaving: it is used to introduce one or more colors in a single row of weaving, as well as to fill larger areas of one color in smaller increments, to avoid the edges drawing in. To carry out this technique, the two wefts must travel in opposite directions. For each pick of weft, the two yarns travel toward each other, meet wherever you choose, and then, when you create the opposite shed, each reverses direction.

Start with each weft coming in toward the center. The wefts meet over a lowered warp thread (a). Bubble, change the shed, and beat. When you turn each weft to go back the other way, one of the wefts must go over the raised warp between the two. It doesn't matter which one you use: your choice may be dictated by which color you want to have travel a bit farther (b). As with turns around the edge warps, take care that each weft wraps cleanly over the warp where it turns — not too tight, but not looped.

Where you decide to have your wefts meet is entirely up to you. Notice, however, that you can change the distance each travels only when they travel toward each other.

VERTICAL COLUMNS

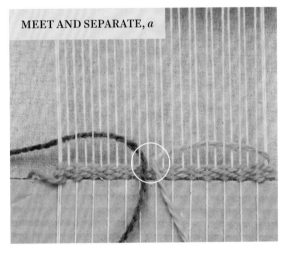

MEET AND SEPARATE, *a*

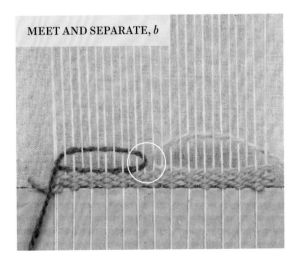

MEET AND SEPARATE, *b*

Getting in Shape

This design features irregularly shaped areas outlined with two picks of a contrasting-color yarn for emphasis. I worked the design out on paper at actual size before beginning the weaving. This drawing is called a cartoon. You could work free-form, but I found it helpful to work from a drawing. Some weavers secure their cartoon under the warp and keep it in place while weaving, but this design is so simple and the loom so small that I found it easier to mark the threads.

Pin the drawing under the warped threads and trace the shapes onto the warp threads with permanent marker.

To achieve the same effect I did, weave all the color blocks as traditional tapestry, even though the shapes are irregular. Keep the weft perpendicular to the warp throughout and complete each color block individually, following the marked design to find where to turn and weave in the other direction.

After finishing each area of color, weave 2 picks of a contrasting color along the edge of the completed block. It's especially important to bubble (see below) the outline picks generously: it usually takes a bit of extra weft to travel the distance caused by the dips and rises in this kind of a design.

Notice that you can never build up an area over an unwoven area of warp, as you would then have no way to reach the lower area to work it and beat in the new weaving. For this tapestry, I began with Oatmeal and worked in a little Toffee with meet and separate (see page 121). I then wove the large Adobe section in the middle, followed by Toffee, and ending with Oatmeal.

BUBBLE, BUBBLE, AND TOIL TO AVOID TROUBLE

Even if you've chosen the proper weft yarn for the warp and sett that you're using, you may find that your weft isn't covering the warp threads completely or that your edges are drawing in. This is probably because you aren't bubbling the weft enough.

Bubbling is a technique used in many kinds of weaving, but it's especially important in traditional tapestry, which requires that the warp be completely covered. (This is true of any weft-faced weaving.) In order to do that, you need to give the weft plenty of room to travel over and under the warp threads. Different setts, as well as different weft and warp yarns or threads, will need different amounts of bubbling, so you will have to experiment whenever you're using new materials. It may surprise you to discover how much it matters to take care of this seemingly small detail in your weaving practice.

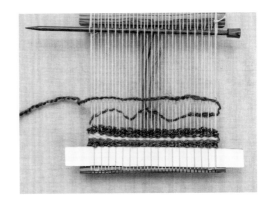

Cross section of path of weft over and under the warp

Playing with Texture

This piece includes looped weft, soumak, and rya knots. Each of these techniques gives you an opportunity to add texture and dimension to your tapestry. Looped weft and rya knots, in particular, can be quite dramatic, depending on how long you make them.

Looped Weft

Looped pin roving and looped yarn create very different effects, but the technique is the same for both.

1. Cut or break a length of yarn or pin roving about twice as long as the width of your weaving. Open the shed opposite the preceding row and insert the measured yarn or pin roving, allowing a 4" tail on the right and the rest of the tail off to the left. (If you are left-handed, you may wish to work from left to right.) Change to a neutral shed (one where no warp threads are raised).

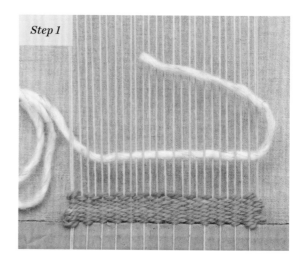

Step 1

2. Starting at the right-hand edge of the weaving, insert the tip of the knitting needle under the roving from the bottom up. Slide the needle through the roving to form a loop and then slide the needle over the next warp. Again, dive down with the needle tip to pick up another loop of roving, working across the warp to the left edge.

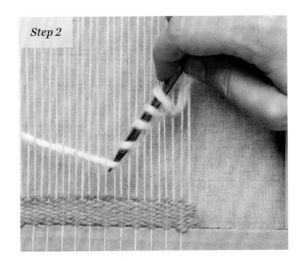
Step 2

3. Continue all the way across the row, drawing in additional roving from the left as needed.

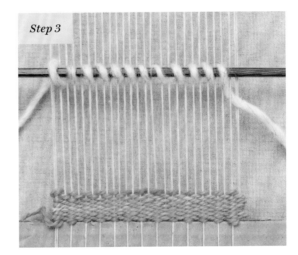
Step 3

4. Change to the opposite shed and throw in a pick of your original weft. Beat in, remove the knitting needle, and again beat to secure the loops.

5. Continue to make rows of loops, alternating with picks of original weft, as desired. When the piece is done, weave the weft tails of the looped weft in on the back.

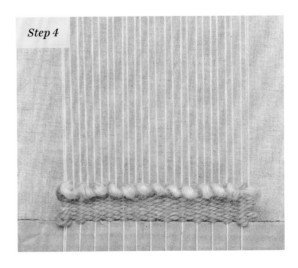
Step 4

Soumak

Soumak is a traditional tapestry technique that creates surface texture. The weft yarn is wrapped around the warp threads as it travels across the row, rather than woven in plain weave. Above the section of looped weft in the tapestry detail shown on page 124 (and in the detail below, at right) are two soumak sections. The one immediately above the looped weft shows 4 rows of soumak woven in Oatmeal: the weft travels over four warps to the left, then back under two to the right. Above that is a variation, this time woven in Adobe (two over and one back).

Continuing with the main-color weft yarn, weave it from the left to the right edge (if it isn't already there). Carry the weft to the left over four warp threads, then wrap it back under and around two. You can also carry the weft over two warp threads and then wrap back under and around one.

When you follow this routine on 2 adjacent rows, the result looks a bit like a column of knitted fabric seen horizontally.

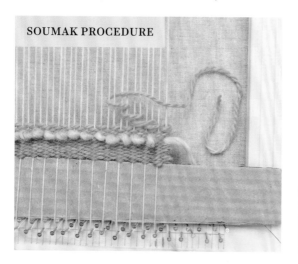

SOUMAK PROCEDURE

COMPLETED SOUMAK

Rya Knotting

The following directions are for creating a short plush fabric with rya knots. You can use this technique to create fringe of whatever length you choose, wherever you choose, along whole or partial rows. If you want the knots on only part of a row, weave as many picks of plain weave needed on each side of the rya knot section to fill the unknotted area. When the rya section is completed, you can again pick up the same sequence of sheds as you wove below it.

For these knots, I used equal amounts of the Adobe and Toffee yarns. Each piece of yarn was about 6".

Step 1

1. Loosely wrap your yarn around your hand about 20 times: you will need more than one wrapping, but this will get you started. Slip the loops of yarn off your hand and cut across the bundle to create a pile of same-size pieces.

Step 2a

Step 2b

2. Lay two pieces of yarn, one of each color, over two warp threads (a). Bring each pair of ends over these two adjacent warps, one on the left and one on the right, and then under the warp and up through the center (b).

3. Pull the ends down to form a knot. Continue in the same way, knotting two pieces of yarn over two adjacent warps all the way across.

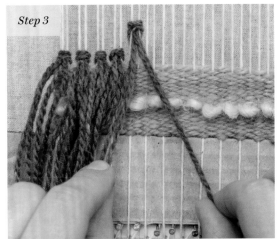

Step 3

4. Raise the shed and weave 1 pick to anchor the knots.

5. Repeat steps 2–4 as many times as desired, alternating the sheds each time.

6. Hold the loom above your work surface with the yarn ends hanging down. Use sharp scissors to trim the ends to the desired length.

The ends in this weaving are about 2" long, but you can make much longer fringe by cutting longer lengths to knot with.

Step 6

Going Free-Form!

Unlike with the first three tapestries, I added yarns with other textures to this design. Except for the bouclé and the Harrisville, all other yarns are handspun, including white and gray Romney and a 50/50 blend of camel/Merino and camel/silk. I also used some unspun, dyed angora locks.

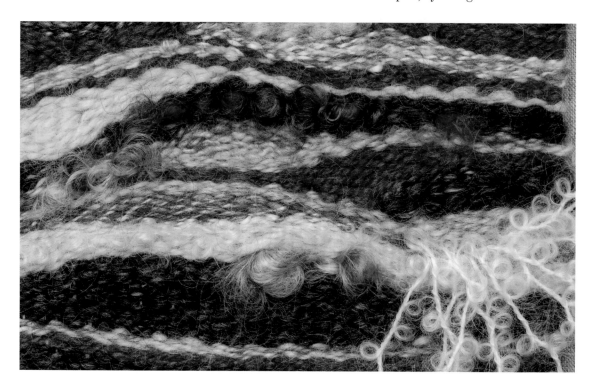

In this tapestry, build up free-form shapes by weaving back and forth. No cartoon or drawing is necessary this time. Keep weaving until you're happy with the shape. The top of each preceding shape will determine the bottom of the next shape. You can manipulate angles and build up areas by weaving shorter distances, then expand an area by weaving all the way across. This approach reminds me of Anni Albers's comment about taking yarn for a walk (see page 3)!

In order to maintain the correct under/over sequence on adjacent picks when you begin a new yarn, it's important to maintain the pattern you've established. To do this, always begin the new yarn where you've just ended a color or shape. Continue the under/over sequence in the same direction as established. It's a bit magical, but as long as you follow that rule faithfully, you can meander from side to side, in short or long sequences, and always be in the correct position to go under or over the next warp.

Note: In spite of this being free-form tapestry, it still adheres to the traditional approach of completely covering the warp threads, so the same rules of finding the warp sett and bubbling (see page 123) apply. In fact, as in Getting in Shape (see page 122), when you carry yarn across a particularly steep path, bubbling is especially critical.

When the shape was as large as I wanted, I threw a pick of white from edge to edge above it to highlight it. Notice the amount of bubbling I gave the white yarn.

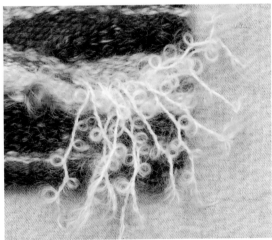

For the small area of bouclé fringe, I used rya knots, but I didn't apply them as thickly or trim them as short as the plush area in Playing with Texture (see page 126).

The three photos above show how to work across fewer warp threads in subsequent rows in order to build up a hill-type shape.

CATCH THE WAVE

I wove the tapestry shown here using worsted weight yarns, both commercial and handspun. The pale yellow, sea colors, and sky are all hand-dyed. With the exception of the wave, which features some looped weft and rya fringe, the piece is woven using traditional tapestry techniques: plain weave and weft-faced. Starting at the bottom, I used the following techniques:

- **FOR THE BEACH:** Alternating picks of pale yellow and white (see Beginning with Two Colors, page 120) create a subtly striped pattern to evoke a sandy beach. I built this irregular section as described in Getting in Shape (see page 122). When the shape was complete, I outlined it with one pick of the white yarn.

- **FOR THE WAVE:** For the frothy wave, I made rya knots (see page 126) along the outlined beach using a wool bouclé. Each knot is made of one length of bouclé knotted over two warps and trimmed to uneven lengths. When the tapestry is off the loom, the strands at the lower right will flow below the edge of the weaving. I secured the knots with another pick of white. The top of the wave is a looped weft (see page 124) done in pin roving; it, too, is secured with a pick of white.

- **FOR THE SEA:** The sea is woven following the technique for Going Free-Form! (see page 128). Note that as you get toward the top of the sea, you need to create shapes that are increasingly horizontal in order to get a clean, straight horizon.

- **FOR THE SKY:** The final section is plain weave. On a frame loom, it's more challenging to get a good shed as you near the top. I removed the shed stick to give myself more room. Be sure to leave enough warp to tie off the ends and weave them in at the back.

REBECCA MEZOFF

Rebecca Mezoff is a contemporary tapestry weaver with a studio in Fort Collins, Colorado. After getting a degree in occupational therapy, Rebecca began studying tapestry weaving with the late James Koehler, a giant in modern tapestry weaving.

Rebecca's work draws from the colors, open skies, and symbols of the southwestern United States. She hand-dyes all her own yarn to get the color gradations she loves and weaves most of her tapestries on her grandfather's Harrisville rug loom. Her work is in various public and private collections, and she teaches classes in her studio, online, and at venues throughout the United States.

In November 2016, Rebecca was the artist in residence at Petrified Forest National Park in Arizona. For a whole month, she was able to do nothing but create art without any preconceived expectations and, as she reports, to be "able to experience the wonder of the painted desert alone at sunrise and sunset." She set a goal of making a small (2" square) tapestry every day. Those she shares on the facing page are paired with photographs of some of the natural and manmade phenomena that inspired her, including the geology of the landscape and pottery shards and hieroglyphs made by the people who once lived there.

LIFELINES, 2016
Hand-dyed wool, 70" × 24"

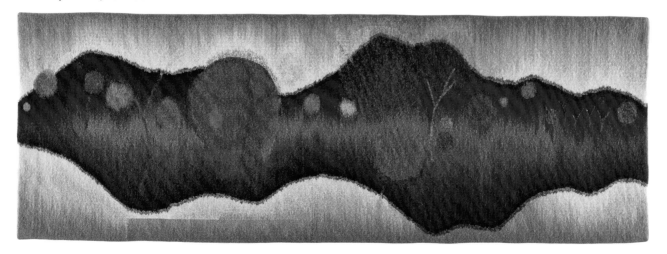

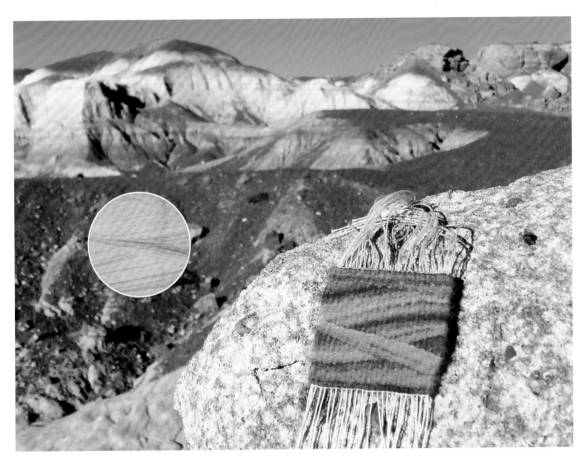

**PETRIFIED FOREST
TAPESTRIES, 2016**

Hand-dyed wool, 2" × 2"

MICHAEL ROHDE

Michael Rohde started weaving in 1973, when he became interested in exploring the construction of cloth. In the years since, his weaving has transitioned from floor rugs to tapestries. Along the way, Michael studied art at the Glassell School of Art at the Museum of Fine Arts, Houston, where he was influenced by the color theories of Joseph Albers and Johannes Itten.

In the early 2000s, Michael left his full-time career as a biochemist so that weaving could be his primary focus. His scientific training has informed his dedication to dyeing the yarn he uses; by keeping meticulous records of his color mixing, he is able to create and re-create his preferred palettes, which gives him more control than if he relied on commercial colors. In recent years he has started using plant-based dyes and colors from other natural elements rather than bright chemical dyes.

Michael's weavings incorporate colorful geometric shapes as a way of interpreting themes such as the effects of human and natural causes on the homes and lives of people. World events, as well as personal observations he makes while traveling, serve as the foundation of his weavings. And while they are filled with meaning, Michael's pieces are also beautiful fiber works of art.

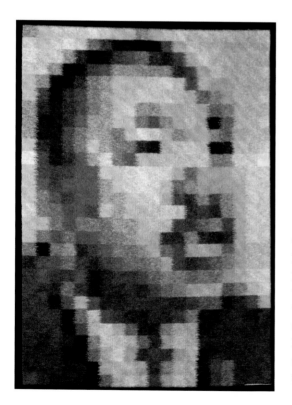

DREAM, 2014
Handwoven tapestry, undyed alpaca,
43½" × 31½"

This stunning portrait of Dr. Martin Luther King, Jr., is part of a collection of handwoven faces of leaders Michael admires. The pieces in the series rely on large pixels to convey the image, making the images seem diffused and, at times, unrecognizable until you squint or look at them differently. I love the way Michael has combined technology and tradition to create this tapestry.

He has had exhibits at the Textile Museum in Washington, D.C., the American Craft Museum in New York City, and the Mingei International Museum in San Diego's Balboa Park, and his work has been included in the State Department's Art in Embassies Program. Michael has also displayed his weavings around the world, including at the International Triennial of Tapestry in Lodz, Poland, and the Janina Monkute-Marks Museum Gallery in Lithuania. He has pieces in the permanent collections of the Art Institute of Chicago, the Racine Art Museum in Wisconsin, and the San Jose Museum of Quilts and Textiles and the Museum of Ventura County, in California.

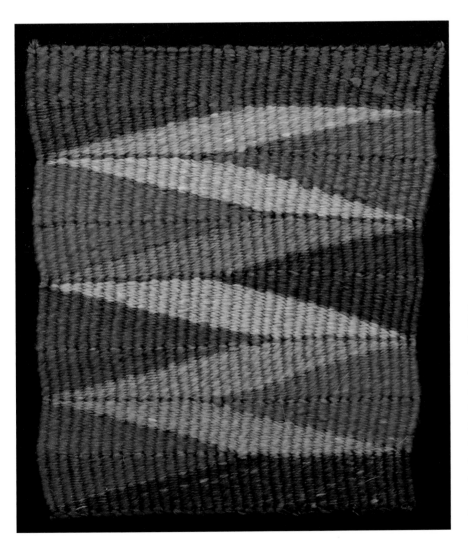

APHRODITE, 2012

Four selvage wedge weave; silk, natural dyes; 5¼" × 5"

This is one of several small weavings done on a portable (handmade) loom Michael uses when he travels. He can frequently be seen with a small cloth tote bag filled with his compact copper loom and hand-dyed fibers for his weft. I love watching these beautiful pieces come to life!

SARAH SWETT

Sarah Swett was born in Brooklyn, moved to Idaho when she was 18, and as she says, currently lives in her imagination. Her work travels the world in books, magazines, and exhibitions. She stays at home telling stories with yarn and munching on cinnamon toast. Sometimes Sarah's tapestries fill a wall, and sometimes they fit in the palm of her hand. "Why?" she asks, and then replies, "I don't know. But there they are: perched on the prairie, rooted to rocks, emerging from the sea, waiting."

The four small pieces below, each no more than 3" square, are among a series of four-selvage weavings of houses that for decades Sarah has woven with wool and linen, iris leaf, and cotton. Four-selvage weaving is a method of warping a loom so that the completed textile has no fringe or hems: it is completely finished when you take it off the loom.

FLAXEN HOUSE, 2018

Handwoven tapestry (four selvage); warp: spindle spun flax; weft: spindle spun flax, cotton; 3" × 3"

RED ROOF INDIGO SKY, 2018

Handwoven tapestry (four selvage); warp: spindle spun flax; weft: spindle spun flax, wool; natural dyes; 2½" × 2½"

THE NEW PINK HOUSE, 2018

Handwoven tapestry (four selvage); warp: spindle spun flax; weft: spindle spun flax and wool; natural dyes; 3" × 2¾"

VIEW FROM THE IRIS SHED, 2018

Handwoven tapestry (four selvage); warp: spindle spun flax; weft: spindle spun flax, paper, cotton, iris leaf; walnut dye; 3" × 3"

HUT ON THE ROCK, 2004

Handwoven tapestry; warp: wool, weft: wool (mostly handspun); natural dyes; 40" × 48"

This large tapestry is one of Sarah's wonderful storytelling pieces, based on a real coracle — a traditional fabric-covered, willow-wickerwork boat that she built with her son — and an imaginary dwelling. She wonders, "How would it feel to live always in such a place, where coracles are transport, your bedroom is a tower, and waves lap at the front door?"

RACHEL HINE

Rachel Hine lives and works in Geelong, Victoria, in Australia. She has always been an artist, ever since someone asked her what she'd like to be when she grew up. Over the last 20 years, Rachel has been devoted to the ancient artform of tapestry weaving. This is a labor of love. After university she took a long break, due to the full-time needs of two small children (now in school), but currently she works in her studio most days.

Lately, Rachel has been focusing on portraiture and the continuum of beauty and femaleness. Looking, observing, and watching from a female perspective are the key elements in all her work. She also pays homage to the postwar weavers of Europe and the techniques they resurrected, which inform the contemporary weavers of today. Whenever possible, Rachel likes to weave spontaneity into her tapestries.

DANI, 2019

Cotton, wool, and silk; 14 cm × 30 cm

The two works shown here have a similar approach, as they both have prominent textural features. Rachel explains, "When I begin work for a new tapestry, I usually make drawings that have a certain feel. Sometimes I want to break out of the conventional rectangular shape of tapestry, and that's when I make some kind of scribble at the bottom of the drawing to indicate a kind of improvisation."

**BETTY BLUE
EYESHADOW,
2017**

Cotton, wool, and silk;
14 cm × 28 cm

PART 2

WEAVING BEYOND THE FRAME

A loom is one of the tools you can use to keep the threads in order while you weave, but there are many ways to intertwine threads in addition to stretching them on a loom. You can weave around almost any shape, and here we have included projects using such objects as bottles and dowels as supports for our weaving. As you fashion each loop, stitch, or row, you also maintain your tension. And depending on the item being created, you can often use the same thread as both the warp and the weft. We're fascinated to see how many different ways a fiber can be interlaced to make interesting patterns, textures, and fabrics. Enjoy the adventure!

BACKSTRAP WEAVING

Many tools for weavers, such as table looms, inkle looms, rigid-heddle looms, floor looms, and even simple frames, are designed to hold and tension a warp for weaving. In contrast, the backstrap weaver provides the tension with his or her own body by positioning the tensioning device — a strap or belt — around his or her waist.

Backstrap weaving has been part of the weaving culture for centuries in widely different parts of the world, from northern Europe to Asia to North, Central, and South America. This type of weaving can be used to create a variety of intricate patterns and weave structures, including warp-faced, weft-faced, and balanced weaves. Although some traditional backstrap weaving is complex, it's possible to adapt and simplify the setup and still create stunning woven articles at little cost and with minimum experience. The simple equipment needed makes the technique uniquely portable. You can roll up your weaving-in-progress, pop it into your backpack or tote bag, and take it along wherever you go.

I used a backstrap setup for both the Leno Scarf (page 147) and the Card-Woven Bookmarks (page 159). —GS

An Overview of the Backstrap Setup

Setting up the backstrap loom is a bit involved, but it is not at all difficult. Both of the following projects that are woven with a backstrap loom include detailed setup instructions. If you've never used a backstrap loom before, though, this overview will give you an idea of how the process works.

1. Measure the warp following the instructions on page 288. Transfer the loop at one end to a rod, maintaining the cross with lease sticks.

2. Attach the rod to a sturdy fixed object, such as a piece of heavy furniture or, if you like weaving outdoors, a tree.

3. Cut the loop at the other end, and thread the warp yarn through the rigid heddle.

4. Slip the backstrap around the back of your waist or hips and attach each end of it to an end of the second rod.

5. Tie the warp to this rod, taking care that all ends are under the same amount of tension.

6. Wind your weft yarn on a shuttle and start weaving!

The weaver from East Timor, above, and the one from Guatemala, at right, are using string heddles and a shed stick instead of a rigid heddle to create the sheds, as we show in the following project. Both weavers, however, are creating tension with a backstrap.

Leno Scarf

Although many traditional backstrap weavers use string heddles (a system of looped strings to raise and lower warp threads) to make the shed (the opening through which they throw the weft), I wove this project using a rigid heddle for this purpose instead. Some weavers in both South and Central America and Scandinavia have used this technique, and many commercially produced backstrap looms today include a rigid heddle.

Using the rigid heddle inhibits the weaver's ability to create some of the intricate colorwork that string heddles and various pickup techniques can make. But because the rigid heddle is easier to set up and weave with, it serves as a practical introduction to backstrap weaving. —GS

DESIGN NOTEBOOK

This scarf features leno, a pickup technique that gives the piece some laciness. It's perfectly fine to skip the leno if you prefer an entirely plain-woven scarf, but weaving leno is much easier than it may seem at first glance. Maybe a little time-consuming, but not at all difficult! See page 154 for an introduction to the technique.

For both the warp and weft of the scarf shown on the facing page, I used Malabrigo Worsted, 100% Merino wool (210 yards/100 g), in colors Indigo and Cuarzo. The warp took 72 yards of Cuarzo (main color) and 54 yards of Indigo (contrasting color); the weft took 100 yards of Cuarzo. For the scarf shown in the step-by-step photos, I used coral worsted weight yarn for the main color and tangerine worsted weight yarn for the contrasting color.

Note that the width of the finished scarf is 25 percent narrower than the on-loom measurement. This resulted in part because of the spaced warps, which drew in during the wet finishing.

Leno Scarf

YOU WILL NEED

- **Warp and weft:** Worsted weight yarn, about 126 yards total for warp and 100 yards for weft
- Waste yarn
- 2 dowels, ¾" diameter and 14" long, with a screw eye inserted into both ends of one of them (see step 6 photo, opposite)
- Lease sticks
- Scissors
- Rigid heddle, 10" wide with 8 holes/slots per inch
- Threading hook
- Sturdy cord, about 1 yard, cut into two 18" lengths, to tie the dowels to a fixed object
- 4 rubber bands
- Backstrap: Twill tape or other non-stretchy band or belt, about 1½ yards long (adjust length according to the size of your waist)
- Stick shuttle
- Fabric strips about 1" wide (for the heading)
- Short blunt-tip tapestry needle
- Pickup sticks or weaving sword, 12" long (for leno)
- Band lock (see page 287) or clamp
- Wool wash, such as Eucalan

MEASUREMENTS

Width in heddle: 8¼"
Finished measurements: 6¼ inches wide by 50 inches long, excluding fringe, after wet finishing

Warping and Setting Up

1. Using the warp-measuring method described on page 288, wind a warp 2¼ yards long. Follow the color order in the chart on page 149. Secure the warp by tying it with small lengths of waste yarn (known as choke ties), at 18" intervals, beginning close to the warp end farthest from the cross (see page 290 for a photo of the cross).

2. Slip the dowel with the screw eyes through the loops at the end of the warp farthest from the cross.

3. Arrange two round or flat sticks (known as lease sticks) in the cross to preserve it and make it easier to pick up the warp ends in the proper order. Cut through the loops at the end of the warp nearest the cross, taking care not to lose the cross. Clamp the rigid heddle to your work table, as shown in the step 4 photo. For instructions on how to make a heddle cradle, see page 286. Lay the warp on the table with the cut ends near the rigid heddle.

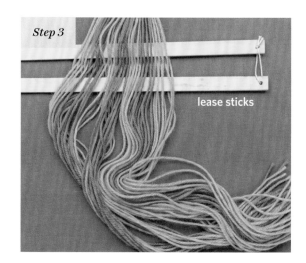

Step 3

lease sticks

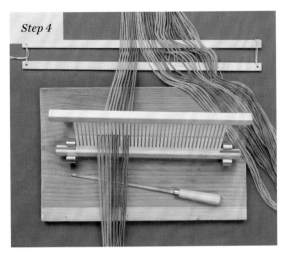

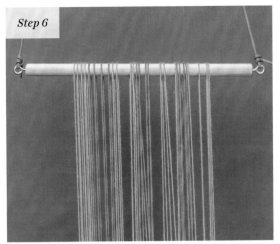

4. Measure the width of your heddle and begin your threading so that the 8¼" warp will be centered on it. Using a threading hook, draw the warp ends through the rigid heddle, inserting one thread end through a slot and the next end through a hole until you have you have 8¼" of threaded warp. Follow the threading chart below, taking care to skip a hole and a slot as indicated.

5. As you complete each color group of warp threads, tie them in a loose overhand knot (see page 291) to prevent the ends from slipping back through the holes and slots. When all the ends have been threaded, remove the lease sticks.

6. Insert a length of sturdy cord into each screw eye on the dowel containing the loop ends of the warp. Tie the cords to a fixed object, such as a heavy piece of furniture; if possible, position the cords so that they are perpendicular to the dowel.

WARP COLOR ORDER AND THREADING CHART

8 MC   4 CC   Skip   4 CC   4 MC   Skip   4 MC   4 CC   Skip   4 CC   8 MC

repeat 2 times

Main color (MC)

Contrasting color (CC)

Skip one hole and one slot

Leno Scarf

7. Sit at a distance from the tied-on dowel so that when you grasp the warp ends and pull the warp taut, there is about 10" of extra length. As you hold the warp taut, push the threaded heddle back to the other (dowel) end of the warp. This will spread the warp and smooth out the warp threads in preparation for tying the cut ends to the remaining dowel. Adjust the threads on the back dowel, distributing them evenly over about 8¼".

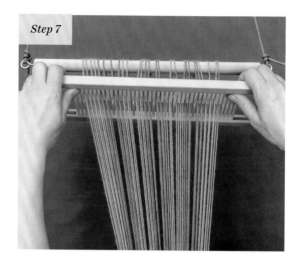

Step 7

8. Attach rubber bands to each end of the remaining dowel, about 1" in from the end. Make an overhand loop at one end of your backstrap and slip it over one end of the dowel, outside the rubber band. Take the strap around the back of your waist or hips and make an overhand loop in the strap at a distance that allows you about 6" between your body and the dowel.

Once you begin weaving, adjust the distance between your body and the dowel to whatever is most comfortable for you.

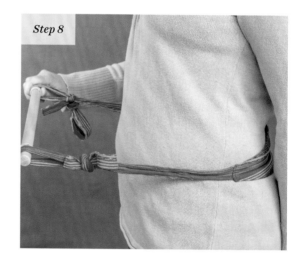

Step 8

9. Beginning with one group of eight warp threads on an outside edge (coral in photo), tie the warp to the dowel in this manner: divide the group in half; take each half over the dowel from front to back, then bring them over the eight warp threads and tie them in the first half of a square knot. (See page 291 for how to tie a square knot.) Move to the other side of the warp, and tie eight warp threads to the dowel in the same manner. Adjust the ties so that the two warp groups are as evenly tensioned as possible.

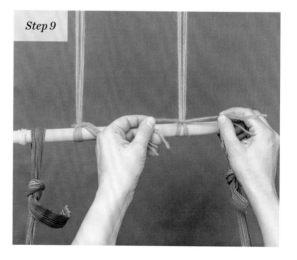

Step 9

WINDING WEFT ONTO A STICK SHUTTLE

If your shuttle has a notch in one of the openings, anchor the weft by tucking it firmly into the notch. Otherwise, hold the tail with your thumb as you begin to wind the weft onto the shuttle. Make the first few wraps over the tail to secure it: if it becomes loose when you're weaving, it can be a nuisance.

Wind the yarn figure-8 fashion along one edge and through the openings at each end of the shuttle. Leave one edge of the shuttle free to serve as a beater, as well as to minimize the bulk of the shuttle. It's often easier to angle the yarn-wrapped edge of the shuttle toward the top of the shed when inserting it through the shed.

10. Continue tying bundles of eight warp threads, alternating from the left to right sides of the warp until you get to the center and the entire warp is tied to the dowel.

11. With the warp under firm tension, run your hand over it to determine whether the tension is equally distributed (a). Make any adjustments necessary, then complete the square knots for each bundle (b).

Step 11a

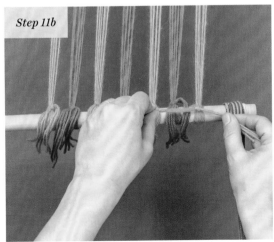

Step 11b

Weaving

12. Wind the main color yarn on a stick shuttle, as shown on page 151. You can comfortably weave with a bundle about 1" thick.

13. Maintaining tension with your body, push the heddle down to lower every other warp thread; this creates the first shed. Insert a fabric strip through the warp (a). (From here on, we'll refer to each insertion with the weaver's term *throw*.) Raise the heddle and throw another fabric strip through the warp (b). Use the heddle to snug, or beat in, the two strips. This motion is done after each throw. As you continue to weave the heading, when the fabric strip is too short to be carried across the entire warp, add another strip, allowing the end to extend an inch or so from the selvage.

A shed is the opening through which you pass the weft. It's made when the warp threads are separated into upper and lower sections.

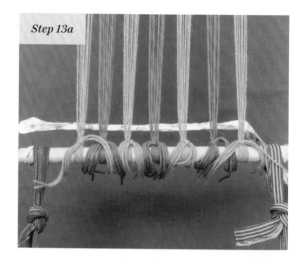
Step 13a

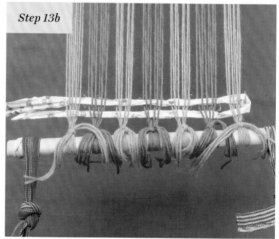
Step 13b

BACKSTRAP-WOVEN SCARF, TAKE TWO

Woven with Swans Island fingering weight Merino/alpaca yarn, this scarf is luxuriously soft. I used a 12-dent rigid-heddle reed. The finer yarn made it a bit more difficult to maintain an even weave and straight selvages, but it was worth it. Although I enjoy weaving on my floor loom, it fascinates me that I can achieve fabric like this using simple backstrap equipment.

I used an off-white yarn here so the hemstitching would show up better. When you hemstitch the edges of your scarf, use your main color yarn.

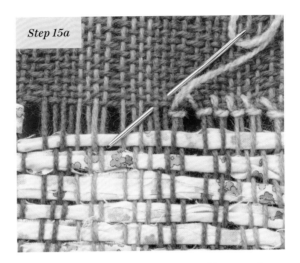

Step 15a

14. Repeat step 13 with two more strips. If the warp still looks uneven, continue to throw in fabric strips until all the threads are evenly spaced. You may need to adjust the tension by tightening or loosening a bundle of warp ends. Now is the time to do it — weaving with uneven warp tension causes problems you may not be able to correct once you've started weaving.

15. Start at the right-hand edge of the weaving and leave a tail about five times the width of the scarf for hemstitching. Using the main color, weave for about 2", and then set aside the shuttle while you hemstitch along the beginning of your weaving.

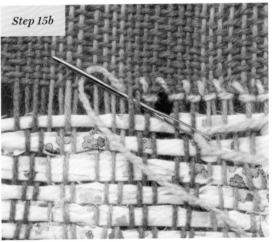

Step 15b

Thread the tapestry needle with the weft tail. Hemstitch over two threads as shown at right: Insert the needle from front to back, two weft threads above the fabric edge, and go under two warp threads, taking the needle on a diagonal from the upper right to the lower left (a).

Take the needle under the two warp threads to the right and through the loop of the working yarn (b). Pull firmly to snug the yarn against the edge, ready to insert the needle again two wefts above the fabric edge and directly between the warp you have just wrapped and the one on its left (c). Repeat a, b, and c across the edge.

Leave a 6" tail of the hemstitching yarn at the left-hand edge of the scarf; when the scarf is finished, you can include this tail in the fringe.

Step 15c

16. Continue weaving until the scarf measures
2½" from the beginning. Keep a light touch,
pushing the weft against the previous row rather
than beating hard. Try to maintain a consistent
pressure each time you beat in the weft. Aim for
achieving about 8 threads per inch — the same
spacing as for the warp. Try also to keep your
edges as straight as possible, not drawing in or
bulging out.

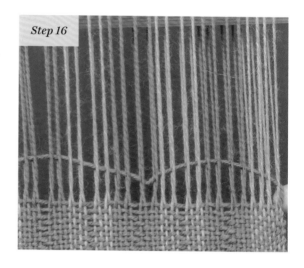

Step 16

Before beating in each throw of weft, push
the thread up at intervals to create what are
known as bubbles, or short, relaxed sections of
the weft. These bubbles allow the weft to travel
under and over the warp threads and help you
maintain straight edges. If you don't give the
weft room for these subtle ups and downs, the
edges of the scarf will likely pull in. Experiment
until you achieve just the right amount of bubbling. You don't want loops at the edges, or
fabric that buckles or shows loops along the surface, any more than you want drawn-in edges!
(For more about bubbling, see page 123.)

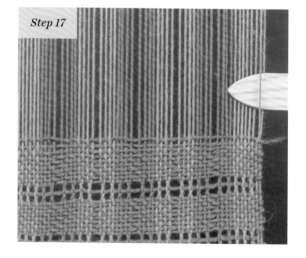

Step 17

Creating the Leno

17. Work your first leno pickup row as follows:
Starting with the rightmost warp thread, take it
under the one to its left, then draw it straight up
and place it on the pickup stick. Continue across
the entire warp, crossing each pair of adjacent
threads in the same manner.

18. Turn your pickup stick on its edge to create a
wider shed through which to insert the weft.
Take care to allow a small loop of weft at the
edge. The main challenge of leno is to give the
weft plenty of room in both the pickup row and
the one after it, so that the edges of your scarf
don't draw in at the leno sections. Remove the
pickup stick and beat the pickup row firmly in;
you may have to give it some encouragement
with your fingers to snug it down into place. In
this particular pattern, you should see a space
of about ¼" between the row before the pickup
and this row.

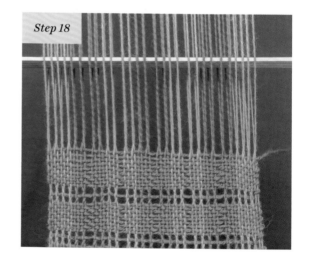

Step 18

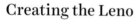

ADVANCING THE WARP

When you have woven about 5", the fell (or edge of the developing fabric), is probably getting uncomfortably far away from you. This means it's time to advance the warp and apply the band lock. Some backstrap weavers leave the warp on the original dowel, place another dowel against it, and roll the fabric around both dowels. They then slip the loops at each end of the dowel around just one of the dowels, which acts as a brake to keep the fabric from unrolling. For a number of reasons, I prefer using a band lock or clamp instead. (See How to Make a Band Lock, page 287, to create one of these.)

It's important to maintain the same even tension across all the warp threads after you advance the warp, and the leno rows in this pattern provide an ideal marker for where to clamp down the band lock.

1. Place your woven fabric on a firm surface, such as the floor, ground, or table. Slide the tied warp ends off of the dowel.

2. Unscrew the wing nuts from the band lock, and position the top piece of the lock just below one of the leno rows, taking care to keep the edge of the lock perfectly positioned along one of the weft threads. The weaving should be centered on the band lock. (If you are not weaving leno, simply align the band lock against a single weft thread.)

3. Take the bottom band-lock piece underneath the weaving, sandwiching the woven fabric between the two band-lock pieces.

4. Insert the bolts and fasten the wing nuts, loosely at first so that you can make any adjustments to ensure that the band lock goes straight across the weaving.

5. Tighten the wing nuts as much as possible, reattach the backstrap loops around the ends of the band lock, and resume weaving. When you want to again advance the warp, you don't need to remove the lock entirely, but do loosen it enough to allow you to slide the fabric back toward you without abrading it or disturbing the alignment.

19. The next row must be woven on the same shed as the row before the pickup row. This locks the cross into place. As with the pickup row, be sure to allow enough weft so that your edges remain straight. Beat in this row firmly, as before. The space between it and the pickup row should be approximately the same as that between the pickup row and the one before it.

20. Weave 8 more rows before working another row of leno. You will have 9 rows between each leno pickup row, and you will always start the leno at the same edge.

Finishing the Scarf

21. Continue weaving until about 12" of warp remains. Plan to weave 2½" of plain weave after the last row of leno. End with the weft coming out on the right-hand edge of the scarf.

22. Cut the weft thread, leaving a tail five times the width of the scarf, and hemstitch as you did in step 15, stitching over two threads, as before. Keep tension on the warp when hemstitching.

23. To remove the scarf from the loom, cut the loops off the dowel at the back and carefully slide the warp ends through the rigid heddle. Loosen the band lock so that you can draw this end of the scarf through it without abrading the fabric.

24. Trim the warp at both ends to about 6" (longer or shorter, as desired). Beginning at one edge of the scarf and holding one strand of fringe in each hand, twist each strand separately as tightly as possible. Before beginning this twist, examine the direction in which the yarn was twisted when it was spun. Working in the opposite direction of that twist, wind the two strands together. Then, holding the ends tight to keep the twist in, make an overhand knot (see page 291) near the end. Let go, and watch the twist wrap the two lengths tightly around one another. Try to give each pair of yarn ends the

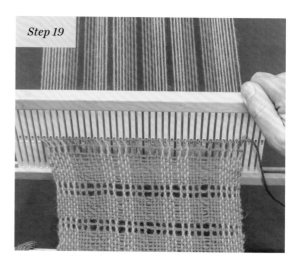

Step 19

When two or more strands of yarn are plied together, they form either an S twist or a Z twist, depending on the direction of the twist, which affects the way the twist slants.

same number of twists so that your fringe is consistently twisted.

Note: The Malabrigo yarn I used is single ply, with a Z twist. Notice that if you twist it counterclockwise, the twist increases. In order to get pairs of yarns to wrap tightly around one another, you must twist them in the other direction from the way they were spun: in this case, clockwise, which creates an S twist.

25. Gently wet finish the scarf in lukewarm water, without agitation. You may wish to add a wool wash, such as Eucalan, to the water. Wrap the scarf in a bath towel and press it to squeeze out excess water. Spread it out on a flat surface to dry.

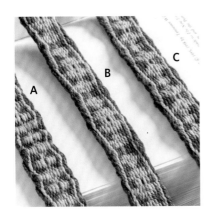

In 1903 in Norway, a Viking ship containing both woven and embroidered textiles, as well as bone tablets used at the time, was discovered in a farmer's field. The restored ship and its contents are in the Museum of Cultural History in Oslo, Norway. These bone tablets are among those discovered on the ship and date back to the ninth century.

Card-Woven Bookmarks

In card weaving, the warp is threaded through holes in each corner of special cards; by turning the cards in various ways, the weaver creates different sheds for the weft. Card weaving (also known as tablet weaving) has a very long history, and card-woven bands — some dating back to 400 BCE — have been found in many parts of Europe. These warp-faced bands have been used as embellishment on larger pieces of fabric, as well as for belts.

The earliest cards were made of a variety of materials, including bone, leather, wood, and metal. Most contemporary card weavers use cardboard cards — even squared-off playing cards. Once threaded, the cards are turned forward a certain number of times and then backward in specified sequences, a process that twists the warp threads so that each new shed (the opening between the raised and lowered warp threads) brings different colors to the surface, thus creating the design. The bands are reversible, with a different pattern on each side.

The warp may be tensioned on any loom, including an inkle, a rigid heddle, or even a floor loom, but it is also simple to provide the tension using a backstrap setup, as this project does. Scandinavian card weavers often use a band lock, and I used one for this project. The steps in the process are similar to those described in An Overview of the Backstrap Setup on page 144, except that in step 3 you thread the warp through the holes in the cards, and in steps 4 and 5, you position the warp in the band lock and attach that to the backstrap. Harrisville Designs makes a small backstrap loom with a band lock (shown on page 163) that is ideal for this purpose, or you can make your own (see page 287). —GS

Card-Woven Bookmarks

DESIGN NOTEBOOK

This project is meant to serve as an introduction to card-weaving techniques. Take care! Once you begin to investigate the seemingly infinite design possibilities of this ancient craft, you may easily become addicted. There are many excellent books on the subject, as well as patterns and advice on the Internet. In this example, all of the cards are turned in unison, but if you get interested in creating more complex patterns, you'll find that you can manipulate the cards in different groupings to introduce new, more complex designs.

The warp measurement given here is enough for weaving three bookmarks. If you prefer to weave only one or two, you can of course measure and cut a shorter warp. Since threading the cards is a bit time-consuming, however, and since you're likely to want to explore other versions of the turning sequence, the extra warp length may be just what you want. In addition, because there is a fair amount of waste (unused) yarn at the beginning and end of the warp, setting up the warp to weave three bookmarks, rather than just one, is more economical.

Experiment with the number of times you turn the cards. In other words, you don't always have to turn the cards four times in one direction and four in the other! For the bookmarks shown on page 159, I wove A in that manner, but for C, I made six turns away and then six toward, and for B, I made eight turns in each direction.

The directions that follow explain how to set up for backstrap weaving. You may also use a rigid-heddle, inkle, or other loom to hold and tension your warp.

I used the following amounts of these pearl cotton colors for the warp:

- Purple, 40 yards
- Green, 36 yards
- Blue, 20 yards

The weft required an additional 25 yards of purple.

YOU WILL NEED

- 12 card-weaving cards
- 2 pegs and 2 C-clamps
- **_Warp and weft:_** 3/2 Halcyon pearl cotton, 100% cotton, about 125 yards total for all 3 bookmarks
- Scissors
- Strong string or cord for scrap
- Backstrap and band lock (see page 287) or clamp
- Stick shuttle
- One 2"-square and two 4"-square pieces of cardboard
- Sewing needle or machine and sewing thread color-matched to the pearl cotton
- Rotary cutter and mat

FINISHED MEASUREMENTS
Three bookmarks, each 1" wide × 16" long, including 2" fringe at each end

Threading the Cards

1. Place the cards in a stack with A and B positioned at the top, and number them 1–12.

2. Following the instructions for How to Measure a Warp on page 288, measure 2-yard lengths of each of the following: 20 purple, 18 green, and 10 blue threads. Lay or hang them out in groups so that they don't tangle.

3. Follow the instructions on page 162 for Reading a Card-Weaving Chart. Use the threading chart on that page for the color order.

Step 1

Note that your cards have a hole in each corner, and each hole is lettered A through D. Note, too, that the lettering on some cards may be ordered differently from those shown here. Be sure to check before following charts from other books or online, as the pattern won't work if the cards are lettered differently from what you are using.

READING A CARD-WEAVING CHART

Card weavers have developed a charting system that shows at a glance which color is inserted in each hole of each numbered card and whether the threads are to be inserted from the front or the back of the card.

The numbers across the top of the chart correspond to the numbered card. The letters running vertically on the left indicate the hole through which each thread is drawn. The arrows along the bottom of the chart indicate whether you insert the thread from the front or the back of the card: when the arrows point up from left to right, insert the threads from back to front; when the arrows point down from left to right, insert the threads from front to back.

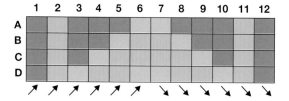

The chart colors correspond to the thread color. For example, as shown below, Card 1 should be threaded from back to front, and each hole is threaded with purple. Card 3 should also be threaded from back to front, with holes A, B, and C threaded with purple and hole D threaded with blue. Card 11 should be threaded from front to back, with all holes threaded with green.

As you finish threading each card, draw the ends out about 10", even them up, and tie them in a loose overhand knot (see page 291). Lay the card face down on the table, with the long, unknotted ends neatly laid out to the left. As you work, try to keep these warp threads from tangling by combing them gently with your fingers. Thread the next card and place it face down on top of the previous one. Be sure to orient the cards so that the letters match up.

Notice that in this chart, the first six cards are all threaded from back to front. Take care to change the threading direction when you reach Card 7.

I like to check the threading of every card before going on to the next step, tying the warp on. Threading errors are never any fun, and much less so with card weaving, which can be challenging to "unweave" and correct.

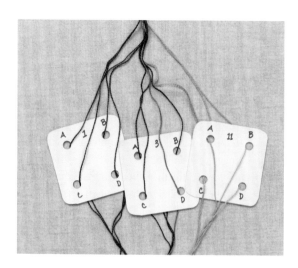

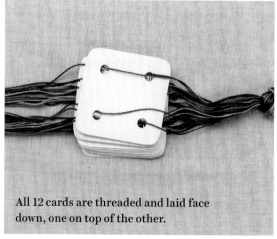

All 12 cards are threaded and laid face down, one on top of the other.

Card-Woven Bookmarks

Tensioning the Warp

4. When all the cards have been threaded, smooth out the long warp and tie the end opposite the cards in a tight overhand knot (see page 291). Use strong string or cord to tie this knot to a fixed object, such as a post, heavy piece of furniture, doorknob, or tree.

5. Holding the near end of the warp firmly, check to see that the cards are arranged with the lettered corners aligned, and with A and B at the top. Continue to keep the warp under tension as you push the cards toward the knotted end of the warp. You will probably have to tease some of the tangled threads into place. The goal is to have the warp completely smooth and untangled so that you can ensure that each thread is under the same tension when you clamp it into the band lock. With the cards still at the far end of the warp and under tension, carefully untie the overhand knots that hold the four threads for each card, and tie the entire group of threads in an overhand knot.

6. Sit a comfortable distance from the far end of the warp with your backstrap in place. Secure the warp in the band lock by placing the other end in the band lock, with the knot toward your body. Bring the cards forward toward you. This may reveal a few threads that need retensioning. If so, undo the knot and adjust as needed.

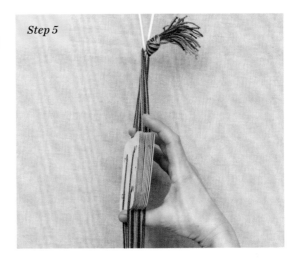

Step 5

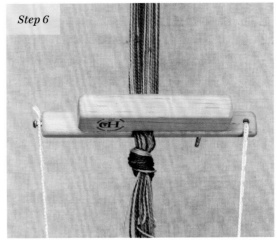

Step 6

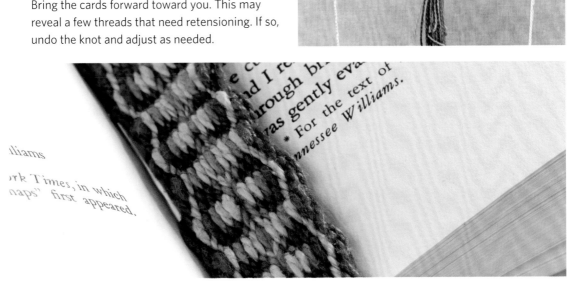

liams

ork Times, in which
naps" first appeared.

Weaving the Band

Begin by weaving a heading that puts all the warp threads in the correct alignment for weaving with the pattern thread. It also gives you a chance to see the pattern begin to develop and to correct any threading errors.

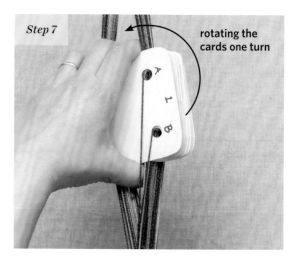

Step 7 — rotating the cards one turn

7. Using cord a bit heavier than your weft thread, you will weave through each of the sheds created by turning the cards in the order indicated by your pattern. (The shed is the opening between the raised and lowered warp threads.) To begin, wind about a yard of cord onto a stick shuttle. Check to ensure that holes A and B are at the top of each card. Holding the bundle of cards lightly in one hand and creating a bit of tension with your body, rotate the group of cards one turn away from you. Pass your fingers through the new shed to clear it completely, then insert the shuttle from right to left and draw the cord through, leaving a 3" tail.

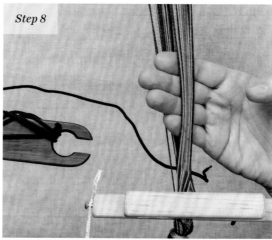

Step 8

8. Change the shed by again rotating the bundle of cards another turn away from you. Clear the shed with your hand, as shown. The photo at the right shows the weaver ready to insert the shuttle from left to right to draw the cord through for the next pass.

    Note: It's important to snug up the weft at the left edge when this pass is completed, as you can see in the step 9 photo below.

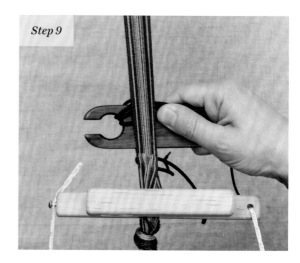

Step 9

9. Change the shed again by rotating the cards, and use the edge of the shuttle to pack in the second weft, as shown. Continue to rotate the cards in the same manner, inserting the weft, changing sheds, snugging the weft up at the edge, and then beating in the previous pick until A and B are again at the top. You will have turned the cards a total of four times.

10. For the next shed, rotate the cards back toward you one turn, and repeat the beating in and drawing the cord through.

11. Continue to rotate the cards toward you one turn for each row of weaving until A and B are again on top. Check to see that the pattern has developed correctly and that the edges are even. Now is a good time to adjust any warp threads with slack in them. Insert the 2"-square piece of cardboard in the last shed to reserve warp for fringe.

12. Wind your shuttle with purple weft thread. It is traditional to use the same color for the weft as the color of the edge threads of the warp, so that the weft blends in with the warp at that point. The goal in card weaving is for the weft threads to be completely covered, making this what is called a warp-faced weaving. Turn the cards away from you and pass your shuttle through from left to right, leaving a 2" tail. Turn the cards again, beat in the previous row, insert the shuttle from right to left, and also lay the tail in this shed. This will secure and hide it.

13. Continue in this manner, following the same pattern described in steps 7–11 (four turns away from you, followed by four turns toward you) until you have woven a band 12" long.

14. To separate this band from the next and to provide warp for the fringe, insert a 4" square of cardboard in one of the sheds before beginning again to weave.

15. Weave the next two bookmarks in the same manner, separating them as in step 14. If you wish, experiment with different turning sequences for the next bookmarks. As described in the Design Notebook on page 160, weave a second bookmark by turning the cards six times forward and then six times toward you. Weave the last one by turning the cards eight times in each direction.

16. When you have woven all three bookmarks, untie (or cut off) the knots at both ends of the piece. Hand- or machine-stitch across both ends of each bookmark to keep them from unraveling. Cut the bookmarks apart in the middle of the unwoven threads reserved for fringe by the cardboard squares. Measure 2" for each fringe and use a rotary cutter to evenly trim the ends.

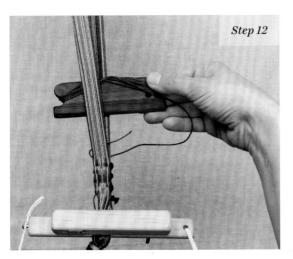

Step 12

JOHN MULLARKEY

John Mullarkey is passionate about teaching card (or tablet) weaving and exploring new ways to make the art form more contemporary. He loves to push this primitive weaving style outside the normal and historical limits to fashion his own interpretation of traditional patterns.

In 2013, John left his software development career to focus on weaving full time. He teaches at conferences and events around the United States, and his students value the patience, clarity, and organization he brings to his classes.

A frequent contributor to several weaving publications, John is also the author of *A Tablet Weaver's Pattern Book*. His creations have been displayed in museums, and in 2010 he won best of show at Handwoven's Not Just for Socks competition. John's Controlled Chaos Vest was selected for the Handwoven/Vav combined international fashion show. The Schacht Zoom Loom is based on John's design.

DIAGONALS WITH HANDSPUN SILK, 2010

1" × 2'

This piece uses a double-faced card-weaving technique called Egyptian diagonals with an original pattern. It is particularly thrilling to see how the same thread arrangement can look so unique by employing different ways of turning the cards.

YELLOW DIAMONDS, 2014

Handspun silk; 1½" × 3'

The technique used for this band is sometimes
called 4 × 4 tablet weaving, but John calls it "Coptic
Diamonds," as similar pattern work has been found
on bands in Egypt that date from the Coptic period.
This is also one of John's original designs; each
of the larger diamonds is unique, and the use of
contrasting colors makes the pattern pop.

FRAMELESS WEAVING

As we've seen, over the centuries different cultures around the globe have invented their own ways of interlacing threads, using a variety of tools and frames to achieve their goals. Even so, there are sometimes surprising similarities in patterns and techniques across time and space.

Weaving can be broadly defined as forming fabric by interlacing threads, whether yarn, fabric strips, plant fibers, or other materials. In some of the projects in this section we explore ways of creating fabric that aren't strictly weaving as we commonly think of it. While the threads in these projects do go over and under each other, we include techniques such as braiding, knotless netting, and Viking knitting, as well as kantha and *sashiko*, which are needle-weaving techniques from India and Japan, respectively.

Lucet-Braid Floor Mat

One thing I've always loved about weaving is that you can weave a sturdy rug one day and completely switch gears the next to create an airy shawl. I found the same delightful diversity is possible with a simple little tool called a lucet.

Like so many tools and techniques in the weaving world, braiding with a lucet has a long history. The Vikings may have been the first to use the lucet at least 1,200 years ago in Scandinavia and other parts of northern Europe.

Today lucets are readily available online. Stephen Willette created the one shown on page 179, where you can also find information about Stephen. Many are beautifully shaped and carved. It's easy to be captivated by their lovely designs, but it's also important to choose one that is comfortable in your hand. The only other thing required to begin braiding with a lucet is yarn — and that can be as lightweight as the Tencel used for the Beaded Bracelet (see page 177) or as heavy as the pin roving used for this small mat. The braiding technique is the same for both projects. It takes about 8 to 10 yards of yarn to make 1 yard of square braid, depending on the thickness of the yarn. For example, the mat required about 10 times the amount of pin roving as the length of braid needed to make the mat. —GS

Lucet-Braid Floor Mat

DESIGN NOTEBOOK

I hand-dyed the pin roving, using Dharma Fiber Reactive Dyes from Dharma Trading Company: Terra Cotta, Guacula (green), Cherrydactyl (raspberry), Mummy Mud Wrap (brown), and Purple People Eater (purple). While you may not wish to dye your roving, predyed material is readily available online, including on Etsy. Have fun dreaming up your own color palette!

I used the following amounts of the dyed roving:

- Terra Cotta, 47 yards

- Green, 37 yards

- Raspberry, 35 yards

- Brown, 33 yards

- Purple, 23 yards

YOU WILL NEED

- 175 yards of pin roving
- Lucet
- Scissors
- Heavy-duty upholstery thread and sewing needle
- Wool wash, such as Eucalan (optional)

FINISHED MEASUREMENTS

22" in diameter

Braiding with the Lucet

1. Draw an 8" tail of yarn through the lucet's threading hole from front to back. Hold the tail against the lucet as you proceed to the next steps.

2. Wrap the working yarn over the front of the right-hand fork and then across to the back of the left-hand fork, around to the front of the left-hand fork, and then across to the front of the right-hand fork, creating a figure 8. Position the last wrap above the loop already on the right-hand fork. Pick up that first loop and draw it up over the working yarn and off the fork to create the first knot.

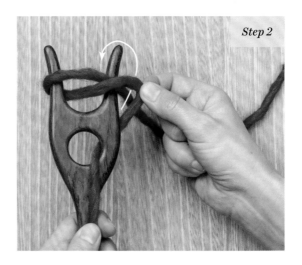

Step 2

3. Pull the tail and the working yarn to secure the knot, as you rotate the lucet clockwise and position the working yarn over the new right-hand fork, above the loop already on it. Pick up the first loop and draw it over the working yarn and off the fork, as you did in the preceding step.

4. Continue as in step 3 until the braid is the desired length. I wove a total of 17 yards of braid, in sections of various colors.

Step 3

5. Finish the braid. After drawing a loop off the right-hand fork, but before rotating again, cut the yarn, leaving an 8" tail. Carefully draw the last loop off the right-hand fork and draw the tail through it to secure it. Remove the remaining loop from the left-hand fork, bring the tail through that, and pull gently to secure.

Step 5

Assembling the Mat

6. Lay the first (center) braided strip on a work surface and arrange it in a spiral. You will notice that the braid is square. It's important to prevent the braid from twisting as you sew the strips together: keep the same plane of the square facing up throughout the assembly.

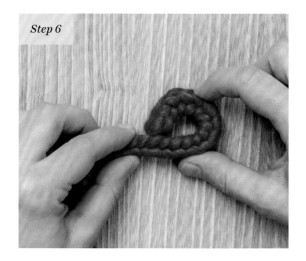

Step 6

7. Thread a doubled length of heavy-duty upholstery thread into your needle and knot the end. Take a small stitch into the side of the braid and then another small stitch into the side of the braid directly opposite. Continue to stitch back and forth between the sides as you build the spiral outward. This technique is called blind stitching. The goal is to keep your stitches hidden within the facing sides of the braid, but also small and close together so that the stitches don't pull apart when the mat is in use.

Step 7

8. When you need to begin a new strip, first butt the end of the new strip to the old and blind stitch the two ends firmly together. As before, take care to line up the planes of the square braids.

Step 8

9. When you have used up the braid or your mat is the size you want, make a few small stitches at the end of the braid and taper it down to make a smooth edge.

10. Block the mat by immersing it in warm water for about 20 minutes to ensure it is thoroughly wet. You can add a capful of Eucalan or other wool wash, if you wish. Place the mat on a large terry-cloth towel and roll the two up together to remove some of the excess moisture from the mat. Lay the mat on a dry towel and use your hands to press it flat and even out any bumps or ripples. Allow it to dry thoroughly.

Step 9

Beaded Bracelet

This delicate bracelet takes surprisingly little time to make. Because the process is both relaxing and meditative, you may find yourself going on to create others for your mother, daughters, cousins, and friends. One of the advantages of lucet braiding is that you don't need to premeasure the yarn before you begin, so you can just keep braiding until you achieve the length you want without needing to join new yarn. —GS

DESIGN NOTEBOOK

Once you learn the lucet braiding technique, it's fun to try it out with a variety of other materials. I used a purple-and-fuchsia variegated 8/2 Tencel for the delicate bracelet shown on the facing page; you need about eight times the desired length of the finished length of the bracelet. You could easily make a longer braid to create a necklace. A single-color yarn is, of course, fine for braiding, but it's especially fun to watch colors change when using a multicolor yarn. You can also braid with silk or pearl cotton in a yardage similar to that of the Tencel that I used. I used a variegated cotton yarn for the bracelet in the step-by-step photos. Choose beads that match or contrast with the thread you use; packets or tubes of beads often come in a variety of analogous colors, which are fun to work with.

Beaded Bracelet

YOU WILL NEED

- Sewing needle and thread
- 21 seed beads, size 8°
- 8/2 Tencel or similar-weight cotton or silk yarn or thread, about 8 yards
- Lucet
- Scissors

FINISHED MEASUREMENT
36" long

Braiding the Bracelet

1. Thread 15 (or more) of the beads onto the yarn and push them down the yarn out of the way until needed.

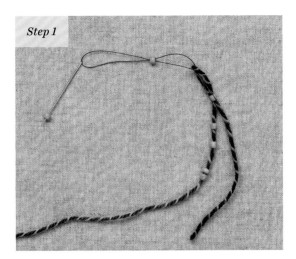

Step 1

Instead of using a beading needle or a dental floss threader, I threaded a 6" length of ordinary sewing thread through a sewing needle. I made an overhand knot (see page 291) to create a loop in the thread, then inserted a few inches of the yarn I was using for the bracelet through the loop. I then used the needle to pick up the beads and easily slide them over the looped sewing thread and onto the bracelet yarn.

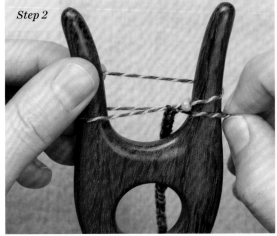

Step 2

2. Following the Braiding with the Lucet instructions on page 173, braid the bracelet yarn for about 6", or until you want to add a bead to the braid. Slide a bead up to the next knot and allow it to be caught up in the braid as you make the next couple of knots. Continue braiding for another 2", then draw up another bead. Repeat this procedure, adding another bead every 2" until the bracelet is the desired length (about 34"). Braid for another 6" before tying off.

3. Tie the 6" tails at each end of the braid together using an overhand knot (see page 291), and then thread three more beads onto each tail, tying them on about 1" apart. Tie the bracelet together above the tails to form a loop. A 34" braid should be long enough to wrap around your wrist four or five times.

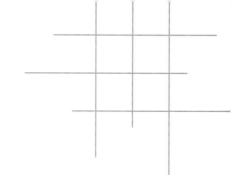

STEPHEN WILLETTE

For more than 40 years, Stephen Willette has handcrafted furniture and cabinets using time-honored methods. Knowing that his work will last for generations, Stephen explains, "I enjoy the creative process of seeing raw materials develop into something that is beautiful and functional."

A second-generation woodworker, Stephen learned to use woodworking tools at a very young age. His dovetail saw, handcrafted in Maine, inspires him to create works that honor that tool's quality and craftsmanship. In turn, he hopes to kindle excellence in the people who use his tools for their craft.

In addition to furniture and cabinetry, Stephen, along with his wife, Linda, creates a line of handsome fiberworking tools, including lucets, tapestry looms, support spindles, and shuttles. He is a juried member of the League of New Hampshire Craftsmen and exhibits these tools widely, including at Vogue Knitting Live and many East Coast fiber festivals and shows. Look him up online to see his tutorials plus examples of work that a variety of weavers and spinners have created using his handsome tools.

LUCET AND BRAIDED BOWL, 2018

Merino wool; 4" × 1½"

"When I work with wood," Stephen says, "I am reminded of my responsibility to use it respectfully and wisely, understanding the need to sustain our natural resources. The natural beauty of the wood never ceases to amaze me, and I enjoy using different woods to contrast and complement each other."

Knotless Netting Bottles

Looping and knotless netting are two ways of weaving a single strand of fiber around itself to create a web. Clay fragments containing twined and netted basketry have been found in central Europe dating from 25,000 years ago. This archeological evidence suggests these are among the oldest known fiber techniques and makes me feel a kinship with weavers through the ages.

Though they create similar-looking fabrics, the netting and looping processes differ. In looping, a single strand of fiber is passed through itself, not necessarily following even rows. Netting is a uniform, mesh-like fabric made by tying knots around a form to create evenly spaced rows. By wrapping the fiber around itself without actually tying a knot, knotless netting creates a strong and very stretchy fabric. Varying the tightness of the loops in these techniques can create a closely woven, dense fabric, a very open mesh, or anything in between. —DJ

DESIGN NOTEBOOK

I like that this technique is not too precise: If the fabric needs to be bigger, I can just make bigger loops or I can make two loops in one loop from the previous row. If the fabric needs to be smaller, I can skip a loop from the previous row or cinch up the loops to be tighter. Netting allows me to be free-form in my process without getting caught up in the details. As you weave your pieces, give yourself permission to play with the sizes of the loops and with the tension. Experiment with what variations you can employ.

I used 5"-tall, 4½"-diameter bottles with small necks. A quick Internet search will provide you with many choices. The size of your bottle — and how tightly you pull your loops — will affect how much twine or cord you need.

Knotless Netting Bottles

YOU WILL NEED

- Scissors
- Hemp twine, 1–2 mm in diameter, or four-ply waxed linen cord, 12–15 yards
- Tapestry needle
- A bottle to work around
- String or sewing thread

TIPS FOR SUCCESS

- Weave this project with the bottle upside down.

- Secure a new length of yarn using a weaver's knot (see page 294).

- Work with manageable lengths of yarn, probably no longer than 40". It is easier to add more yarn as you go than to work with a piece of yarn that is too long and gets tangled as you work.

- Clean the bottle after finishing your weaving if you used waxed linen, as the bottle will be smeared with wax. Use a damp paper towel to clean the glass in the open spaces of the netting.

- Snip and gently remove the strings you used to secure the bottom of the net to the bottle neck.

1. Cut a manageable length of yarn, about 40" long. Make a slip knot (see page 293) with the yarn.

2. Wrap the short tail from the slip knot a couple of times around the circle formed by the slip knot to make the base row.

3. Thread the needle with the long length of yarn, leaving about a 6" tail.

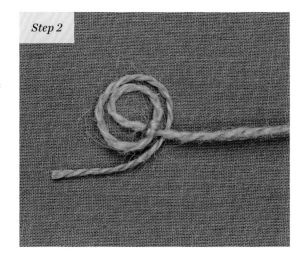

Step 2

4. Work the beginning rounds:

ROUND 1: Make 5 loops in the circle of the slip knot. To make a loop, take the needle from top to bottom behind the base row. Move the needle behind the base row (a) and over the working thread as it came out of the previous loop (b). Snug up the thread until you have the size loop you want (c). (5 loops)

I made the loops about ½" in diameter on the blue hemp version and about ¾" on the purple waxed linen version on page 185.

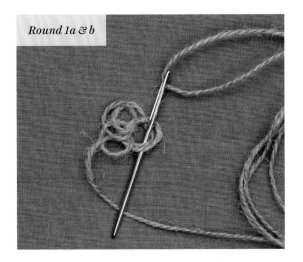
Round 1a & b

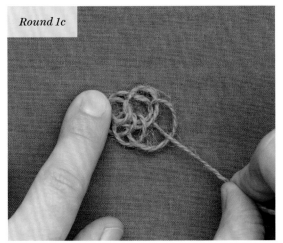
Round 1c

ROUND 2: Make 2 loops in each loop from the previous round. (10 loops)

ROUND 3: Make 1 loop in each loop from the previous round (this is also called working a round even).

ROUND 4: Make 2 loops in each loop from the previous round. (20 loops)

ROUND 5: Work 1 round even.

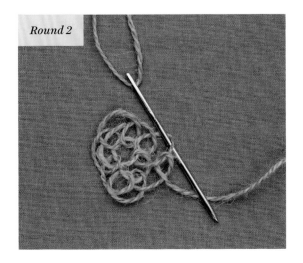
Round 2

Netting the Sides

5. Center what you've woven on the bottom of the bottle. Use four strings to tie it in place so it doesn't move around while you continue working.

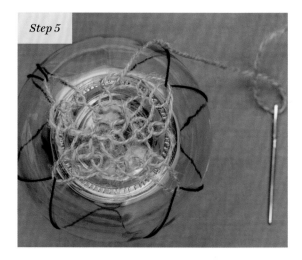

Step 5

6. Work in even rounds up the sides of the bottle. As the girth of the bottle grows, increase the size of the loops. As the bottle gets narrower toward the top, draw the loops tighter.

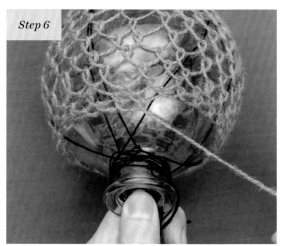

Step 6

7. When the netting is as high on the bottle as you wish, cut the yarn and secure the tail by carefully threading it back through the previous few loops. I prefer not to tie a knot as that can make a visual distortion on the edge of the weaving.

Step 7

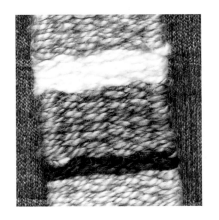

Bow-Loom Woven Belt

Bow looms are very simple weaving devices made by stringing the warp threads on a flexible stick. When warped, the loom looks like an archery bow. The weaving creates narrow bands, which many people adorn with beads.

Many cultures have used bow looms through the centuries: some northeastern Native American tribes used the bow loom to weave with porcupine quills to decorate necklaces, bracelets, and belts. Tribes also used wampum belts, or rows of beads woven together, as historical markers, ceremonial gifts, status symbols, and currency. In Thailand, bow looms have been used to weave ornate headdresses.

One contemporary version of the bow loom is made with a wooden dowel, duct tape, paper clips, and a piece of cardboard or stiff sponge. I put my own twist on this bow loom design and used some items from the local hardware store.
—DJ

DESIGN NOTEBOOK

- I used a fiberglass stake 48" long for the bow.

- The back scratchers I used have seven teeth (and six openings between the teeth) so I planned for six warp threads.

- For my weft yarn, I chose various shades of black, gray, blue, beige, and white.

- For best results, make the belt at least 8" longer than your waist measurement.

Bow-Loom Woven Belt

YOU WILL NEED

- 6 small zip ties
- 2 extendable back scratchers
- Fiberglass stake like those used on "for sale" signs or for garden stakes (found at home improvement stores)
- Scissors
- Painter's tape
- **Warp:** 5/2 cotton, 100% cotton, 10–12 yards

- Cardboard/shirt box strip trimmed to 1" × 5"
- Pocket comb
- Long blunt-tip needle
- **Weft:** 3/2 pearl cotton, 100% cotton, in multiple colors, about 100 yards total
- Two 1½" D-rings
- Sewing needle and thread

Making the Bow Loom

1. Use three zip ties to attach each back scratcher to an end of the stake. Align the teeth on both back scratchers so they face the same direction. Trim the tails of the ties, then wrap painter's tape around the stake and the handles of the back scratchers to smooth out the bumps from the zip ties.

2. Cut lengths of warp yarn that are several inches longer than the stake. You will need the same number of warp threads as there are spaces in between your back-scratcher teeth.

3. Tie the warp threads together with an overhand knot (see page 291) close (1"–2") to one end. Position the knot on the concave side of the back scratcher.

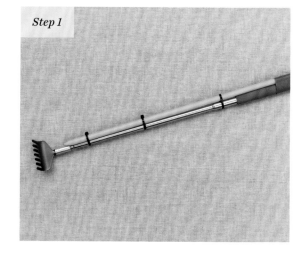

Step 1

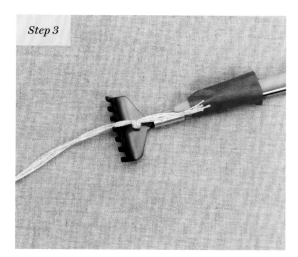

Step 3

4. Separate the warp threads, placing one in each opening between the teeth and coming over the smooth back side of the scratcher.

5. Stretch the warp threads along the stake to the smooth side of the back scratcher at the other end. Make sure the teeth of both back scratchers are facing the same direction.

6. Bring the warp threads over the smooth side and place them in order through the openings between the teeth. Pull the warp threads to have even tension, then tie a tight bow with all the threads.

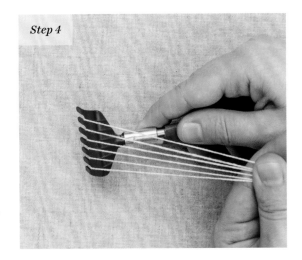

Step 4

It can be tricky to keep the threads in order and in the correct opening while you tie a bow and try to maintain an even tension on all six threads. Be patient and take your time on this step. This is the base for the rest of the project, and getting it right will make everything easier from here on.

7. Pull the warp threads tight, making the fiberglass stake bend and bow.

8. Pull again until the warp threads are very taut, making sure the six threads are evenly tensioned.

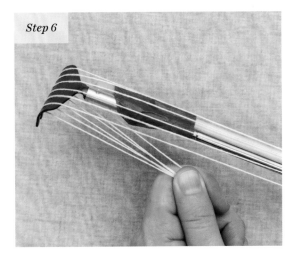

Step 6

TIPS FOR SUCCESS

- Snug each weft row tightly against the previous row to cover the warp threads completely.

- The length of the stake limits the longest possible length that you can weave the belt. You can make a belt that's shorter than the stake, though: simply stop weaving when you reach your desired length.

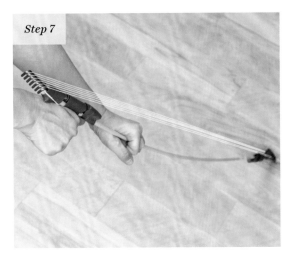

Step 7

9. Tie a square knot (see page 291) on one end of the stake to secure the tension in place. The loom is now ready to weave on.

Setting up the Loom for Weaving

10. Cut the cardboard strip into two sections, each about 2½" long. At the end of the loom closest to you, weave the first strip in an under/over pattern across the warp threads. Then weave the second strip in the opposite pattern, over/under. This forms a base for you to weave against.

11. Lay the pocket comb into the warp threads a few inches above the cardboard. Make sure the warp threads are evenly spaced in the teeth.

12. Secure the comb on the warp by adding painter's tape on the tips of the comb teeth. This will keep your warp threads evenly spaced as you are weaving and prevent the fabric from drawing in too much. You will weave between the cardboard strips and the comb. Move the comb up as your weaving progresses.

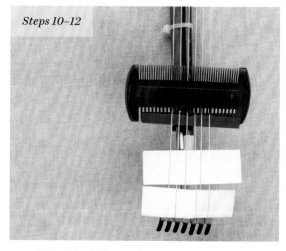

Steps 10–12

I used the side of the comb with wider spaces and threaded in every third slot so there were two empty spaces between each warp thread.

This bow loom is long and can be a bit awkward to use until you get the hang of it. I placed a chair about 4 feet away from the working end of the loom and hooked the back-scratcher teeth over the back of the chair. This held the loom in place when I was starting out. As my weaving progressed, I moved that chair closer to me.

Weaving

13. Thread the needle with the weft thread, then use the needle to weave over and under the warp threads. Push the weft into place with the needle as you would with a tapestry beater. Snug the weft thread up close to the edges so there are no loops sticking out from the edges, but be careful to not pull too tight, which can cause an indentation in the edge.

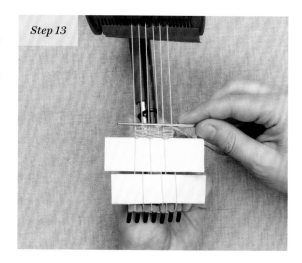

Step 13

14. Weave the entire length of the loom, switching colors as you like. I randomly used weft colors from the chosen palette and varied the length of the stripes in no particular order. Be sure to snug each weft row against the previous row. Leave any weft tails hanging from the sides to be woven in later. Begin each new weft thread on the opposite side of the warp that you finished with the previous thread.

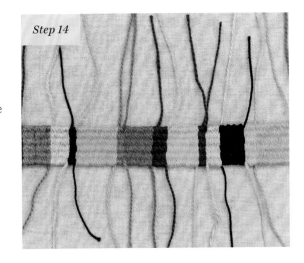
Step 14

You want a weft-faced structure, meaning the weft threads should completely cover the warp threads. Using the specified yarns, I wove 57 ends (or rows of weft) per inch of weaving.

Finishing

15. After the belt is woven, remove the comb and untie the knots that are behind the back scratchers at both ends of the loom.

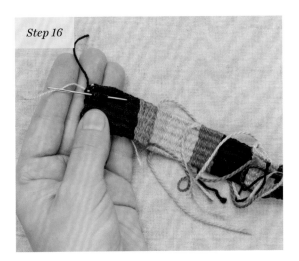
Step 16

16. Take the belt off the loom. On the ends of the belt, bury the warp thread tails by weaving them back into the fabric following the warp threads. This will make a firm, secure end that doesn't need to be hemmed.

17. Position the two D-rings on one end of the weaving and fold the belt end over the flat side of the rings. Stitch the belt end in place with the sewing needle and thread.

18. Bury the weft tails by needle-weaving them into the fabric following the warp threads.

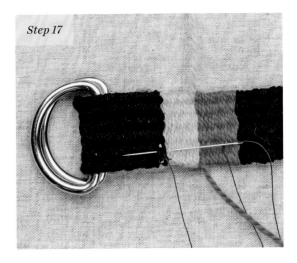
Step 17

Wire Necklaces

Evidence of trichinopoly chain, more commonly known as Viking knitting, dating from the eighth and ninth centuries has been discovered in Scandinavia and the British Isles. Although the common name includes "knitting," this is, in fact, a type of weaving that ancient Vikings used to make jewelry, charms, clothing adornments, and other decorative items.

The chain is woven around a form, usually a dowel, so that the finished piece has a hollow center. After removing the dowel, you pull the chain through a series of increasingly smaller holes in a hardwood rectangle known as a draw plate. (An Internet search will offer selections for draw plates. Look for one with a wide variety of size openings.) Each pull through the draw plate makes the chain more compact and rigid. Compressing the overlapping chain layers sometimes results in a completely new and interesting surface. The finished piece is a flexible yet sturdy ropelike cord.

Because many variables affect how long the final piece will be after pulling, it's difficult to say how long to make your original chain. The final chain will be anywhere between 130 and 200 percent longer than what you take off the dowel. The pulled length depends on the wire used, how many loops (or petals) are in the starter, how tightly the rows are pulled together, and many other factors. It's always best to weave the chain longer than you think you might need because you can cut off some length, but you can't add length after it's taken off the dowel.

The following pages include instructions for three different necklaces, each one using a slightly different method. —DJ

Rainbow Necklace (page 195)

Choker Chain (page 201)

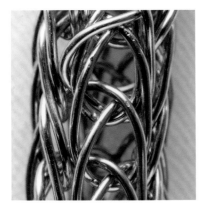

Freya Chain (page 202)

Wire Necklaces

YOU WILL NEED

- 24-gauge wire (for starting petal), 1 yard, plus wire specified for necklace of your choice
- Piece of wood or stiff cardboard, 1"–1½" high (optional)
- Dowel, pencil, or Allen wrench to work around; about ⅜" in diameter and 6"–10" long
- Rubber band or masking tape
- Awl

- Draw plate (with openings from ⅜" to ¹⁄₁₆")
- Needle-nose pliers
- Wire cutters
- Pliers
- Jewelry findings
- Kumihimo diameter braid sizing tool (optional)
- Epoxy
- 2" mini spring clamps (optional)

TIPS FOR SUCCESS

- Add more loops to your beginning petal to result in more loops in each subsequent round and a denser chain.

- Use an awl to even out the size of the loops as you make them. Insert the awl into the loop and carefully tug whatever side needs to be expanded. Use caution, as an awl is usually very sharp.

- Weave the first couple rows without worrying too much about the quality of your weaving, as the beginning of the chain will be hidden in the findings.

- Slide the woven area (including the rubber band) up and off the dowel as the weaving progresses, keeping only a couple of woven inches on the dowel. This will prevent the weaving from becoming too tight around the dowel to slide it off.

- Use care when pulling the chain through the draw plate so you do not hurt yourself. The chain can suddenly come through the plate, and you may hit yourself. Goggles are a good idea. And pull toward your chest, not your face.

Rainbow Necklace

This version of a Viking knit necklace (seen at the bottom of the facing page) is a wonderful beginning project. Its loose weave lets you easily practice the technique. You then pull the chain through the draw plate several times until you end up with a very narrow cord.

DESIGN NOTEBOOK

My chain was 21" long after weaving but 52" long after repeatedly pulling it through the draw plate. The wire tails are trapped in the core of the chain, essentially hidden from view. Since the finished thin necklace was lightweight and a bit kinky, I added a couple of glass donut beads to give the piece some weight.

I used nine colors of 28-gauge wire, and about 2 yards of each color. The clasp on my necklace is a 3.2 mm magnetic kumihimo clasp; Since the diameter of your finished chain may vary depending on the smallest hole you use on your draw plate, I recommend waiting until the chain is finished to determine the correct size for your findings.

ADDITIONAL SUPPLIES

In addition to the materials listed on page 194, you will need 18 yards total of 28-gauge copper wire and, if desired, one or more large donut beads or a pendant.

The Petal (or Starting Point)

1. With the 24-gauge wire, make 4 even loops (each 1"–1½" long) with the wire, leaving tails 4"–6" long at the beginning and the end. You have just made a 4-loop petal.

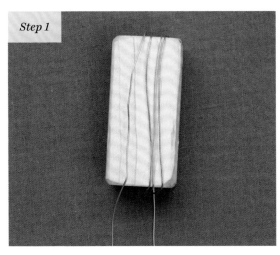

Step 1

You can wrap the wire around a piece of cardboard or wood, or around your fingers, to get even loops.

2. Securely wrap one end of the wire around one end of the loops to firmly hold them together.

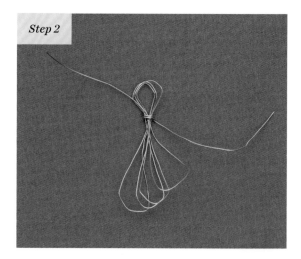

3. Center the connected hub of the petal on the end of the dowel with the loops hanging down around the dowel. Space the 4 loops evenly around the dowel, and fasten them to the dowel with a rubber band or piece of masking tape. With the awl, pull the loops so they are evenly spaced.

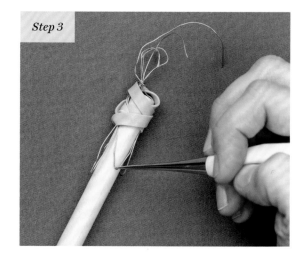

Weaving the Chain

4. Decide the order you will use the colors. Cut a piece of the 28-gauge weaving wire about 1 yard long of the first color. This will result in about 1" of woven chain. Hold the beginning tail of about 2" of the weaving wire down the side of the dowel and pointing away from the petals. Take the working end of the weaving wire and push it from right to left through the 1st loop of the first petal and back out over itself.

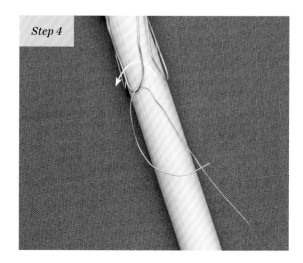

5. Take the wire to the petal on the right of the 1st petal. Pass the wire through this petal from right to left and then back over itself. Repeat step 5 until you are at the beginning loop.

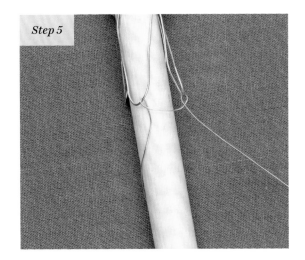

6. Take the working end of the wire from right to left under the twist from the 1st loop, and bring it back out over itself, then travel from left to right to the next loop.

7. Repeat step 6 for all subsequent rounds. After each loop, pull the wire to snug it up and make the twist tight, keeping the tension on the loops as even as you can. Leave about ⅛" between each round of loops.

8. Continue weaving until you get to the end of the 1 yard length you cut of the first color. This will be about 1" of woven chain.

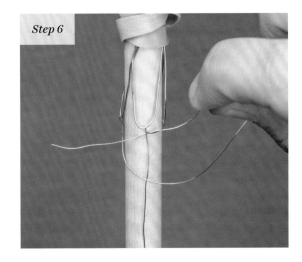

Adding a New Length of Wire

9. Push the wire end you've been weaving with through the twist from right to left as usual. Bend the wire down the dowel, away from the finished loops. Cut a new piece of wire about 1 yard long (in the next color you want to use) and insert the new tail in the opposite direction (left to right) of how you normally work under the twist.

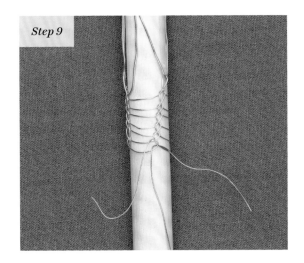

10. Bend the new tail down and twist it together with the final end of the previous working wire, keeping the twist snug up against the previous row. Then bend both ends together down the dowel and away from the finished weaving. Use the needle-nose pliers to help twist the ends into place.

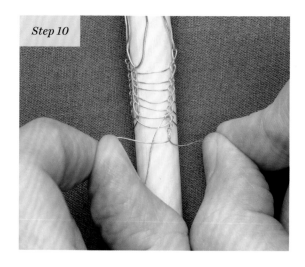

Step 10

11. Work around the dowel, catching the tails with the twist as you work that loop in the rotation. These tails will be in the center of the tube and will not be noticeable after the piece is pulled through the draw plate.

Continue weaving with 36" lengths of wire, making about a 1" woven area with each of the nine colors, then repeat the colors in opposite order. You will have 2" of the ninth color in the middle of the chain. Leave the final end of wire hanging loose so you can use it to attach the findings.

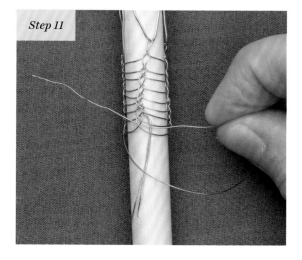

Step 11

Finishing

12. After weaving all the sections, slide the piece completely off the dowel.

13. Insert the beginning of the chain through the first hole in the draw plate so that the chain will easily fit through. Using the pliers to grip the petal wire along with the beginning couple of rows, pull the chain through the hole. Try to pull with an even and consistent pressure on the chain.

14. Repeat step 13, pulling the chain through progressively smaller holes in the draw plate until the cord is the diameter you want it to be.

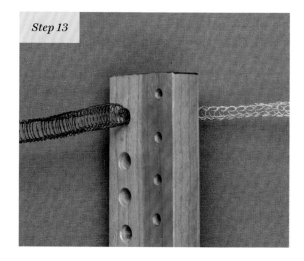

Step 13

15. Using the wire cutters, take out the petal wire.

16. With the pliers, compress the ends of the chain so they will fit in your findings. Use findings that are large enough to put the end of the chain in but small enough that it won't wiggle around. If you use a kumihimo diameter sizing tool you will be able to determine exactly the size of finding you need. Just insert the finished chain in the series of holes until it fits easily; this is the diameter of your chain.

17. Following package directions, use epoxy to glue the ends of the chain into the findings. Be sure to use epoxy in a well-ventilated area.

18. Allow the epoxy to dry fully before testing the clasp.

19. If desired, slide the donut beads or pendant onto the chain.

I like to use mini spring clamps to secure the chain in the findings while the epoxy dries. This helps make sure the finding is not jostled or moved from its position on the chain.

Step 15

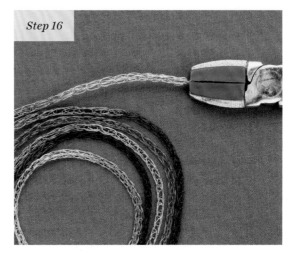

Step 16

Step 18

Choker Chain

Sometimes when I wear an open collar, I love to have a choker that fits snugly around my neck. This intricate-looking chain makes a beautiful statement all by itself, but you can also add a Free-Form Pendant (see page 55) onto the choker!

DESIGN NOTEBOOK

I used a 5 mm snap-together kumihimo clasp but find it best to wait until the chain is completed to determine the correct size for the finding. I suggest you weave the choker to be longer than you think you need because you can always cut off some length, but once you remove the chain from the dowel, you can't add to the length.

ADDITIONAL SUPPLIES

In addition to the materials listed on page 194, you will need about 20 yards of 28-gauge silver-toned art wire.

1. Follow steps 1–8 from Rainbow Necklace (page 195) but do not change colors; use only silver-toned art wire for the chain.

2. Weave until the chain is about three-fourths as long as you want your finished choker to be, then slide the piece completely off the dowel. When planning how long you'd like your finished chain to be, remember that the findings will add some length to the choker. My finished length is 13½", and I wove 9" before removing the chain from the dowel and adding 1" with the clasp. Again, it is possible to trim the chain if it is too long, but it cannot be made longer once taken off the dowel.

3. Follow steps 13 and 14 from Rainbow Necklace (page 195) to pull the chain through the draw plate. When pulling through the draw plate, do not make this chain too thin and flimsy.

4. Follow steps 15–18, from Rainbow Necklace to secure the jewelry findings onto the finished choker.

Freya Chain

This variation produces a stiffer chain than the previous two versions. You begin in the same manner but after the first round of looping, move up 2 rounds and push the working wire under the twist. This makes a denser tube that will not elongate as much when pulled through the draw plate, resulting in a thicker chain. Freya was the goddess of love and fertility in Scandinavian mythology, so I named this piece in her honor.

DESIGN NOTEBOOK

I used an 8 mm magnetic kumihimo clasp, but find it best to determine the correct size for the finding when the chain is completed.

ADDITIONAL SUPPLIES

In addition to the materials listed on page 194, you will need about 50 yards of 28-gauge silver-toned art wire.

1. Follow steps 1–6 for Rainbow Necklace (page 195).

2. Work the 2nd round into the same loops of the petal as the 1st round, but do not pull the loops as tight on the 2nd round. This will create some space between the loops in round 1 and round 2.

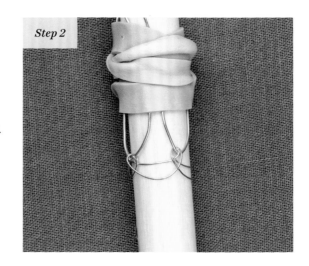

Step 2

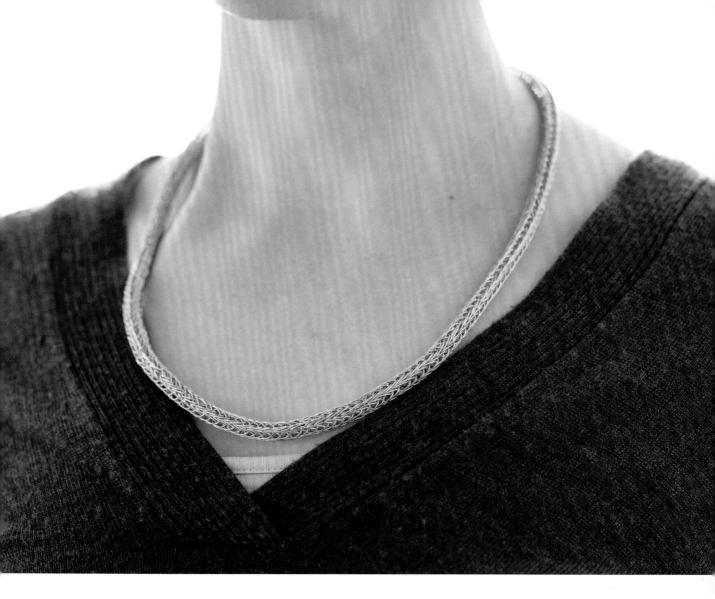

3. On the 3rd round, loop into the twist on the 1st round rather than into the twist on the 2nd round.

4. Repeat step 3, always working into the 2nd round above so you go around two twists rather than one twist.

5. Weave the chain until it is about 17" long.

6. Finish by following steps 12–19 (pages 198–199).

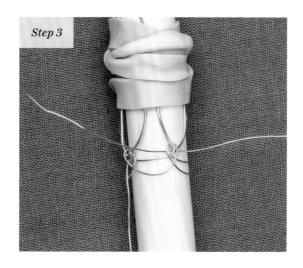

Step 3

FREE
AND EASY

Some projects do not require any loom at all. In the Small Treasure Bag with Twisted Draw Cord and Free-Form Vessels (pages 207 and 213, respectively), the fiber or wire twists around itself, building layer upon layer to create a vessel. The other two projects in this section feature needle weaving on fabric, which feels very free-form since the fabric is not stretched on a loom or encased within an embroidery hoop. It can be challenging to begin such a project since there is no form to build upon or frame to guide your efforts. But it is so fascinating to watch something grow from nothing. You have the freedom to shape the stitches to your liking.

Small Treasure Bag
with Twisted Draw Cord

I love when I can employ one technique to make very different things. The Knotless Netting Bottles project (page 181) calls for an open structure woven around a form. For this project, I used the same method, but without a form to weave around, and I pulled the loops fairly tight. A wonderful thing about looping is that it does not unravel like knitting or crochet will. So if you get a snag in the project or miss a stitch, there is no need to worry about it falling apart. It makes an extremely strong and durable cloth. —DJ

DESIGN NOTEBOOK

The instructions that follow explain how to make a very functional bag that is great for small tools or other treasures. Of course you can expand the project to make any size bag you'd like. Just keep increasing the number of loops per round until you have the diameter you want, then keep going up until you have your desired length. No matter what size you make this bag, it's a great "take along" project, since the stitches do not unravel and you can easily work on it in short bursts with no ill effects on the pattern.

One versatile thing about this process is that you can change yarns whenever you like. I used Rowen Hemp Tweed, a blended yarn of hemp and wool, in three colors. Work with 30"–36" lengths of yarn. Here is the yardage required for each color:

- Color A, 75 yards
- Color B, 49 yards
- Color C, 20 yards

Small Treasure Bag

YOU WILL NEED

- Worsted weight yarn, about 150 yards
- Large-eyed tapestry needle
- Scissors
- Hanger and pencil to help make the twisted cord

TIPS FOR SUCCESS

- Work this bag from the bottom up.

- Place a short piece of a different color yarn or a stitch marker at the beginning of a round to keep track of where to start the next round. Move the yarn scrap up as you get to the next round.

- Try making a 16-Cord Kumihimo Braid (page 25) to use as the drawstring instead of a twisted cord.

Bag

ROUND 1: With color A, make a slip knot (see page 293). Make 5 loops around the slip knot. To make a loop, take the needle from top to bottom behind the base row. Move the needle behind the base row and over the working thread as it came out of the previous loop. Snug up the thread until you have the size loop you want. (5 loops)

ROUND 2: Make 2 loops in each loop of the previous round. (10 loops)

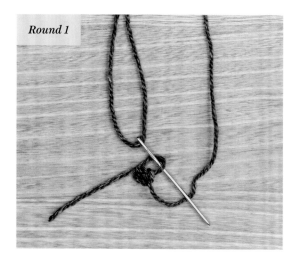

Round 1

Round 2

ROUND 3: Make 2 loops in each loop of the previous round. (20 loops)

ROUND 4: Work 1 loop in each loop of the previous round (also called working even).

ROUND 5: Work 2 loops in each loop of the previous round. (40 loops)

ROUND 6: Work 1 loop in 1 loop and 2 loops in the next loop of the previous round. Repeat around the full round. (60 loops)

Work even until the piece measures 3½".

STRIPED ROUNDS: Change to color B, attaching the new yarn with a weaver's knot (see page 294) and work even for 1".

Change to color A, attaching the new yarn with a weaver's knot, and work even for 1¾".

NECK ROUNDS: Change to color C and work even for 1 round.

Work 1 round as follows: Make 2 loops in one loop from the previous round, then skip 1 loop from the previous round. Repeat this pattern all the way around this round. This creates small holes in the fabric to thread the drawstring through. (60 loops)

Work 1 round as follows: [Make 1 loop in one loop from the previous round] twice, then work 2 loops in next loop from the previous round. Repeat this pattern all the way around this round. (80 loops)

FINAL ROUNDS: Work 2 rounds even, then cut the yarn and weave in the tail.

Striped Rounds

Neck Rounds

Drawstring

1. Decide what color you'd like the drawstring to be and cut a piece of that yarn 4 yards long, then fold it in half so it's 2 yards long.

2. Tie an overhand knot (see page 291) in the end with the tails and slip that over the hook of a hanger that is hung up. Keep the folded end of the yarn toward you.

3. Insert a pencil in the loop and twist vigorously in one direction.

4. When the yarn starts to kink up from being twisted, double the cord back on itself, matching up the end you are holding with the end at the hook of the hanger. Don't allow the cord to twist on itself yet. Loop the fold where the pencil was over the hanger hook.

5. With one hand, carefully hold the folded end that previously was the middle point. With the other hand, pinch the cord a couple of inches from the end you are already holding. Be sure to keep the cord straight and under tension as it is

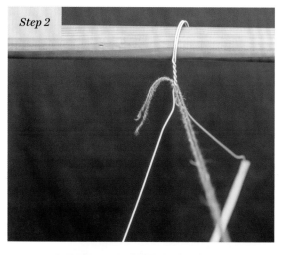

Step 2

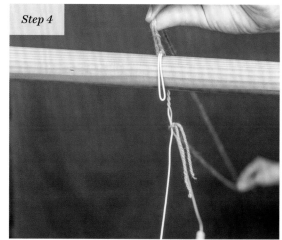

Step 4

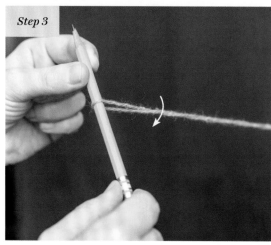

Step 3

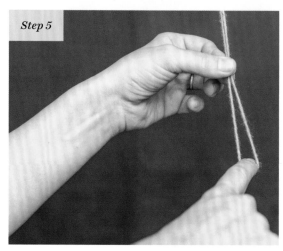

Step 5

stretched from the hanger. Release the folded end, allowing the cord to twist back onto itself.

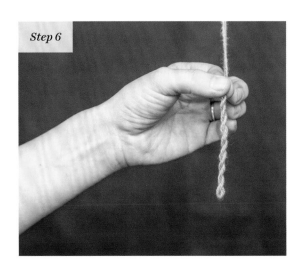

Step 6

6. Move your pinch closer to the hanger a few inches at a time, allowing the twist to work its way up the cord.

7. Tie an overhand knot in the end of the cord and slip the other end off of the hanger. The finished cord will be about 32" long.

8. Thread the cord through the bag's open loops to make a drawstring.

Small and Simple (page 214)

Free-Form Vessels

In these two looping projects, creating vessels with wire gives the finished pieces enough structure and body to be freestanding objects. One of the joys of working with wire is that it is its own needle. Additionally, the ends do not unravel and only need to be bent into place as you finish working with a strand. And since the wire is malleable, you can moderately manipulate the shape to conform to your vision once the piece is finished. —DJ

Free-Form Filigree (page 217)

Small and Simple

For this project I used 24-gauge wire, which is pretty stiff, doesn't easily break, and firmly holds its shape. Sometimes I use this small vessel to hold my business cards when I'm teaching or at shows. If it happens to get smashed in transit, I can easily bend it back into shape and it looks as good as new!

YOU WILL NEED

- 24-gauge copper wire, about 20 yards
- Round-nose pliers

- Wire cutters or scissors you can use for cutting wire (I used some inexpensive kids' scissors from the office supply store.)

Looping the Bottom

SETUP: Start with a piece of wire about 30" long. Beginning at one end and using the pliers, make a small circle about a ½" in diameter and circle around it two times.

ROUND 1: Make 5 half-hitch loops (see facing page) around the foundation circle. Your loops should average about ¼" in diameter.

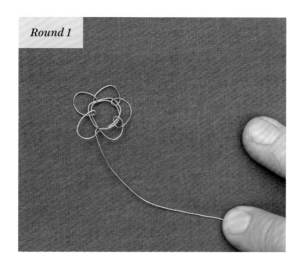

Round 1

ROUND 2: Make 2 loops in each of the 5 loops you made in round 1. (10 loops)

ROUND 3: Make 2 loops in each loop you made in round 2. Each loop in this round and throughout the rest of the project will measure slightly more than ⅛" in diameter. (20 loops)

ROUND 4: Make 1 loop in the 1st loop and 2 loops in the next. Continue in this alternating manner around this round. (30 loops)

ROUND 5: Work 1 loop in each loop from the previous round. (30 loops)

ROUND 6: Work 1 loop in each of the first 3 loops and 2 loops in the next loop. Continue in this alternating manner around this round, ending with 2 single loops. (37 loops)

ROUND 7: Work 1 loop in each loop from the previous round. (37 loops)

ROUND 8: On the next round, work 1 loop in each of the first 3 loops and 2 loops in the next loop. Continue in this pattern around this round, ending with a single loop. (46 loops)

HALF-HITCH HOW-TO

To make a half-hitch loop, bring the wire from top to bottom under the wire that creates the bottom of the circle (a). Then bring the wire back over the working loop (b) and pull toward you to tighten the loop (c).

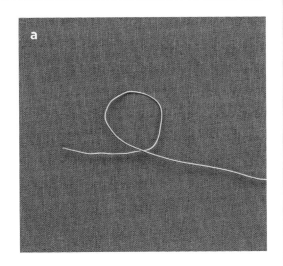

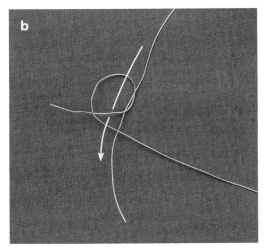

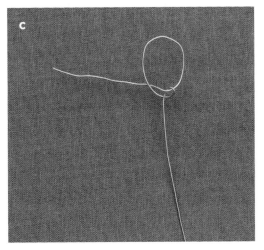

ROUND 9: Work 1 loop in each loop of this round. (46 loops)

ROUND 10: Work 1 loop in each of 4 loops and 2 loops in the next loop. Continue in this pattern around this round, ending with a single loop. (55 loops)

ROUND 11: Work 1 loop in each of 6 loops and 2 loops in the next loop. Continue in this pattern around this round, ending with 6 single loops. (62 loops) The piece should now measure 4½"– 5" diameter, depending on how tight you pulled each loop.

TURNING ROUND: Work 1 loop in the 1st loop and 2 loops in the next loop. Continue in this pattern around this round. (93 loops)

Looping the Sides

SETUP: Bend the previous row up to begin making the sides of the vessel. You will now turn the piece upside down and work with the bottom of the vessel facing up while moving down the sides.

ROUND 1: Work 1 loop in 1 loop, then skip 1 loop. Continue in this pattern around this round, ending by working 1 loop. (47 loops)

Work even until the vessel is about 2¼" tall.

Finishing

Cut the wire and tuck in the tail. Smooth the end with the pliers. If desired, press the top part of the vessel toward the center so the top edge angles in and is slightly smaller in diameter than the bottom.

Setup

Free-Form Filigree

This piece is decorative and fun. I chose to weave the vessel with very lightweight wire, giving it a lacy, ethereal look. One of the charms of this piece is the asymmetry of the ruffle at the top. The tiny seed beads around this delicate object's top edge add to its whimsy. Because this technique is meant to be free-form, my instructions do not specify an exact number of loops in each row. Your numbers will vary based on how you make your loops. Although the directions advise how many loops to increase or decrease in each round, feel free to improvise, giving your vessel your own unique style and shape.

YOU WILL NEED

- 30-gauge copper wire, about 20 yards
- Wire cutters or scissors you can use for cutting wire (I used some inexpensive kids' scissors from the office supply store.)
- Round-nose pliers
- About three hundred 2 mm seed beads

To make a half-hitch loop (see page 215), bring the wire from top to bottom under the wire that creates the bottom of the circle (a). Then bring the wire back over the working loop (b) and pull toward you to tighten the loop (c).

Looping the Bottom

SETUP: Start with a piece of wire about 30" long. With one end, make a small circle about ¼" in diameter and circle around it two times.

ROUND 1: Make 6 half-hitch loops around the circle. For this project your loops should average about ⅛" in diameter.

ROUND 2: Work 1 round even, making the loops slightly larger than those you made in round 1.

ROUND 3: Work 2 loops in each loop from the previous round.

ROUND 4: On the next round, make 1 loop in the 1st loop and 2 loops in the next loop. Continue in this pattern around the round.

ROUND 5: On the next round, make 1 loop in each of the next 2 loops and 2 loops in the next loop. Continue in this pattern around the round.

ROUND 6: Work 1 loop in each loop of this round.

TURNING ROUND: Work 1 loop in the 1st loop and 2 loops in the next loop. Continue in this pattern around the round.

TIPS FOR SUCCESS

- Keep track of the beginning of each round by tying a small piece of yarn or placing a knitting stitch marker around the 1st loop in the round.

- Use round-nose pliers to straighten and even out the loops after completing each round. Gently tug on the most recent round of loops while being careful not to pull too hard and undo the loops.

- Use wire pieces no longer than 36" to prevent tangles.

- Work each wire length until you have only about 1" remaining. Join new wire as follows: Turn the end of a new wire length down about ¾" and hook that from right to left on the last twist of the old wire. With round-nose pliers, twist the tail of the new wire around the existing wire a couple of times. Clip the tails.

- Each time you add a new length of wire, go back to the join at the beginning of that wire and press it between the pliers to mash down the wire ends that may be poking out.

- If you are adding beads, don't put all your beads on at once. Start by slipping a few beads on the wire, then just add more as needed by sliding the beads down to their spot in the piece.

- Refine the vessel's shape once it is completed by bending the wire to suit your vision.

Joining a new length of wire

new wire ←

Free-Form Filigree

Looping the Sides

SETUP: Bend the previous row up to begin working the sides of the vessel. You will now turn the piece upside down and work with the bottom of the vessel facing up while moving down the sides.

SIDE ROUNDS: Work even rounds until the sides of the vessel are about 3" long. As you work down the sides and move toward the neck, gradually pull the loops slightly tighter to decrease the diameter of the vessel.

Shape the Neck

ROUND 1: Work 1 loop in the first 3 loops, then skip 1 loop. Continue in this pattern around the round.

ROUND 2: Work 1 loop in each loop around, pulling the loops a bit tighter than in the previous round.

ROUND 3: Make 1 loop in the 1st loop and 2 loops in the next loop. Continue in this pattern around the round.

ROUNDS 4 AND 5: Work 2 rounds even (1 loop in each loop), making the loops in the 2nd round slightly bigger than in the 1st round.

Shape the Ruffle

ROWS 1 AND 2: Work 1 loop in each loop halfway around the vessel. Turn the vessel and work back in the opposite direction, working 1 loop in each loop, but do not go all the way to where you started the beginning of this round.

RUFFLE ROWS: Work back and forth, decreasing the number of loops in each row by not going all the way back to the end of the previous round until the widest portion of the ruffle measures about 2". Make one ruffle or more, depending on your own inclination.

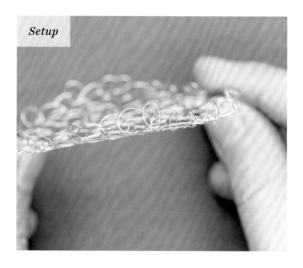

Setup

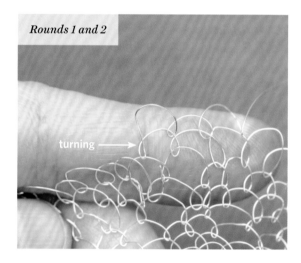

Rounds 1 and 2

turning →

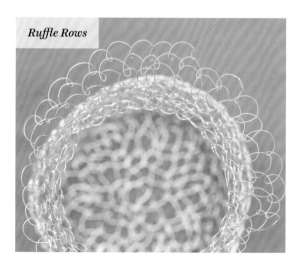

Ruffle Rows

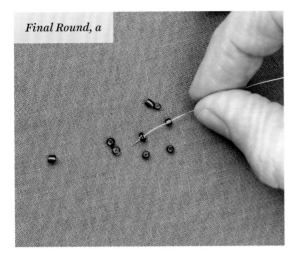

Final Round, a

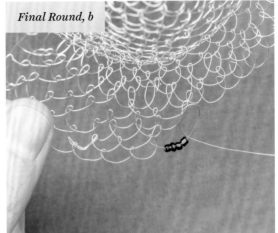

Final Round, b

FINAL ROUND: You will now work the final round of loops with beads. With the working end of the wire, slide three or four beads onto the wire (a), then in place as you make each loop (b). Add more beads on the wire as you need them. You will work 1 loop in each loop around the entire top edge, sliding beads in place as you go.

After completing the full round with beads, cut the wire and use your pliers to bend the end into the previous loop.

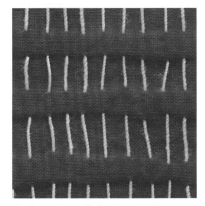

All in a Row (page 226)

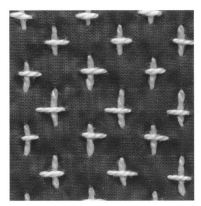

Compact Parallels (page 226)

Crosses (page 227)

Thoughtful Threads Note Cards

In this age of email and texts, receiving a handwritten note is a treat. It's especially charming to get one on a handmade card. All three of the following patterns use the slow stitching needlework style, with each version a bit more challenging than the previous one. Making all three proved a wonderful way to learn this tradition and gave me lots of practice regulating my stitching. I got into the weaving spirit by pushing my needle up and down, in and out of the fabric, creating designs in the cloth. —DJ

DESIGN NOTEBOOK

My inspiration for the Thoughtful Threads Note Cards and Stitched Project Bag (page 229) came from two traditional Asian methods of reusing cloth to make new and improved fabric. *Sashiko* is a Japanese stitching style that became a popular domestic craft more 400 years ago, but has origins well before then. Kantha is a style of stitching that originated in eastern India and the surrounding areas, perhaps as far back as 500 years ago. Both methods incorporate linear stitching on cloth in ways that share some similarities with both embroidery and quilting, but that also relate to the basic over/under flow of weaving. I find it fascinating that such similar styles of stitching were developed in different times and parts of the world and that I can use them as inspiration for my projects in modern times.

I have come to think of the threads making up the cloth as the warp and my stitching thread as the weft. By following the grain line of the woven threads in the cloth, my stitching goes over and under as with other weaving. While many designs are possible in each method, I find the grid-like patterns appeal to me the most, as they resemble weaving in the regular interlacement of the threads. I purchased a few fat quarters at the fabric store and used those as the basis of my projects.

YOU WILL NEED

- Piece of stiff paper that is larger than your card
- Medium-weight fabric, ironed (One fat quarter will make 4 cards.)
- Scissors
- Photo frame cards
- Fabric marking pencil (I like a mechanical fabric-chalk pencil.)
- Ruler
- Long stitching needle (A *sashiko* needle works best.)
- Size 3, 5, or 10 crochet cotton (3/2, 5/2, or 10/2 pearl cotton)
- Washcloth
- Iron and ironing board
- Fabric glue (optional)

General Instructions

1. Using the stiff paper, make a template that is slightly smaller than the front of your card.

2. Trace the template on the fat quarter as many times as possible. Cut the rectangles apart.

3. Center the opening in the card on the fabric. Using the fabric marking pencil, mark the outline of this area.

4. Using the fabric marking pencil and ruler, draw parallel lines on the fabric. Specifics for each pattern follow on pages 226–227.

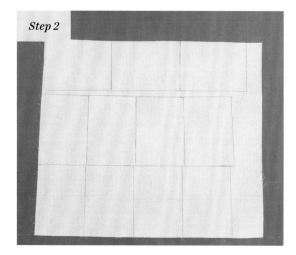

Step 2

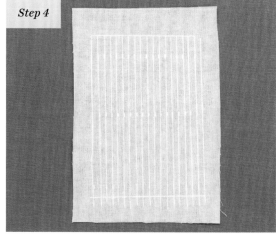

Step 4

5. Thread the needle with a piece of crochet cotton about 20" long. (Much longer than that and the thread tangles and becomes difficult to work with.)

6. Follow the first line using a running stitch; try to keep the length of the stitches and the unstitched areas evenly spaced on the line.

7. After the 1st row is stitched, move to the 2nd row, following the spacing of the stitches on the 1st row.

8. Stitch the remaining rows, always following the spacing set by the 1st row.

9. Use a damp washcloth on the fabric to help the disappearing chalk lines fade away.

10. Iron the fabric if it has puckered a bit.

11. Most cards have adhesive tape to attach the fabric under the opening. Sometimes a bit of glue will help hold the fabric in place. Use just a small amount of glue; otherwise the paper may crinkle.

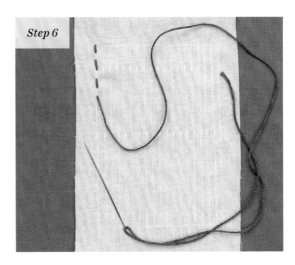

Step 6

Step 11

TIPS FOR SUCCESS

- Carefully iron the fabric before stitching to remove any fold marks or wrinkles.

- Measure carefully as you stitch the 1st row to keep the spacing of the stitches the proper length. Once you have completed the 1st row of stitching, it's easy to follow the spacing for the remainder of the project.

- Keep the knots at the ends of the rows to make a cleaner join when adding new lengths of thread.

- To keep the fabric from puckering, avoid pulling the stitching too tight.

All in a Row

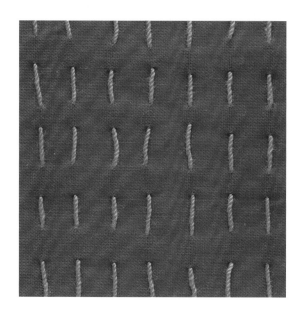

Set up the fabric by following the General Instructions steps 1 and 2 (page 224).

1. Draw parallel lines ⅜" apart. Extend the lines about ½" beyond the area marked for the opening on the card.

2. Following each line, sew a running stitch, making the length of each stitch slightly more than ¼" and the space between the stitches slightly less than ¼".

   Follow the General Instructions steps 7–11 to finish.

Compact Parallels

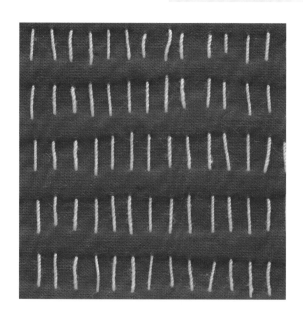

Set up the fabric by following the General Instructions steps 1 and 2 (page 224).

1. Draw parallel lines ³⁄₁₆" apart. Extend the lines about ½" beyond the area marked for the opening on the card.

2. Following each line, sew a running stitch, making the length of each stitch ¼" and the space between stitches about ³⁄₁₆".

   Follow the General Instructions steps 7–11 to finish.

Crosses

Set up the fabric by following the General Instructions steps 1 and 2 (page 224).

1. Draw parallel lines ¼" apart. Extend the lines about ½" beyond the area marked for the opening on the card.

2. Following the first line, sew a running stitch, making the length of each stitch ¼" and the space between the stitches ¼".

3. For the second line, use the same spacing as the first line, but sew where the open spaces fell in the first line and leave open spaces where the stitches are in the first line. In other words, stagger the placement of the stitches.

4. Alternate stitching the lines as in steps 2 and 3 above.

5. Turn the piece a quarter turn and place a ¼" stitch crossing each existing stitch.
   Follow the General Instructions steps 8–11 to finish.

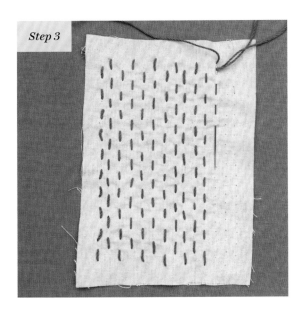

Step 3

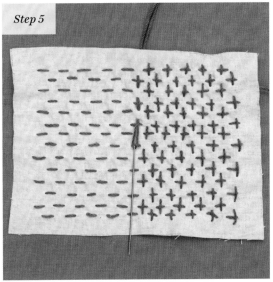

Step 5

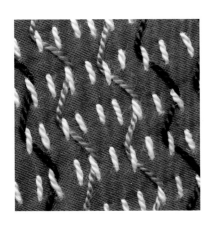

Stitched Project Bag

Having a small bag to corral essential tools for a particular project makes it easy to bring the project with you everywhere you go, giving you something to do whenever you're waiting for an appointment or looking to fill some spare time. Of course, any bag will do, but a beautiful handmade bag is such a pleasure to use. When working the final stitches on this bag, I was especially pleased to weave the thread over and under the previous stitching. —DJ

DESIGN NOTEBOOK

I used gray (color A), apple green (color B), light green (color C), turquoise (color D), black (color E), and purple (color F) crochet cotton on this purple version. For the green bag shown in the how-to photos, I used variegated gray (color A), variegated pink (color B), lavender (color C), variegated red (color D), teal (color E), and dark gray (color F).

Stitched Project Bag

YOU WILL NEED

- Iron and ironing board
- Medium-weight cotton fabric, one fat quarter
- Quilter's gridded ruler
- Scissors
- Fabric marking pencil (I like a mechanical fabric chalk pencil.)
- Size 5 crochet cotton (5/2 pearl cotton), 7 yards each of 6 colors
- Long sewing needle
- Sewing thread and needle or sewing machine

- 24"–28" drawstring cord (To make your own drawstring, see 16-Cord Kumihimo Braid, page 25.)
- Safety pin

FINISHED MEASUREMENTS
8" wide × 9½" long

Setup

1. Wash, dry, and iron the fabric. Then trim it to be 15½" long × 19" wide.

2. Use the fabric marking pencil to draw a 1½" seam allowance along each short edge of the fabric. Then mark the foldline down the center of the 19". If desired, mark the top casing and bottom hem allowances.

3. With the fabric folded on the center fold line, measure and mark 1¼" in from the left and right edges on both faces of the bag. This should leave a space measuring 5½" across that is centered on each face of the bag. This will be your design area. It is easier to do the stitching *before* sewing the bag together, so measure carefully to make sure your design will be centered.

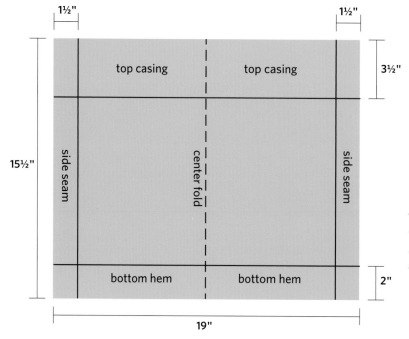

The finished bag will be folded in half, so each side is 8" wide after allowing for the 1½" seam allowance on each edge.

4. Measure 5¼" from the top (3½" for the top casing and 1¾" blank above the design) and 3½" from the bottom (2" for the hem and 1½" blank below the design). Then mark the design inside the 5½" × 6¾" area on both sides of the bag with the chalk pencil. I made 9 rows per each 1½" horizontally across.

Stitching the Bag

5. Using the long sewing needle, stitch four groups of 9 rows each in the following color order, starting from the top: color A, color B, color C, and color D. There are 16 stitches and 15 open spaces across the 5½".

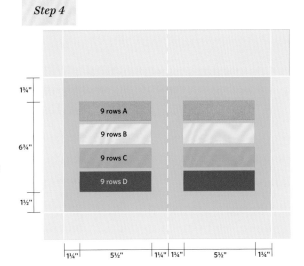

Step 4

6. After the basic grid is stitched with the four colors, weave in the second design with color E and color F, following the chart. Start with the color E stitches, then work the color F stitches.

Step 6

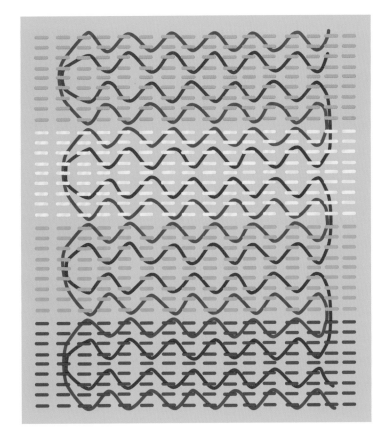

Let your needle travel through the existing stitches, going under the designated stitch and alternating which side of the stitch you enter from.

Stitched Project Bag

Assembly

7. Fold the side and bottom edges of the bag ½" and ½" again to the inside and iron.

8. With the right sides together, fold up the bottom of the bag ½" to the inside and press. Then turn the bottom in again ½" and press. Stitch across the bottom.

9. Line up the edges and sew the side seam, stitching ¼" from the turned-under edge of the pressed-in fold. Stop 3½" from the top of the bag.

10. Fold in the top edge ½" and press. Then turn the top down again 1½" from the first fold and press.

11. Make a casing in the center of the fold by stitching ⅜" from the top and bottom of that fold.

12. Stitch the side seam above and below the casing to connect the sides of the bag at the top. Leave the center of the casing open for the drawstring.

13. Tie a knot in both ends of the drawstring and attach a safety pin to one end. Thread the safety pin through the casing, pulling the cord through and out the other side of the casing. Remove the safety pin and center the drawstring.

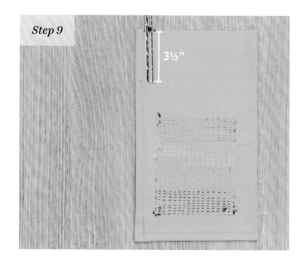

Step 9

3½"

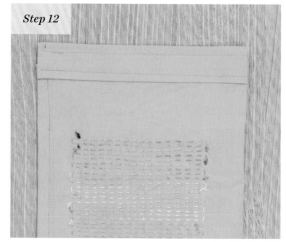

Step 12

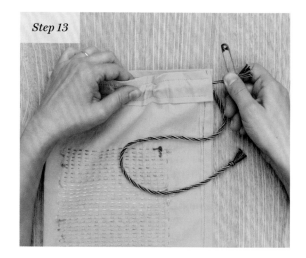

Step 13

To make your own drawstring, see
16-Cord Kumihimo Braid, page 25.

ROCK, PAPER, RIBBON!

In the projects that follow, we leave looms behind and weave on, or with, some everyday materials: stones, paper, and ribbon. We begin with stone, then offer several paper-weaving techniques, and conclude with two projects using ribbon.

Gathering stones — wet and gleaming from the ebb and flow of the waves on a sunny day at the beach — is the idea of paradise for many people. If you've ever come home with pockets laden with your prizes, you may enjoy the creative process of weaving around each one to make them just a bit more special. They can even become useful items as paperweights or coasters. (See Stone-Age Weaving on page 237.)

Paper opens a whole new world of weaving both two- and even three-dimensional items, like the baskets and stars on pages 247–269. You can choose to use the most ubiquitous of papers — newspaper, brown craft paper, maps, sheet music, or even pages from used books, as Deborah did for her baskets (pages 247–253). On the other hand, it's also a pleasure to explore specialty papers with lovely textures and colorful patterns. Some of the projects that follow are traditional paper crafts, while others use paper as a substitute for classic versions done with straw or other natural materials.

Ribbons have many uses, both decorative and functional: they can adorn a young girl's hair or embellish a gift or serve as weft for lavender wands (page 271). And because ribbons are sturdy and have even edges, they make strong weaving strips for baskets and containers (page 254), as well as a spectacular table runner (page 275). Ribbons are also available in a wide variety of colors, textures, and widths. Once you see all the variations of a woven project you can make with different ribbons, the process can become habit forming.

Stone-Age Weaving:
Paperweights

While there is evidence of weaving as far back as 25,000 years ago, that particular weaving is not what this project is about! This weaving is for anyone who can't come back from the beach or forest without a pocketful of stones. Decorated stones can be enjoyed simply as decoration, but if you can find the right shape, you can create unique paperweights or coasters embellished with a bit of weaving. —GS

DESIGN NOTEBOOK

Although this is a very simple project, not every stone makes a good foundation for weaving. It's difficult to weave across very round, smooth stones, so choose one with a bit of "toothiness" along the edges or with notches where you can anchor the thread. Somewhat squared-off stones also work well.

For the stones on the facing page, I used #2 sport weight Euroflax linen, 100% wet spun linen (270 yards per 100 g), color #2544 Teal. Linen works especially well for this project because it's not as slippery as many cottons or wools. I used five warps for these stones, but you may have more as long as you start with an odd number. As you can see in the photo on the facing page, you can create a symmetrical, starlike pattern, an asymmetric pattern, or a symmetrical one with two pairs of warps parallel at right angles to single warps. The stone will "tell" you how to arrange the warps!

Paperweights

YOU WILL NEED

- Linen thread or yarn, 1½ yards
- A flat stone, approximately 3"–4" in diameter
- Bent-tip tapestry needle
- Clear-drying white glue (optional)
- Swarovski flatback beads in Pacific Opal (optional)

1. Lay the length of yarn straight across your work surface. With the side of the stone you want as the top facing up, place the stone about 10" from one end of the yarn.

2. Gather the ends of the yarn and cross them on top of the stone as you would with a ribbon while wrapping a package. Experiment with the positioning until you find the points on opposite sides of the stone where the yarn won't slip when tied. These will be the points at which the stone is narrowest or where there may be small indentations that will catch the yarn.

3. Take the ends of the yarn to the back of the stone and tie them tightly in a square knot (see page 291). Run each end under the crossing to draw the center together. Tie them with another square knot.

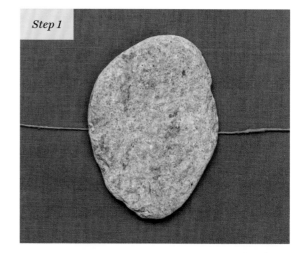

Step 1

Step 2

Step 3

4. Thread the long end of the yarn through a tapestry needle and bring it to the front of the stone. Take it under the point where the yarns cross and use a half-hitch knot (see page 292) to draw the crossed yarns tightly together.

5. Note that you now have five warp threads. This odd number makes it possible to weave under and over around the center in a spiral fashion. Weave around until you like the size of your circle, probably 7–10 times, but the choice is yours. You can choose to beat the weft in tightly as on the stones on page 236, or leave a bit of air between the rows as shown here.

Step 4

Step 5

6. Take the yarn under the woven circle to the opposite side and make a double half-hitch knot (see page 292) around the nearest warp thread. Take the yarn to the back of the stone and use a double half-hitch knot to secure it to the center. Note that you can create both symmetrical and asymmetrical patterns with your warp arrangement. The stone will determine what design will make the weaving most secure — and pleasing!

    Optional: Use a drop of clear-drying white glue to affix a bead at the center of the weaving.

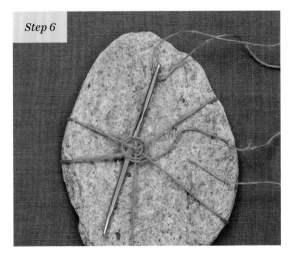

Step 6

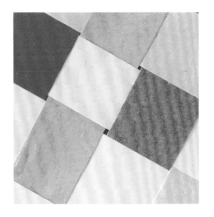

Greetings!

Many young children are introduced to weaving using construction paper. This totally free-form style of weaving is done without any loom or frame and can help kids develop dexterity and discover how colors interact. Although paper weaving can be very simple, it can also be quite complex, depending on the patterns and shapes employed.

The greeting cards shown here are satisfying to make for those special occasions when a store-bought card doesn't feel quite right. Make several so that you have a stash ready for any occasion. —GS

DESIGN NOTEBOOK

Although the plain-weave pattern of this design is quite simple, the use of color gradations gives it a more sophisticated look. I used Aitoh origami papers in shades of dark red to pink (the Red Shade package includes 12 red shades and tints), but you may want to use another range of colors in your own custom design.

Greetings!

YOU WILL NEED

- 1 package of origami paper (forty-eight 5⅞" squares)
- Ruler
- Self-healing mat
- Rotary cutter or hobby knife
- Pen or pencil
- Glue stick

- Photo frame cards, black with a centered opening of 3¼ inches by 4¾ inches

FINISHED MEASUREMENTS
5" wide × 7" long

A LITTLE COLOR THEORY

A pure color (or hue) can be changed to a shade by adding black or to a tint by adding white. When you're mixing paints or dyes, you can obviously create infinite gradations of any color, but the commercially printed origami papers I used offer you an opportunity to play around with shades and tints. As you see in the photos below, you begin to weave with mid-range colors at the middle and then move outward using increasingly darker strips at the upper right and increasingly lighter strips at the lower left. In this way, you achieve something like a rough color wash across your paper weaving.

1. Choose 8 to 10 different shades and tints of paper and lay them out in order, progressing from the darkest shade at the left to the lightest tint at the right.

2. Using the ruler, self-healing mat, and rotary cutter, measure and cut ten ½" strips to use vertically. (See Tips for Success opposite.) You may need to place two strips of the same color next to each other to have enough strips for the required width. Set these aside, placing them in the gradated color order.

Step 1

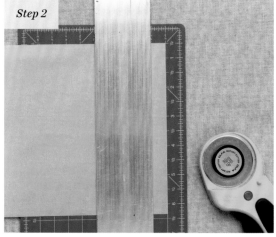

Step 2

TIPS FOR SUCCESS

- You can use scissors to cut the strips, but I have found that a rotary cutter or hobby knife is not only faster and easier on your hands, but the results are also more even. Place the paper on the mat, position the ruler along the cutting line, and make a clean, straight cut with the rotary cutter or knife.

- To ensure tight joints, fold back (without creasing) the strips that will go over the next strip, apply a dab of glue to the strips that will be under the new strip, lay in the new strip and apply a dab of glue where each upper strip will lie over it, and fold the upper strips back down.

3. Measure and cut seven ½" strips — as in step 2, one or two of each shade — to use horizontally. Set these aside, again maintaining the color order as in step 2.

4. Pick up the middle horizontal strip and lay it on your work surface. Mark the center with a pencil. Glue the fifth vertical strip perpendicular on the horizontal and with its right edge touching the center mark. Glue the sixth vertical strip under the horizontal, to the right of the center, and parallel to the fifth vertical strip.

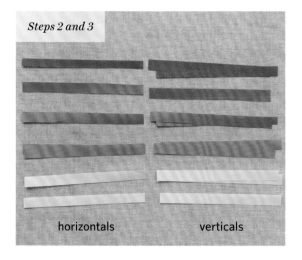

Steps 2 and 3

horizontals   verticals

Step 4

5. Weave in and glue strips horizontally and vertically, maintaining the color order you set up, so that the colors of both the warp and weft become lighter as you weave toward the left and bottom and darker as you weave to the right and top. Butt the strips together as tightly as possible, and glue each strip to secure it.

6. Trim the woven piece so that it fits into the slot in the photo frame card.

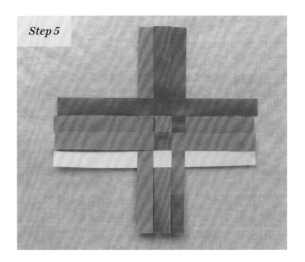

Step 5

AND NOW FOR SOME CURVES

Not all of your warps need to be cut on straight lines. For this variation, I used two Japanese rice papers. I cut the lighter-colored "weft" into ½" strips, which I wove through three wide "warps" that I cut freestyle. You can shape and cut your warp in an infinite variety of ways.

After cutting the warp pieces apart, position them side by side just as they appeared before being cut, and weave the strips through them in the usual under/over fashion. To provide stability while you're weaving. tape the top edge of the paper warps to a larger piece of paper. I don't use any glue in a piece like this, but after trimming it to the size that fits in the card opening, I tape around all four sides on the back to stabilize it.

HELEN HIEBERT

Helen Hiebert confesses to being obsessed with paper. She enjoys working with, designing, and making paper by hand, and she loves to design paper projects and share them with everyone.

Helen runs a professional papermaking studio high up in the Colorado Rocky Mountains, where she creates artists' books and unique handmade papers, designs paper projects, and develops and records online classes, including "Paper Weaving." She also writes a weekly blog called *The Sunday Paper*, which is a treasure trove of ideas and inspiration having to do with this amazing material. To help keep hand-papermaking traditions alive, Helen produces *Paper Talk*, a monthly podcast featuring oral histories from papermakers of our time.

In 2013, Helen gave herself a challenge: over 100 straight days, she would make 100 paper weavings, each featuring two distinctive papers. Look her up online to find out more about this project and Helen's other work.

TARGET, 2017
Embossed purple momigami and orange tairei paper; 12" × 12"

WOVEN PAPER LANTERN, 2017
Green mingei and yellow tatami paper; 6" × 4" × 4"

Brown Bag Basket (page 248)

Studded Brown Paper Basket
(page 251)

Map Basket (page 253)

Ribbon Basket (page 254)

Hold It!
Paper or Ribbon Baskets

I find it exciting to create beautiful and functional objects out of items that could easily be discarded or thought of as useless. Two of these baskets were woven using brown paper grocery bags, one is made of a paper road map, and one is made of ribbon. The basic structure of each is the same, but I've used different thicknesses of paper and different finishing techniques to make each basket unique. Small variations can result in fairly different results. Try all four versions and see what modifications and outcomes you can discover! Then look around to see what other items you can turn into baskets — photos, magazines, colored paper, and more! —DJ

TIPS FOR SUCCESS

- If the paper bag or map is wrinkled, iron it to smooth it out before cutting the strips.

- Mark your measurements for cutting on the printed side of the bag, then fold the printed side inward so it will be the inside of the strips.

- Use straight pins or paper clips to hold the strips in place while weaving. These prevent the strips from slipping around and hold them firmly in place.

- Overlap the end of the horizontal strips a couple of inches. If they are too long, just trim them.

- For the Ribbon Basket, coat sewing thread with beeswax to make it stronger and less likely to tangle.

Brown Bag Basket

This basic basket is fun to make and can be quite useful. One sits on my desk organizing index cards, sticky notes, and small notebooks. Another lives on my craft table holding a box of straight pins, small scissors, fabric marking pens, a permanent marker, a tape measure, and an eraser. It's a wonderful catch-all that reuses a paper bag and takes only a little time to put together!

YOU WILL NEED

- Scissors
- 1 brown paper grocery bag
- Ruler
- Bone folder (helpful but not absolutely necessary)

FINISHED MEASUREMENTS
4½" wide × 4½" long × 3" deep

Preparing the Paper

1. Cut down the seam on one side of the bag.

2. Cut along the fold around all sides of the bottom to make one long, flat rectangular piece of paper. Discard the bag bottom.

3. From the long rectangle, cut 16 strips that are 1" wide × 14" long and 5 strips that are 1" wide × 21" long.

4. Fold the strips in half lengthwise so they are ½" wide and double thickness.

5. Press the fold line with the bone folder to achieve a crisp edge. If you don't have a bone folder, something like the side of a letter opener or the edge of a butter knife will work.

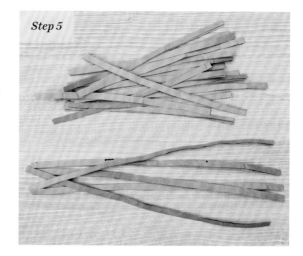

Step 5

Weaving the Basket

6. Lay out eight of the 14" strips next to each other vertically with the ends even.

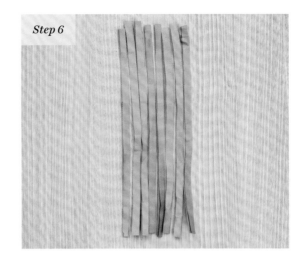
Step 6

7. In the center of the vertical strips, insert a 14" strip horizontally so it goes over one strip and under the next all the way across.

8. Insert a second 14" strip horizontally into the vertical strips, but this time go over the vertical strips that you went under in the previous row and under the strips that you went over.

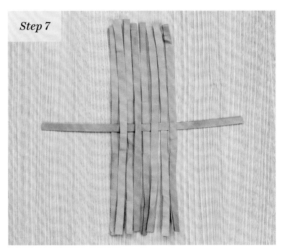
Step 7

9. Repeat steps 7 and 8, moving outward from the center and working your way first above and then below that horizontal center strip.

10. When you have used all of the 14" strips, the woven area should form a square in the center of the vertical and horizontal strips. This will be the bottom of the basket.

As you weave in the strips, snug them together so they touch the previous row.

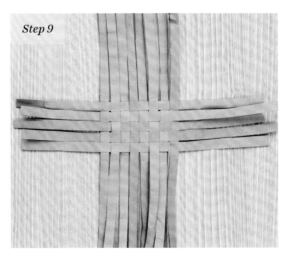
Step 9

Brown Bag Basket

11. Fold the side strips up from the bottom, being careful to keep the bottom grid tight. Pinch and fold the strips as they turn the corner from the bottom to help hold the shape of the bottom square.

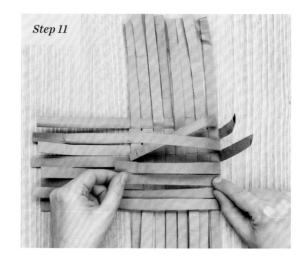

Step 11

12. Insert one of the 21"-long strips horizontally, alternating over and under, to begin forming the sides of the basket. Use paper clips to help stabilize the strips you're weaving, then reposition the clips as you move along.

13. Repeat step 12, but weave over the strips you went under in the previous row and under the strips you went over. Continue in this manner, working up the sides and tightening the individual strips as you go along so you pull up any slack. Overlap the beginning and end of each strip as you weave each round.

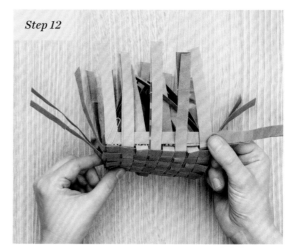

Step 12

14. Weave as high as you want the basket to be. This example is 5 horizontal strips high.

15. Go back and tighten up all the strips again, working any slack to the top edge of the basket.

Finishing

16. Trim both ends of the 16 strips, fold them over, and tuck them into the previous row.

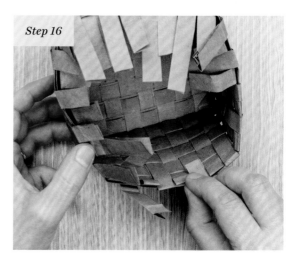

Step 16

Studded Brown Paper Basket

This basket is made with three layers of paper, so it is more rigid than the Brown Bag Basket.

YOU WILL NEED

In addition to all of the materials listed for the Brown Bag Basket (page 248), you will need a second brown paper grocery bag, an awl or sharp needle, and 32 mini fasteners (tiny round brads).

FINISHED MEASUREMENTS
4½" wide × 4½" long × 3" deep

Preparing the Paper

1. Follow steps 1–3 for the Brown Bag Basket (page 248) except cut the 16 strips to be 1½" wide × 14" long, and the 5 strips to be 1½" wide × 21" long.

2. Fold the strips lengthwise by turning ½" down, then ½" down from the opposite side to create strips that are ½" wide and three layers thick.

Weaving the Basket

Follow steps 6–15 for the Brown Bag Basket.

Finishing

3. Trim the strips so that they extend ½" from the top edge of the basket.

4. Fold each end over the top and down the other side, then secure with a paper clip.

5. Use an awl to poke a hole in the center of the final square on each strip.

6. Insert a mini fastener and spread the brad sides to secure the end of each strip .

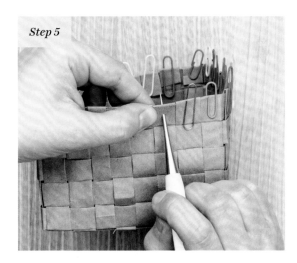

Step 5

Step 6

Map Basket

An old map makes a delightful basket. The various colors of towns, lakes, roads, and words result in fascinating patterns. And if you use a map that has guided you on a trip, the basket also serves as a pleasant reminder!

YOU WILL NEED

- Scissors
- 2 road maps
- Ruler
- Bone folder (helpful but not absolutely necessary)
- Paper glue

Preparing the Paper

1. Follow steps 1–3 for the Brown Bag Basket (page 248), except cut the 16 strips to be 1" wide × 21" long, and cut 11 strips that are 1" wide × 25" long.

2. Fold the strips in half lengthwise so they are two layers thick and ½" wide.

Weaving the Basket

Follow steps 6–15 for the Brown Bag Basket, except make this basket 9 or 10 horizontal strips high.

Finishing

3. At the top edge of the basket, trim the end of each side strip to be less than ½" long.

4. Fold the side strips over and glue them down.

5. Wrap a ½"-wide strip around the top row of the basket, and glue it on the outside of the basket all the way around.

6. Glue another ½" strip around the top edge on the inside of the basket.

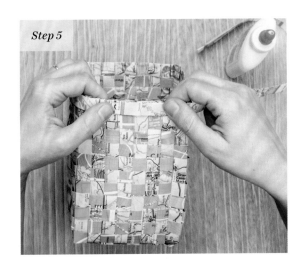

Step 5

Ribbon Basket

This fun rendition of the basket is more flexible than the others — and quite attractive. To make it even more decorative, I sewed 2/0 Czech glass E beads around the top after I was finished weaving. If you like this method, try using narrower ribbon or folded fabric or perhaps felt. For the basket at the bottom of the facing page, I used teal (color A), apple green (color B), and purple (color C), and for the version in the how-to photos below, I used melon (color A), pink (color B), and brown (color C).

YOU WILL NEED

- ⅝"-wide ribbon, 5 yards each of colors A and B, and 7 yards of color C
- Ruler
- Scissors
- Straight pins
- Sewing needle and thread
- Beeswax (optional)
- 32 beads

MEASUREMENTS
6" wide × 5½" long × 6" deep

Preparing the Ribbon

1. Follow the steps 1–3 for the Brown Bag Basket (page 248), except cut the 16 strips (8 strips each of colors A and B) to be 20" long, and cut 9 strips (of color C) that are 25" long. You will be working with the ⅝"-wide ribbon, so there's no need to fold lengthwise.

Weaving the Basket

2. Follow steps 6–15 for the Brown Bag Basket (pages 249–250, weaving as high as you want the basket to be. This example is 9 horizontal strips high. Use straight pins to hold the strips of ribbon in place while you work on the basket. Use color A as the vertical strips and color B as the horizontal strips when weaving the base of the basket. Color C will be woven as the basket sides.

Finishing

3. Cut the ribbons at the top so each one extends for 1½" above the basket.

4. Double fold the ends of the ribbon at the top of the basket and pin in place with straight pins.

Step 4

5. Run the sewing thread through the beeswax to strengthen the thread and keep it from tangling. Working across the top of the basket, add a bead to the center of each vertical ribbon while you stitch the folded edge down.

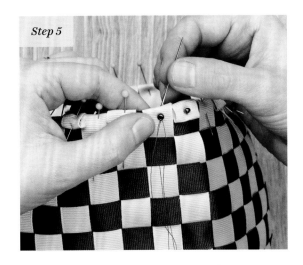

Step 5

Danish Stars and Wreath

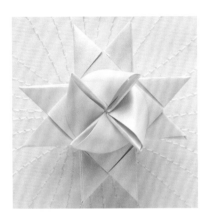

Many years ago, a dear friend taught me to make this classic star. Because she is Danish, I've always called them "Danish stars," but they are also known as Moravian, Froebel, and German stars.

One star makes a lovely, simple tree ornament or package decoration. If you find yourself enjoying the process, you might want to weave enough to make a wreath. In the one shown on the facing page, I linked 16 stars together to form the wreath, with an additional lone star hung through the center as a little pendulum. —GS

DESIGN NOTEBOOK

I created the stars on the facing page with Snow White pearl-finish paper strips from Paplin Products; the paper used for the step-by-step photos is Froebel's Moravian Star Strip Quilling Paper, which is slightly wider but not as shiny. I used to cut my own paper strips from ordinary printer's paper, but I was pleased to discover that pre-cut strips are available from a variety of online sources. The precut paper is much nicer, and the strips are much more even!

Danish Stars and Wreath

YOU WILL NEED

- For each star: 4 paper strips, each ½" × 25"
- White sewing thread and sewing needle

FINISHED MEASUREMENTS

- *One star:* 2" in diameter

- *17-star wreath:* 8" in diameter

1. Cut each end of each strip on the diagonal to form a point. Fold each paper strip in half widthwise.

   Note: In the photo below, the ends appear to be cut into a pennant shape. This is because you are seeing each strip after it has been folded, and the diagonal cuts cross over one another.

2. Interlock the four strips as shown, and then draw them together to bring the folded ends to the center, locking them to form a tightly woven core.

3. Starting at the upper left, fold the top strip down.

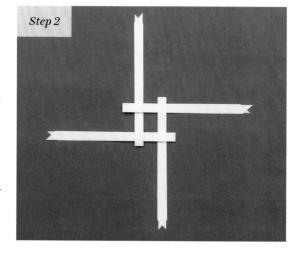

Step 2

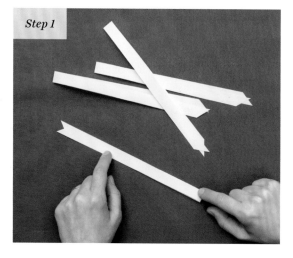

Step 1

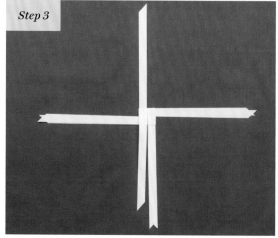

Step 3

4. Fold the top strip on the left over to the right.

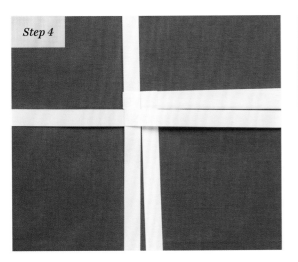

5. Fold up the top strip on the lower right.

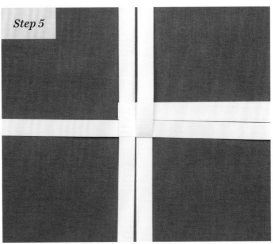

TIPS FOR SUCCESS

- Make very crisp folds and try to keep strips exactly parallel or perpendicular as you work.

- Take care to begin exactly in the center wherever a diagonal fold comes from the center. Not only will your stars be more symmetrical, but you'll also find it easier to insert strips through the various folds while you're working.

- If you have difficulty pushing the strip through in any of these steps, fold the tip to make it stiffer and pointier.

folded up

6. Fold the top strip on the right over to the left, threading it under the top left strip.

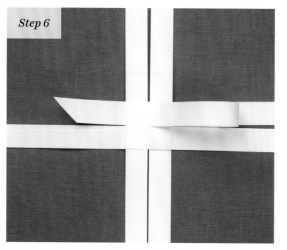

7. Fold the top right strip to the back to form a diagonal from the center.

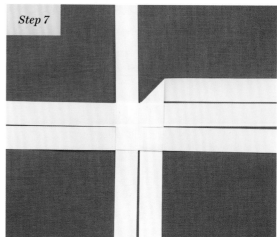

8. Fold the same strip you worked in step 7 to the front to form a triangle above the horizontal strips.

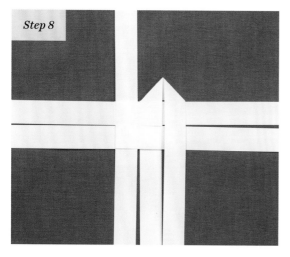

9. Fold the triangle in half to match up the diagonals. Tuck the end through the strip below, and pull down to lock it in place. Push it over to the left until it touches the center vertical strip.

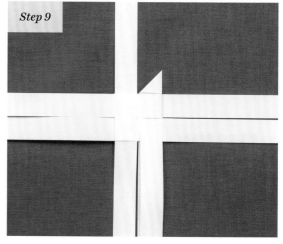

10. Turn the piece counterclockwise and repeat steps 7–9 at each corner. Note that on the fourth corner, you will have to lift one of the strips out of the way to find the slot formed by the strip below. You now have a four-pointed star.

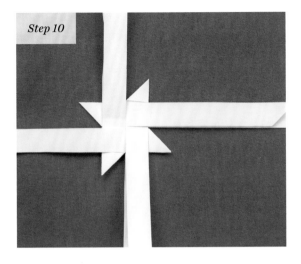

Step 10

11. Turn the piece over and repeat steps 7–9 at each corner until all corners have been woven in and you have an eight-pointed star. Lay the piece out so that all eight strips are positioned fully extended.

Step 11

12. Push the top right strip out of the way over to the left. Fold the bottom right strip up and make a diagonal fold down from the center. Bring this strip around and insert it under the strip at the left (a). Push it all the way through: it will emerge from the star tip at the top left. Snug

it up to the edge of the strip, forming a gentle curve and creating the point (b).

As you become more experienced, try to coax the strip around without first folding it, so that the surface is more curved than actually folded.

Step 12a

Step 12b

13. Turn the piece clockwise and repeat with the next strip. Continue in this way until you have completed four three-dimensional points on one side.

14. Turn the piece over and repeat steps 12 and 13.

Step 13

15. When all eight strips are woven in and you have four star points on each side, trim off each end close to the fold, taking care not to cut the fold itself. Give the strip a little tug to pull it out a bit before you trim it. When it's trimmed, it will relax back and be hidden between the folds.

16. Insert a 12" length of white sewing thread in a sewing needle, and stick the needle between two of the flat star tips at the center. Draw the thread up to create a loop about 4" long, and tie the ends in an overhand knot (see page 291).

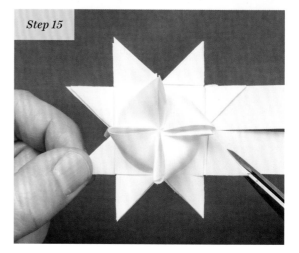

Step 15

WREATH

1. Make 17 stars as described on pages 258–262.

2. Interlock 16 stars in the following manner, reserving the 17th star for the center. Notice that the pairs of flat star tips are spaced differently: one pair measures about 1¼" across the base; the other, a little less than 1". Notice also that the inside edges of the wider pair are folds. These folds provide a space for you to push the tips of another star into. To join two stars, always insert a wider pair into a corresponding wide pair. You may use glue to anchor the tips in place, but you may also find that they interlock nicely without glue.

3. To provide thread for hanging the wreath, repeat step 16 on each fourth star around the wreath using 12" lengths of thread. Rather than making a loop with the threads, however, tie each one to the star with a square knot (see page 291) at the end of the thread. Tie a 14" thread to the 17th star; it will hang a bit below the wreath. Gather all five threads at the ends and tie them in an overhand knot (see page 291).

Swedish Stars

Like Danish stars, this is a traditional Scandinavian technique. You can make these stars in a wide variety of sizes, depending on the length of the paper strips you use. It's fun to use different papers for these stars as well. White is elegant and classic, but I've also used a variety of colors as well as printed origami paper. You could even use found papers, such as maps, sheet music, and pages from a book or magazine. —GS

DESIGN NOTEBOOK

The two stars shown on the facing page are made with different lengths of paper (8"and 7"), but all of the strips are ½" wide. I used 10 strips for each star. For the step-by-step photos, I used Maggicoo Star Origami Paper, available in precut strips, 1 cm × 24 cm (about ½" × 9½"). I cut these strips into 7" lengths.

Swedish Stars

YOU WILL NEED

- 21 paper strips, each 7" × ½"
- Glue stick

Weaving the Stars (make 2)

1. With the first paper strip laid vertically on your work surface, find its center and put a dab of glue on it. Find the center of a second strip and place it on top of the first strip and at a right angle to it, gluing it in place.

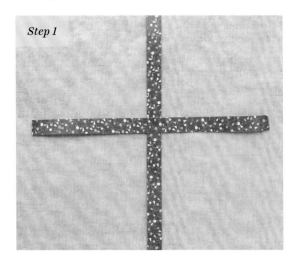

Step 1

2. Lay down two more vertical strips, one on each side of and parallel to the first, positioning them over the first horizontal strip. Glue them in place. Take care to butt the corner joins exactly.

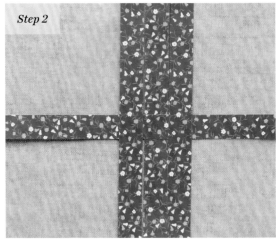

Step 2

3. Weave and glue a strip above and below the first horizontal, keeping edges butted tightly as before. Note that these will each go over the two outer vertical strips and under the center one. Add a dab of glue to the center verticals as well.

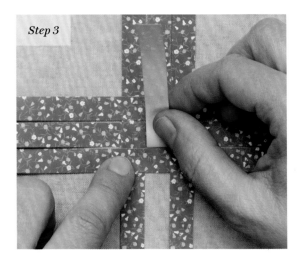

Step 3

4. Weave in four more strips in the same way, one on each side of the three verticals and one on each side of the three horizontals.

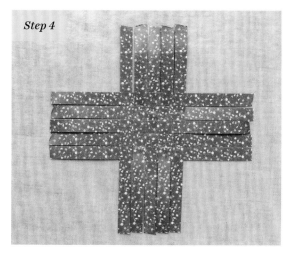

Step 4

5. Working at a corner, roll one strip from each side of the corner to the back, and overlap the ends of the strips at right angles as shown. Use a dab of glue to hold the ends in place.

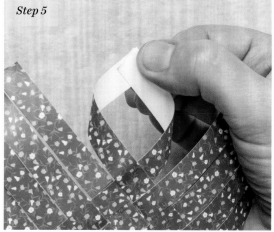

Step 5

6. Repeat step 5 using the next two strips at the same corner.

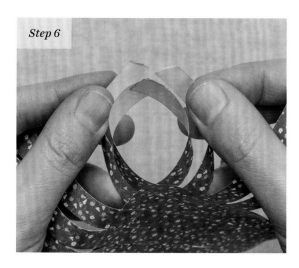

Step 6

7. Repeat steps 5 and 6 at each corner.

Step 7

Swedish Stars

Joining the Two Stars

8. With wrong sides facing, position the two stars so that the center squares are offset.

9. Draw each remaining strip (the center strips) through to the tip of the other star, and glue it to both layers of corner strips.

Step 9

10. Trim each tip to make a point.

Step 10

11. To create a hanger, glue the remaining strip into a loop and glue that inside one of the star points.

Step 11

Scents of Summer:
Lavender Wand

For me, lavender's sharply sweet scent evokes hillsides awash in lilac color. Over the centuries, this popular herb has been used for everything from a medicine and a relaxant to an aphrodisiac. Its most practical use is for scenting stored linens to deter moths and other pests, and an old-fashioned woven lavender wand is the ideal package for this purpose.

To make this wand, it's important to use freshly cut lavender, with stems as long as possible, since the stems must be supple enough to bend and withstand being used as warp for the narrow ribbon weft. Plants that are still in bud, rather than fully in flower, are easier to work with, but either stage is suitable. If you can't work with the stems soon after cutting, they may be stored for a day or so in a jar of water in the refrigerator. —GS

Lavender Wand

YOU WILL NEED

- 13 or more freshly cut stems of lavender, at least 12" long (Be sure to use an odd number of stems.)
- Florists' tape

- ¼"-wide satin ribbon, 3 yards
- Short blunt-tip tapestry needle
- Scissors

1. Remove the leaves along the stems below the flower clusters. Gather the stems together in a bouquet, with the flower tips even across the top. Tightly wrap florists' tape around the stems just beneath the flower clusters to bind them snugly together. Make about three wraps, then trim the tape.

Step 1

The stems can be slightly uneven at the bottom; you will trim them when the wand is complete.

2. Carefully bend each stem over the tape, folding the stems neatly at the edge of the tape. At the same time, gather the stems neatly around the base of the flowers, arranging the stems as evenly as possible around the flower heads. When all the stems are bent over, secure them with another few rounds of florists' tape just beyond the flower tips. Push the stems out around the flowers to form a ball shape.

Step 2

3. Thread the ribbon through a tapestry needle, insert it between two stems, and draw the ribbon through, leaving a 3" tail. Weave under and over the stems, taking care to keep the shiny side of the ribbon facing out. Keep the ribbon smooth as you weave around. Although the first round or two of weaving can be frustrating, as the stems tend to slip around each other and hide in the flower heads, the weaving becomes much easier after it is established — really!

6. Trim the ribbon, leaving a 24" tail. Use the tail to make a double half-hitch knot (see page 292) at the bottom of the flower heads to secure the weaving (a), spiral the ribbon down the length of the trimmed stems, and then spiral back up again (b). Cut another 24" length of ribbon and use it along with the remaining spiraled ribbon to tie a bow. Trim the stems even with the bottom ribbon.

Step 3

Step 6a

4. As you continue to weave under and over the stems around the flower heads, nudge the ribbon up to cover the stems at the top of the wand. At the same time, pull on the tail to help smooth that first row of weaving. Once the weaving is secure, hide the tail inside the flower cluster.

5. Continue to weave until you reach the base of the flower clusters. I like to spread the stems a bit once the top rows are secure to make it much easier to see what you're doing as you continue weaving.

Step 6b

7. Store in a warm, airy place for about two weeks until the flowers and stems are dry. You may want to tighten and smooth the ribbon again before use, as the weaving tends to loosen when the stems are dry.

Tumbling Blocks Triaxial Table Runner

Most traditional weaving is done with two elements (warp and weft) that intersect at 90-degree angles. In triaxial weaving, however, there are three elements that intersect at 30- and 60-degree angles, which creates a dramatic-looking fabric that appears to have three layers and allows for more color exploration. Because triaxial weaving results in stable and shear-resistant fabric, the technique is often used in basketry. This project explores a combination of pattern and color that results in a three-dimensional-looking design. —DJ

DESIGN NOTEBOOK

- For someone with a weaving background, it can be challenging to visualize the unexpected way these parts intersect. I must admit that I walked away after the first few times I tried this process, but I came back again and again because I was intrigued with the possible patterns. When it finally clicked for me, I realized I'd been making it way more difficult than it actually is. Once I got the rhythm, it was exciting to see how the pattern developed, and the process seemed easy. I absolutely love the three-dimensional look of the finished piece, and I'm happy that my persistence paid off.

- For the photos on the facing page and page 283, I chose maroon (color A1), purple (color A2), black (color B), and turquoise (color C) for my four 1"-wide ribbons. I used the same color scheme for the step-by-step photos except there melon is used instead of turquoise for color C.

- Instead of a foam board, I used my knitting blocking board. It has a 1" grid block printed on the surface, and I drew the 60-degree angle lines on it with a permanent marker.

- The flat wooden needle I used is 15" long.

Tumbling Blocks Triaxial Table Runner

YOU WILL NEED

- Long ruler
- Scissors
- Medium-weight fusible interfacing, 1 yard
- Foam board at least 14" wide × 28" high
- Painter's tape
- Fine-tip permanent marker
- 30/60 triangle or quilter's tool with these angles marked
- 1"-wide ribbon, one 21-foot roll of each of 4 colors
- Straight pins

- Long flat wooden needle with large eye
- Iron and press cloth
- Black duck cloth, ½ yard
- Sharp sewing needle
- Black sewing thread
- 1½"-wide black ribbon, one 21-foot roll

FINISHED MEASUREMENTS
11" wide × 22" long

Preparing the Work Surface

1. Measure and cut the fusible interfacing to be 20" wide × 28" long.

2. Cover the foam board with the fusible interfacing, making sure to place the adhesive side facing up. Tape the interfacing edges down on the board and carefully flatten out all wrinkles to make a smooth surface on the front of the board.

3. Using the ruler and marker, draw vertical parallel lines 1" apart on the interfacing. If you are using a blocking board with a 1" grid already marked, the lines should already be visible through the interfacing.

4. Draw a horizontal line in the center of the board, at 90 degrees to the vertical lines.

5. Draw lines at 30 and 60 degrees radiating from the center of the lines you made in step 3. It is helpful to draw several lines over the length of the interfacing to guide where the ribbons will be placed as you work.

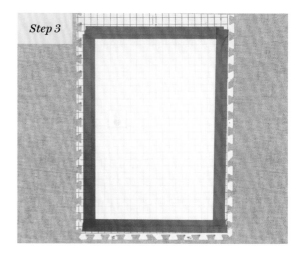

If you can see the 1" grid through the interfacing, there's no need to draw the measurement lines.

6. Draw a rectangle that is 10" wide × 18" high around the weaving area. Your piece will be woven in this area with a small margin on each side.

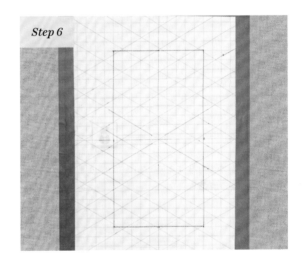

Step 6

Weaving Layer 1

7. Cut six 24" ribbon pieces in color A1 and four 24" ribbon pieces in color A2.

8. At the top of the marked weaving area, center the six color A1 ribbons. Place two color A2 ribbons to the left and two color A2 ribbons to the right of the A1 ribbons. The ribbons should almost, but not quite, touch each other and should extend about 2½" over the top and bottom edges of the weaving area. Pin the ribbons in place across the top. This is the first layer.

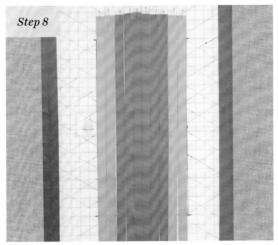

Step 8

Weaving Layer 2

9. Cut one color B ribbon 5" long and two color B ribbons in each of the following lengths: 15", 14", 11", 9", and 7". Set these aside and cut twelve 16"-long color B ribbons.

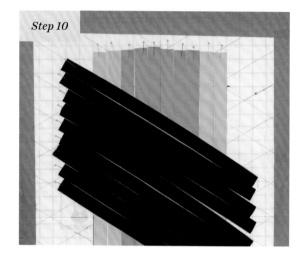

Step 10

10. Starting on the top left, pin eight to ten 16" color B ribbons down the side of the weaving area, allowing them to extend 2½" outside the marked pattern area. Again, they should almost, but not quite, touch each other. Place the pins straight up and down so the ribbon can pivot.

11. Starting with the top ribbon, weave it through the vertical ribbons at a 30-degree angle going over 1 and under 2 of the vertical ribbons all the way across the grid. As you weave in the ribbons, angle the pins to follow the diagonal direction from the upper left to the lower right.

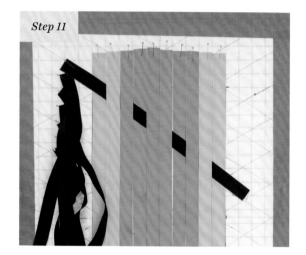

Step 11

12. On the 2nd row, to maintain the pattern, start by going under 1 first, then repeat the sequence over 1, under 2 the rest of the way across.

13. On the 3rd row, go under 2, then over 1 and under 2 all the way across.

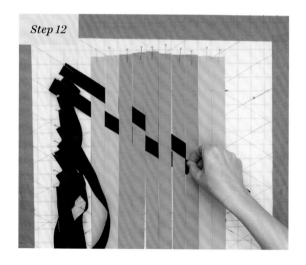

Step 12

14. Repeat the pattern in steps 11–13 for the length of the piece.

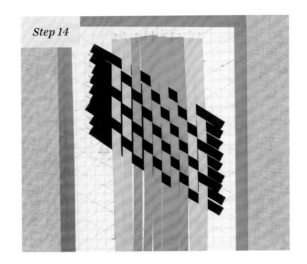
Step 14

15. As you reach the bottom left and upper right corners of layer 2, you'll need the progressively shorter pieces of ribbon you cut in step 9. Go back and fill in the corners with the shorter pieces of ribbon, maintaining the pattern.

Weaving Layer 3

16. In color C, cut twelve 16" lengths of ribbon, one 5" length, and two each of the following lengths: 15", 14", 11", 9", and 7".

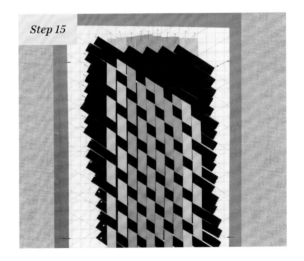
Step 15

17. Beginning around the center of the right, go under 1 and over 2 of the vertical weavers. Sometimes they are a bit hard to see because they are covered by layer 2. Use the very long wooden needle to pull the ribbon through the previous two layers.

Look for the vertical ribbon you are going under and you'll see a color B angled ribbon on each side of it. Go under the color B ribbon on both sides along with the vertical ribbon as shown at right.

When you go over the two vertical ribbons, you will see only colors A1 and A2 as the front of the pattern block, as it will be partially covered on the sides by the color B ribbon from layer 2.

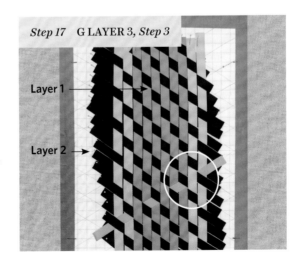
Step 17   G LAYER 3, Step 3
Layer 1 →
Layer 2 →

18. Entering from the right, continue weaving under 1 and over 2 vertical ribbons.

19. When you've woven in all the areas that are full width, go back and fill in the upper left corner and lower right corner with the shorter pieces of color C ribbon.

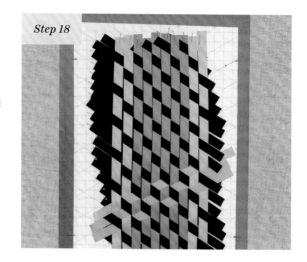

Step 18

Assembly

20. Pin around all edges of the woven piece, making sure to anchor the ribbons to the interfacing but not to the foam board. Remove the tape that holds the interfacing to the board.

21. Remove the weaving from the board, carefully keeping the ribbons in their proper places.

22. Place the weaving face down on an ironing board. Iron, following the directions for your interfacing. Use press cloths above *and* below the weaving to avoid having the interfacing stick to either the iron or the ironing board.

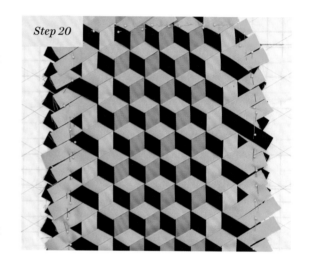

Step 20

23. When the piece is completely dry, use the marker to outline on the interfacing side the edges of the woven area. Remove the pins and trim the piece to be ½" longer than the pattern area on all sides. The piece should measure 11" × 19".

24. Cut the duck cloth to be ½" bigger than the woven piece on all sides. If the measurements are followed as above, the duck cloth will be 12" × 20".

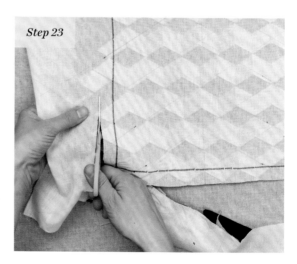

Step 23

25. Center the weaving on the duck cloth, then pin the duck cloth to the interfacing side of the weaving.

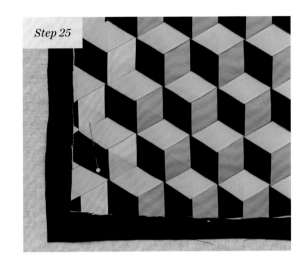

26. Turn up the ½" overlapping edge of the duck cloth to cover the edges of the right side of the weaving. Before folding, trim the corners of the duck cloth diagonally so there is not much bulk on the corners. Pin in place.

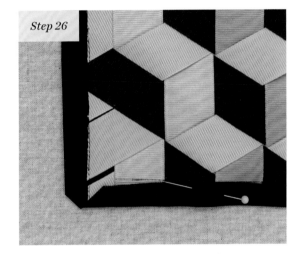

27. Whipstitch (see page 302) into the raw edge of the duck cloth. As you stitch, smooth the ribbon ends to even out any slack or trim any excess.

28. Press the edges.

29. Cut two lengths of the 1½" ribbon to cover the short edges of the runner. Position each ribbon to overlap a right-side edge by ¾", making sure to cover the raw edge of the duck cloth.

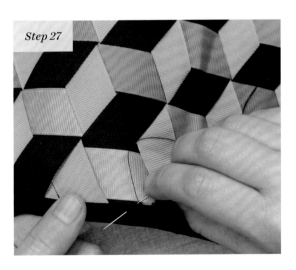

30. Whipstitch the ribbons onto the right side of the runner.

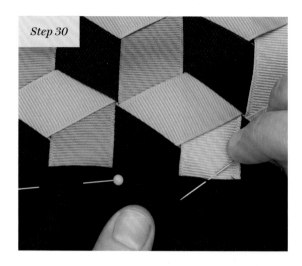

Step 30

31. Turn the edging ribbons to the back side of the runner, making sure to keep the edges straight and even. Hand-stitch in place.

32. Cut two lengths of the 1½" ribbon long enough to cover the long sides of the runner plus 2". Position each ribbon on the runner to overlap one long right-side edge by ¾", making sure to cover the raw edge of the duck cloth and the wide ribbon at the short ends. Leave an extra 1" sticking out from each end.

Step 31

33. Fold under the 1" excess on each end to make finished edges.

34. Hand-stitch the ribbons onto the face-up side of the runner.

35. Turn the edging ribbons to the back side of the runner, making sure to keep the edges straight and even. Hand-stitch in place.

36. Iron.

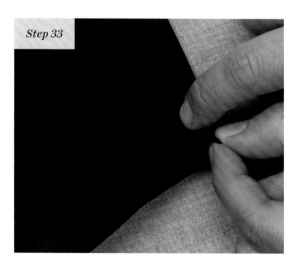

Step 33

ACKNOWLEDGMENTS

We are deeply appreciative of all those who have been part of our creative lives over the years, as well as those who have been part of the process that has made this book happen. We thank

- Those at Storey whose skill and creativity have helped to bring our book to life: Michal Lumsden, editor; Alethea Morrison, art director; Jennie Jepson Smith, production designer; Mars Vilaubi, photographer; Hartley Batchelder, prepress specialist; Caroline Burch, production director; Anastasia Whalen, publicist. Special thanks to Storey's publisher, Deborah Balmuth for her wise support, encouragement, and friendship.

- Our family and friends who contributed materials and encouragement that were essential to creating the various projects in the book: Sara Steege Campainha, for her God's eye; Paul Steege for materials used in Branching Out; Richard Steege, for designing and making the band lock and heddle cradle; Bill Jarchow for assembling and organizing all Deborah's equipment; Cheryl Creach, for her advice and faith in Deborah.

- The many weavers who shared their knowledge and inspired us, including Abbie Hatton, Gwen's first weaving teacher; Rebecca Mezoff, consummate tapestry weaver; Bodil Wilson, who helped Gwen make her first Danish star; Arlene Mead, Regina Vorgang, and Michael Rohde, Deborah's studio mates who offer endless support and motivation.

- And, as always, our family, whose love buoys us through all the ups and downs of writing a book. Their inspiration and encouragement are priceless treasures that we value beyond words.

APPENDIX

HOW TO BUILD A SIMPLE FRAME LOOM

You can use canvas stretcher strips, or bars, to create a sturdy but simple frame loom. Designed for stretching canvas in preparation for oil painting, these strips are available at art supply shops and many websites. The directions below are for a frame with 32" sides, but you could easily make one smaller or larger.

For some weaving projects, such as the Carry-All (page 89), you'll need to hammer in nails along the top and bottom to space the warp, but for the Twined Parachute-Cord Mat (page 81), spacers are not necessary. The strips shown here have a tongue-and-groove system at each corner.

YOU WILL NEED

- 4 canvas stretcher strips, each 32" long
- Rubber mallet or hammer
- Four 2" × ⅜" flat corner braces and 16 screws to match
- Screwdriver
- Hammer and finishing nails (optional)

---

1. Slide the strips together at each corner, and give the pieces a few taps with a rubber mallet or hammer to secure them.

2. To provide stability, screw a flat corner brace on the back of the frame at each corner. Take care to use screws that are short enough not to protrude through the wood.

Step 1

Step 2

3. If your project requires nails along the top and bottom of the frame to space the warp threads, use finishing nails, set in a zigzag fashion to avoid splitting the wood. For the Carry-All, the warp threads are spaced ½" apart; you may need a different spacing, depending on what you are weaving. The 28" opening of this frame required 116 nails. (If you add nails for projects like the Carry-All, you can still use the loom for projects like the Twined Parachute-Cord Mat that do not require nails; simply work around the nails in that case.)

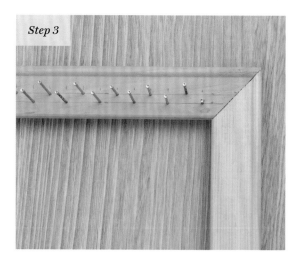

Step 3

HOW TO MAKE A HEDDLE CRADLE

Rigid-heddle looms have notches to support the heddle and keep it upright while you are threading it. To stabilize a rigid heddle without such support, you can make this simple tool.

YOU WILL NEED

- 2 grip clips (used for holding brooms and other tools against a wall)
- 1 piece of wood measuring 8" × 12" (or about 2" longer than your heddle)
- Screwdriver

Affix the grip clips about 8" part, centered widthwise, on the wood. Position the clips so that they face each other, making it easy to slip the heddle into them.

HOW TO MAKE A BAND LOCK

A band lock is used to secure one end of the warp when using the backstrap weaving technique (see page 143). It's important that the wood pieces you use for this tool are smooth and not at all warped, so that they hold all of the warp threads without allowing them to slip. The 12" length shown here is adequate for an 8"-wide scarf; if you wish to weave something wider, use a piece of wood long enough to accommodate the width.

machine screw and wing nut

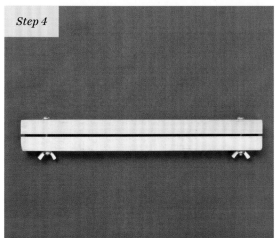

Step 4

YOU WILL NEED

- Sandpaper
- 2 pieces of 1"× 1" wood, 12" long
- Ruler
- Pencil or pen
- Drill with ¼" bit
- 2 machine screws, 2" × ¼", with wing nuts to fit

---

1. Lightly sand the two pieces of wood and lay them on a worktable, one on top of the other, with the ends aligned.

2. Measure and mark drill holes 1" from each end and centered widthwise.

3. Using a ¼" drill bit, drill through both pieces of wood.

4. Insert the machine screws through both pieces of wood, and use the wing nuts to tighten them down.

HOW TO MEASURE A WARP

For many of the projects in this book, the warp is stretched directly on the loom, frame, or an object. Although you need to know approximately how much yarn you'll use in total, the separate lengths do not need to be individually cut prior to warping the loom. The yarn is stretched either around the loom or back and forth around notches or pegs that help create tension on the individual threads.

For some types of looms, like multi-harness floor looms as well as for a few projects in this book (including the Leno Scarf and Card-Woven Bookmarks on pages 147 and 159, respectively), however, all the warp threads must be measured and aligned *before* placing them on the loom. On these looms, if your warp is too short, you will run out of warp threads before you finish the project. And if your warp is too long, there will be extra thread left at the end of the project, which is wasteful and can be expensive. So for these types of looms, you need to know the necessary length and how much will be lost to "loom waste" caused by tying the threads to the loom and evening out the tension and spacing. You also have to allow for shrinkage and take-up, meaning how much length is lost in the final project by the warp threads traveling over and under the weft threads.

It is important to keep the warp threads in the correct order as you wind the warp. To do so, wind the warp around warping pegs or use a warping board, as described below.

YOU WILL NEED

- 3 warping pegs and 3 clamps
- 2 dowels or slats to preserve the cross. Known as "lease sticks," these should be slightly wider than the width of your project, with a hole drilled through them at each end so you can tie them together.
- Warp yarn
- String for the choke ties and to fasten the lease sticks together

---

1. Determine the length of the finished project, including any fringe or hems. You need to add some extra length for shrinkage, as well as for the ends of the warp that are unweavable. This extra length is known as "loom waste."

2. Position three warping pegs as follows: place two at a distance equal to the length you've determined your warp should be in step 1; place the third in between those two, about 15" from one of the pegs. This third peg will help you create what is called the cross: you carry the warp yarn over one side of this middle peg when traveling from one end peg to the other, and carry the warp yarn under the other side of the middle peg when returning to the first end peg, thus creating a figure 8. You will insert the lease sticks through this cross, so that when you are threading, you can lift the warp threads off in the order you wound them on without tangling.

3. Determine the number of warp threads you need for your project. (See Calculating Yarn Requirements on page 290.)

CALCULATING LENGTH OF WARP

Most warps will become slightly shorter (shrinkage) when you wet finish them; the warps also lose some length as they go over and under the weft yarn (take-up). The amount of take-up and shrinkage depends on the fiber you are using, as well as its thickness. It's usually safe to add 5 to 10 percent to the desired finished length to allow for take-up and shrinkage. However, some yarns may shrink more or less depending on the fiber used. Before embarking on a large project, make a small sample with the project yarn to assess the amount of actual shrinkage.

Additional loom waste occurs at both ends of the warp and includes any ties that you make to anchor the warp, as well as the areas close to the ties where you are no longer able to get a shed. For example, if you are weaving a 2-yard-long scarf, with a 4" fringe at each end, the finished length of the project will be 80". Add to that 10 percent loom waste for shrinkage, which gives you 88". We like to add another 20" for the loom waste at the beginning and end of the warp. A 3-yard warp should be perfect for this project.

Go Figure

72" (2 yards) finished scarf +
8" of fringe (4" at each end) **=**
80" total project length

80" × 10 percent for shrinkage **= 8"**

80" total project length + **8"** shrinkage
+ **20"** loom waste = **108"**,
or **3 yards** warp

4. Place your ball or cone of warp yarn on the floor below the end peg nearer the middle peg and tie the warp yarn to this end peg.

5. Take the warp yarn over the middle peg and around the peg at the other end. As you come back to the first end, take the warp under the middle peg and then to the end peg. With this path complete, you have wound on the first two warp threads.

6. Continue this figure-8 path until you have wound on the number of threads you need for your warp.

7. Before removing the measured warp from the pegs, use a 6" length of string to tie a tight knot around the loop at the end of the warp away from the cross. If you have a long warp (2 yards or more), make additional ties, called choke ties, at 18" intervals along the warp. These ties should be tight, as their purpose is to keep the warp ends from slipping. Use additional 6" lengths of string to make four loose ties at the cross: one on each side of the two pegs where the warp separates around the peg.

8. Cut the loop at the end of the warp nearer the cross, lift the warp off the pegs, and lay it out on your work table.

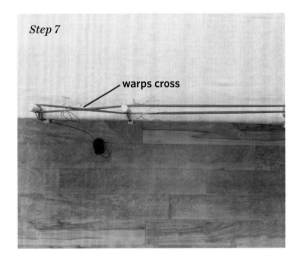

Step 7

warps cross

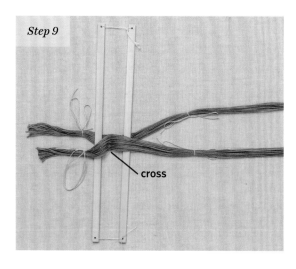

Step 9

cross

9. If you are threading your warp through a heddle, as for the Leno Scarf project on page 147, run lease sticks through each side of the cross to preserve it (where your ties are). Tie the lease sticks together as shown. It is now safe to remove the ties at the cross and spread the warp evenly between the sticks.

10. Proceed according to project directions.

CALCULATING YARN REQUIREMENTS

If you are planning your own project, determine the amount of warp yarn you need by multiplying your warp length (see Calculating Length of Warp, page 289) by the number of threads per inch and then by the width of your project. As with warp length, there is some shrinkage and take-up in the woven width, so add another 10 to 15 percent to account for this.

For example, if you want your scarf to be 8" wide, add another inch to that for shrinkage, so the scarf is 9" wide on the loom. For a yarn that you work at 8 warp threads per inch, multiply 9 (width in inches) by 8 (ends per inch) by 3 (warp length in yards). The result is that you need 216 yards of warp yarn.

Go Figure
9 (width of scarf in inches) **× 8** (ends per inch) **× 3** (yards of warp length) = **216 yards** of warp yarn

To estimate the amount of yarn needed for the weft, multiply the length of the scarf in inches (*not* the length of the warp) by the width of the scarf by the number of rows (picks) per woven inch.

For example, for a 72"-long scarf, you need to weave 80" to allow for 10 percent take-up and shrinkage. If your on-loom width is 9" woven at 8 picks per inch, multiply these three figures to obtain the weft yardage requirement.

Go Figure
80 (length of weaving in inches) **× 9** (on-loom width in inches) **× 8** (picks per inch) **= 5760 ÷ 36 = 160 yards** for the weft

SIX KNOTS FOR WEAVERS

Weavers need to use many knots in many different situations. Here are some of the most useful — and easiest to learn! The project instructions suggest which to use for what purpose.

Overhand Knot

This simple knot is useful for joining two ends quickly and securely. Although it serves the same purpose as the sliding knot, it is larger and not as easily hidden, and therefore should be used only where it won't show in the finished weaving.

1. Position two (or more) lengths of yarn parallel to each other with their tail ends aligned. Make a loop, taking the tail ends from the right and laying them over the working yarn on the left.

2. Reach through the loop and draw the ends through.

3. Pull the ends tight to form the knot.

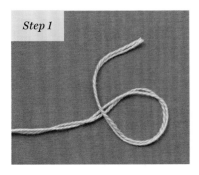

Step 1

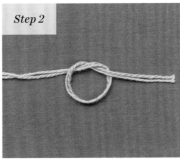

Step 2

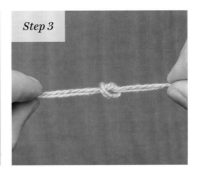

Step 3

Square Knot

This is an extremely common and useful knot. It holds quite securely, and it is also easy to untie, if necessary, by pulling up on one of the ends and sliding the knot off the other end.

1. Working with two strands of yarn, cross and wrap the left-hand end over the right.

2. Cross and wrap the right-hand end over the left.

3. Pull the ends together to tighten.

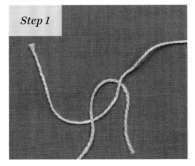

Step 1

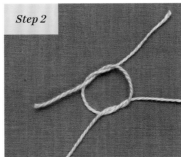

Step 2

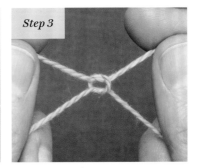

Step 3

Half-Hitch Knots

A half-hitch knot may be made around another strand of yarn or around a structure such as a loom frame or dowels from which a warp is suspended in backstrap weaving.

Leaving at least a 4" tail, wrap the end of the yarn around the structure or yarn that you are attaching it to. Tie a knot by taking the tail end over the working yarn from right to left (a). From the back, take the tail through the loop formed by the wrap (b).

To make a double half-hitch knot, tighten the first half-hitch and again take the tail end over the working yarn from right to left (c). From the back, take the tail through the new loop (d).

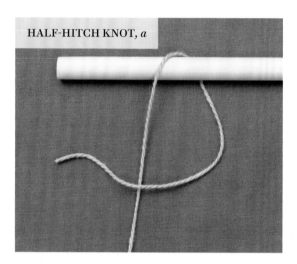

HALF-HITCH KNOT, *a*

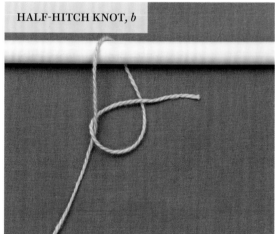

HALF-HITCH KNOT, *b*

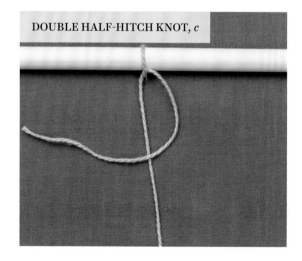

DOUBLE HALF-HITCH KNOT, *c*

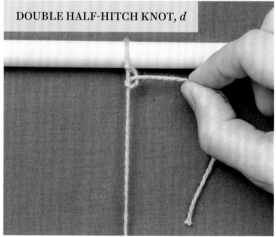

DOUBLE HALF-HITCH KNOT, *d*

Sliding Knot

This knot is useful for joining new lengths of yarn that you need to hide on the back of a piece.

1. Overlap the old and new ends by about 4". Using the new tail, tie one half of a square knot (see page 291) around the old tail.

2. Tie the old tail around the new tail in the same way (a). Pull on each yarn to draw the knots together (b). Trim the ends.

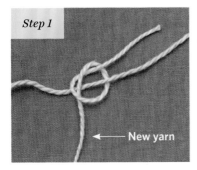

Step 1

← New yarn

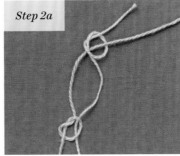

Step 2a

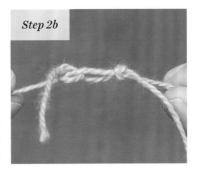

Step 2b

Slip Knot

This knot is very useful for getting projects started. It holds the yarn in place but can easily be undone by pulling on the short tail.

1. Make a loop with the yarn with the long end coming from the left, then make a clockwise circle with the short end staying on top of the long end.

2. With the index finger and thumb of your dominant hand, reach down through the opening in the loop and grab the short tail just after it goes over the loop. The short tail will wrap around the yarn by going over the loop and then coming from under it.

3. Hold the long piece of yarn and the end of the short tail in your nondominant hand and pull the yarn from the short tail up through the loop so the loop traps the ends of both lengths of yarn.

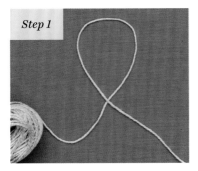

Step 1

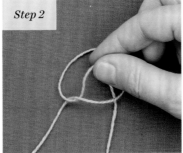

Step 2

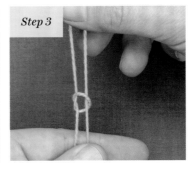

Step 3

Weaver's Knot

This is a strong knot that does not come undone easily and has a slim profile. It is good to use when the join needs to be invisible.

1. With the working yarn, make an open loop with the short end underneath. Then make a narrow loop with the new yarn.

2. Poke the new yarn loop up through the working yarn loop. Feed the short tail of the working yarn through the new yarn loop.

3. Holding all of the yarn and tails securely, pull to tighten the knot. Trim the tail.

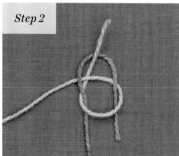
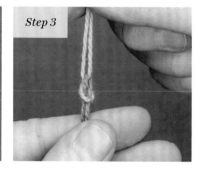

Step 1 — Working yarn / New yarn

Step 2

Step 3

COMMONLY USED MATERIALS

Needles

Needles come in a wide variety of sizes and shapes. Here are some of the common ones we use in this book.

Sewing needle

Blunt-tip embroidery needle

Sharp embroidery needle

Short blunt-tip tapestry needle

Bent-tip tapestry needle

Long blunt-tip tapestry needle

Sashiko needle

5" long needle for using with pin looms

Yarn Sizes

Sometimes very similar yarn goes by different names, depending on what craft you are practicing. These images (shown at actual size) will help you identify the size of yarn referenced for each project.

Sewing thread

C-Lon thread

Linen warp

Linen thread

10/2 pearl or size 10 crochet cotton

5/2 pearl or size 5 crochet cotton

Cotton warp

Sport weight yarn

Hemp twine

3/2 pearl or size 3 crochet cotton

Light worsted weight yarn

A GLOSSARY OF WEAVING TERMS

AWL. A tool with a very sharp point often used for making holes in leather, wood, or other thick materials.

BACKSTITCH. A stitch that is doubled back on the previous stitch.

BACKSTRAP. A weaving technique in which one end of the warp is attached to a fixed structure, such as a tree or piece of heavy furniture, and the other end is secured by a bar, band lock, or clamp that is attached to a belt or strap around the weaver's waist; the weaver adjusts the warp tension by moving his or her body as needed.

BALANCED WEAVE. A weave in which the warp and weft are equally spaced and both are apparent. See also *Plain weave*.

BAND LOCK OR CLAMP. A tool consisting of two bars or pieces of wood that are clamped together to secure and help tension the warp; it is used in this book for card weaving and other backstrap techniques. See page 287 for instructions on making your own.

BEAT. The act of pushing the newest length of weft yarn against the already-woven fabric. This can be a very light push or a determined beat depending on the nature of the project. A variety of tools are used for this act, again depending on the project and the loom.

BLIND STITCH. A sewing stitch often used by upholsterers to join two pieces invisibly.

BOAT SHUTTLE. A device used to pass the weft through the shed easily. It gets its name because it looks like a small boat.

BONE FOLDER. A dull-edged knifelike tool used to fold and crease paper or other materials.

BOUCLÉ. A two-ply yarn created by keeping one strand under tension while a second strand is loosely plied around it, making loops of whatever size and spacing are desired by the spinner.

BUBBLING. The process of pushing the weft upward in an arc (or several arcs) above the fell before being beaten in. This provides the weft enough length to travel over and under the warp threads without drawing the fabric in at the edges. It is particularly important in weft-faced weaves, such as traditional tapestry, where the warp must be completely covered. For an illustration, see page 123.

BUTTERFLY. A method of packaging, or preparing, relatively long lengths of weft yarn to make them more manageable for weaving. It gets its name because of its butterfly shape. For instructions on how to make butterflies, see page 37.

CARD WEAVING. An ancient form of weaving in which warp threads are drawn through holes in a group of cards. The cards are then manipulated in such a way that the warp threads twist around each other to create patterns.

CARTOON. An actual-size drawing that may be pinned under the warp when weaving a tapestry; it serves as a template to follow while weaving.

CHOKE TIES. Small lengths of yarn or string tied tightly at intervals around a measured warp to keep it aligned.

C-LON THREAD. A type of very strong nylon thread often used for beading.

CONTINUOUS WARP. A warp that does not need to be measured before it is wound onto the loom. Instead, the beginning end is tied to the top (or bottom) of the loom and then wound from top to bottom and back continuously until the desired width is achieved.

CROCHET COTTON. Tightly spun cotton thread frequently used for crochet. This comes in many sizes designated by numbers (for example 3, 5, 8, 10, 12). The higher the number, the thinner the thread.

CROSS. When measuring a warp, the cross is formed by winding the thread or yarn between three pegs in a figure-8 pattern to maintain the order and prevent tangling. The cross isolates four groups of threads, and it is secured by tying each of the groups with a separate piece of yarn or thread. For photos, see pages 289 and 290.

DENTAL FLOSS THREADER. Usually made of a plastic loop with a tail that resembles a noose, this was designed to thread dental floss under orthodontic braces, fixed bridges, and dental implants. These are frequently used by crafters to thread beads onto yarn or string.

DRAW PLATE. A rectangle of hardwood with a series of progressively smaller holes used to tighten and lengthen a Viking knitted chain (see page 193). After taking a Viking knitted piece off the dowel it is

made on, the piece is pulled through the draw plate hole that is only slightly smaller than the diameter of the chain. The piece is then pulled through each next smaller hole until the chain is the desired diameter. Each pull makes the chain stiffer and more compact, and each pull also compresses the overlaps so it sometimes achieves a completely new and interesting surface.

ENDS PER INCH. The number of warp threads (or ends) required for each inch of the width of the fabric. This number varies depending on the thickness of the warp yarn and/or the desired density of the finished fabric. Sometimes abbreviated as "epi." See also *Sett*.

FAT QUARTER. A piece of fabric frequently used by quilters that generally measures 18" × 21".

FELL. The edge of the developing fabric.

FLAT CRIMP CLOSURE. A jewelry tool with small toothlike protrusions that folds over the ends of a piece and is crimped or pressed into place.

GAUGE. The thickness or size of wire, typically for purposes in this book ranging from 24 to 30 gauge. The higher the number, the thinner the wire.

HEADING. After the warp is tied onto the loom, the several shots (or picks) of weft thrown to align the warp threads at the desired number of ends per inch.

HEDDLE. A wire or string suspended on a frame or shaft of a loom; eyes, or openings in the center of each wire or string, receive the warp threads and allow them to be raised or lowered as the heddle is moved. See also *Rigid heddle*.

HEDDLE HOOK. A tool used to draw the warp threads or yarn through the openings in the heddles when warping a loom. See also *Threading hook*.

HEMSTITCH. A decorative stitch in which a specified number of adjacent threads are drawn together to help secure the edge of handwoven fabric. For an illustration of how to do this, see page 153.

INKLE LOOM. A frame loom, usually used to weave narrow, warp-faced bands. String heddles raise designated warp threads to create the shed and form a pattern.

JEWELRY FINDINGS. Small supplies used in jewelry making, often attached to the ends of pieces to enable them to be held together. They include headpins, jump rings, clasps, cones, and more.

JUMP RINGS. Rings used to attach closures and other parts of jewelry together.

KUMIHIMO DIAMETER SIZING TOOL. A disk with openings into which cords, braids, or chains can be inserted to determine the diameter. This tool helps to match the cord to the appropriate jewelry finding.

LEASE STICKS. Two round or flat sticks that are positioned in the cross in order to preserve it while threading the warp through heddles or a rigid heddle.

LENO. A weaving technique that creates a lacelike effect. It is achieved by twisting adjacent warp threads before the next pick of the weft.

LOBSTER CLAW. A popular type of jewelry closure.

LOOM. A device on which warp threads are attached to maintain a consistent tension and order and to support the warp threads, thus making it possible to weave the weft through the warp.

LUCET. A hand-held, two-pronged device on which yarn or fabric strips are looped in order to create a four-sided braid.

MAT BOARD. Made from cardboard or similar material, this is a surface that can be pinned into. Sometimes it is a foam-like center with a cardboard-like material on both sides.

OMBRÉ. The gradual blending of one color to another.

PEARL COTTON. A type of cotton thread that is highly mercerized and tightly plied. It comes in many sizes including 3, 5, 10, 20; the higher the number, the thinner the thread. If there is a slash mark and an additional number (as in 5/2 or 10/2), the number after the slash indicates how many plies the thread contains. In this example, the "/2" means that two threads were twisted together to make the finished yarn.

PAINTER'S TAPE. A type of tape that can easily be removed and leaves no sticky residue. It is frequently blue.

PICK. One length of weft yarn across the warp threads. May also be called a row, shot, or throw. See also *Throwing the weft*.

PICKS PER INCH. The number of weft rows per woven inch. Sometimes abbreviated to "ppi."

PICKUP STICK. A smooth, flat stick with a pointed end (or ends), used to select warp threads to create the desired shed.

PIN ROVING. A long, narrow bundle of fibers that have been prepared in such a way that the individual fibers do not lie parallel to the bundle, but are random, thus creating a loftier material; roving is not twisted or plied. It may subsequently be spun, but it may also be used as is for such techniques as braiding with a lucet (see page 173), incorporating into a tapestry as weft (see page 124), or even knitting.

PLAIN WEAVE. The simplest weave structure, plain weave is achieved by passing the weft over one warp and under the next, alternating that order in the next row. In a balanced plain weave, the weft and warp are equally spaced and both are apparent.

RIGID HEDDLE. A piece of equipment with alternating slots and holes in the uprights through which the warp threads pass. The rigid heddle can be raised and lowered, thus allowing the weft to pass

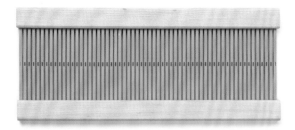

over and under various groups of warp threads as desired.

RUNNING STITCH. An easy sewing stitch consisting of a line of small, even stitches that run in and out through the fabric. The stitches do not overlap.

RYA KNOT. A type of Ghiordes knot applied to a warp in order to create fringe or pile; traditional Scandinavian rugs or throws often consist of 1"–3" pile. For an illustration of how to make this knot, see page 126.

SELVAGE. The edge warp threads on each side of woven cloth.

SETT. A reference to the number of warp ends per inch in a fabric. See also *Ends per inch*.

SHANK. A protrusion that provides a small amount of space between a button and a garment. It allows space for the fabric to lay without causing the garment to bunch up around the button.

SHED. The opening made when the warp threads are separated into two layers — an upper and a lower — through which the weft is passed.

SHED STICK. A dowel or stick used to create the opening for the weft to travel through.

SHOT. See *Pick*.

SHUTTLE. See *Stick shuttle*.

SOUMAK. A traditional tapestry technique in which the weft yarn is wrapped around the warp threads as the yarn travels just above the fell, rather than being woven in plain weave. For an illustration of how to do this, see page 126.

SQUARE KNOT. A symmetrical, double knot that is secure but easy to untie; also known as a reef knot. For instructions and an illustration of how to create a square knot, see page 291.

STICK SHUTTLE. A tool around which the weft thread or yarn is wound and which carries the weft from side to side through the warp threads to weave the fabric.

STRING HEDDLES. Loops through which the warp may be threaded in order to lift warp thread combinations that create opposing sheds.

TAIL. The end of yarn, usually 4"–6" long, that is set aside for tying off or weaving in after a weaving is completed.

TAKE-UP. The length warp threads lose as the weft threads cross over and under them.

TAPESTRY. Traditionally, a weft-faced, plain-weave structure with a discontinuous weft.

TAPESTRY BEATER. A tool used to beat in the weft in order to help cover the warp in tapestry weaving. You may use a pronged tool specifically created for this purpose, a tapestry bobbin, or even a table fork.

TAPESTRY BOBBIN. A tool that the weft is wrapped around so it can be easily passed through warp threads.

TAPESTRY NEEDLE. A blunt-tip needle with a wide eye, useful for weaving yarn tails in after a piece is completed; it may also be used to carry the weft through the warp.

TENCEL. A form of rayon consisting of cellulose fibers (usually bleached wood pulp); Tencel is the brand name for lyocell.

TENSION. The tautness of the warp threads; it is created by the weaver's body when a backstrap is used or by special braking devices on various kinds of table and floor looms.

THREADING HOOK. A tool with a hooked tip that makes it easy to draw warp threads through a heddle. See also *Heddle hook*.

THROWING THE WEFT. The act of passing a weft thread through the shed in the warp. See also *Pick*.

WARP. The yarn or threads that form the foundation for a piece of fabric; the warp threads run vertically from the weaver to a fixed object or back beam of a loom. The word *warp* can also refer to a single warp thread. As a verb, *warp* can refer to setting up the loom by stringing the warp threads onto it.

WARP-FACED WEAVING. A weave structure in which the warp yarn completely covers the weft threads, such as in card weaving.

WARPING PEG. A stable device positioned for winding and measuring warp threads of a consistent length. In this book, we recommend using three warping pegs for this purpose (see page 288).

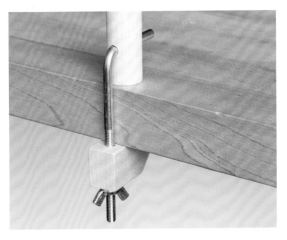

WEAVE. Interlacing of lengthwise and crosswise threads in such a firm, regular way as to make a complete piece of fabric.

WEAVE STRUCTURE. A description of the way the warp and weft yarns in a weaving relate to each other. See, for example, *leno, plain weave, weft-faced weaving*, and *warp-faced weaving*.

WEFT. The yarn or threads that are woven across and through the warp threads, from left to right and then from right to left.

WEFT-FACED WEAVING. A weave structure in which the weft yarn completely covers the warp threads, as in traditional tapestry.

WET FINISHING. Immersing woven fabric in water to complete the intermingling of the fibers. During this process, the warp and weft fibers bloom and some inconsistencies in the weaving even out. Allow the woven fabric to soak for 20 minutes, then let it air dry.

WHIPSTITCH. A sewing stitch that passes over the edge of the fabric. This is sometimes referred to as a blanket stitch.

METRIC CONVERSION CHART

WHEN THE MEASUREMENT GIVEN IS	TO CONVERT IT TO	MULTIPLY IT BY
inches	millimeters	25.4
inches	centimeters	2.54
inches	meters	0.0254
feet	meters	0.3048
yards	centimeters	91.44
yards	meters	0.9144
ounces	grams	28.35
pounds	grams	453.5
pounds	kilograms	by 0.45

SPOTLIGHT ARTISTS

DEB ESSEN
www.djehandwovens.com

HELEN HIEBERT
https://helenhiebertstudio.com

RACHEL HINE
www.rachel-hine.com

TAMMY KANAT
www.tammykanat.com

REBECCA MEZOFF
https://rebeccamezoff.com

MARILYN MOORE
www.marilynmooreswired.net

JOHN MULLARKEY
http://malarkycrafts.com/

MICHAEL ROHDE
www.michaelrohde.com

SARAH SWETT
www.afieldguidetoneedlework.com

STEPHEN WILLETTE
www.stephenwillette.com

INDEX

FILL YOUR FIBER CRAFTING LIBRARY
WITH MORE STOREY BOOKS

by Syne Mitchell

This best-selling guide covers everything you need to know to master the craft of rigid-heddle weaving. Choose a loom, set it up, and get started with a variety of fun techniques to produce beautiful and colorful results.

by Sarah Anderson

Discover the fun and satisfaction of creating your own specialty yarns from basic 2-ply to spirals, bouclés, crepes, and novelty styles. Step-by-step instructions and photographs feature 80 distinctive yarns.

by Jillian Moreno

Walk through every phase of yarn construction with step-by-step photos showing how to select the fiber, establish a foundation, and achieve the desired structure, texture, and color patterning. In addition, 12 original knitting patterns showcase handspun yarn.

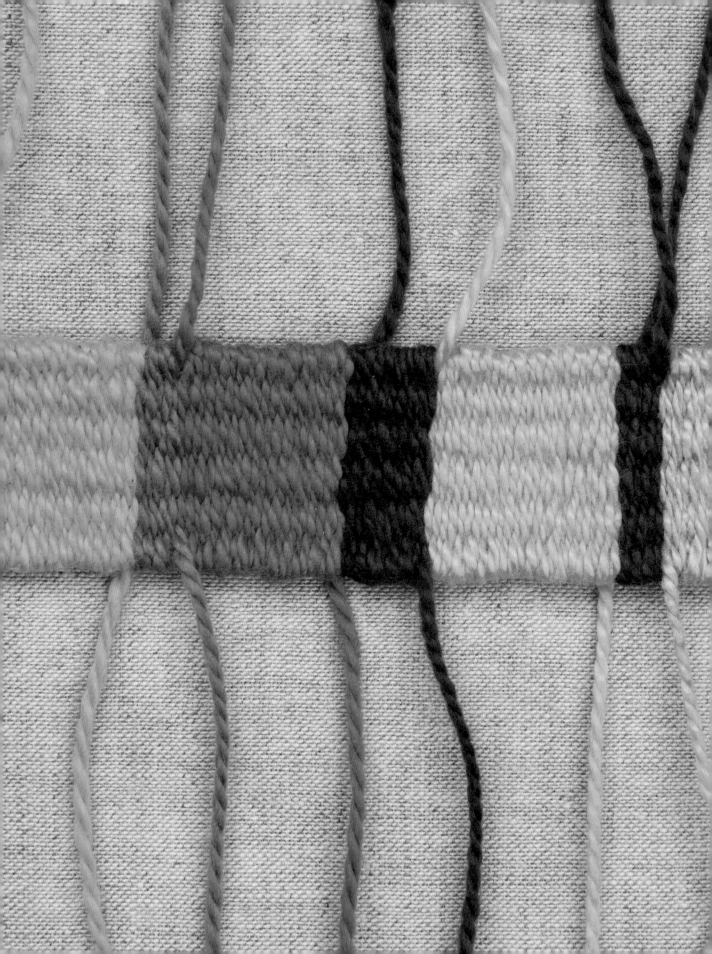